The Irrational Jesus

To General Theological Seminary,

On this day, February the 8th, 2017. May full humanity, and joyous, faithful irrationality be yours to the Glory of God.

The Irrational Jesus

Leading the Fully Human Church

❦

KEN EVERS-HOOD

FOREWORD BY
L. GREGORY JONES

CASCADE *Books* · Eugene, Oregon

THE IRRATIONAL JESUS
Leading the Fully Human Church

Cascade Books
An Imprint of Wipf and Stock Publishers
199 W. 8th Ave., Suite 3
Eugene, OR 97401

www.wipfandstock.com

PAPERBACK ISBN: 978-1-4982-2048-4
HARDCOVER ISBN: 978-1-4982-2050-7
EBOOK ISBN: 978-1-4982-2049-1

Cataloguing-in-Publication data:

Names: Evers-Hood, Ken. | Jones, L. Gregory, foreword.

Title: The irrational Jesus : leading the fully human church / Ken Evers-Hood ; foreword by L. Gregory Jones.

Description: Eugene, OR : Cascade Books, 2016 | Includes bibliographical references and index.

Identifiers: ISBN 978-1-4982-2048-4 (paperback) | ISBN 978-1-4982-2050-7 (hardcover) | ISBN 978-1-4982-2049-1 (ebook)

Subjects: LCSH: Christianity—Economic aspects. | Economics—Religious aspects—Christianity. | Game theory—Decision making.

Classification: BR115.E3 E93 2016 (paperback) | BR115.E3 E93 2016 (ebook)

Manufactured in the U.S.A.   11/08/16

I dedicate this book to the inner Esau and inner Jacob wrestling inside all of us. Here's hoping our Esau discovers patience and our Jacob finds humility—all before Rebekah gets fed up with them both and heads to Vegas.

Contents

Foreword

Dan Ariely, Karl Barth, and Jane McGonigal walk into a bar . . .
Sounds like the beginning of an intriguing joke, a variation on a theme. But this joke would likely fall stillborn, as there are few people in the world who could recognize the incongruity of all three characters finding themselves in a bar together. Not exactly your typical "a rabbi, a priest, and a minister" or even, for Catholics, "a Dominican, a Franciscan, and a Jesuit."

Who are Dan Ariely, and Karl Barth, and Jane McGonigal, and why should we care if they walk into a bar together? Well, Ken Evers-Hood believes that fruitful theological imagination, insightful understanding of human beings, and a promising future for congregational ministry are likely to result from their conversation. And, with Ken's intoxicating sense of humor and earthy incarnational approach, of course they would meet in a bar.

In Evers-Hood's deft rhetorical hands, the result of this conversation among Ariely, Barth, McGonigal, and many others is a fascinating book that ought to be read not only by pastors but also by theologians, economists, and others. Why? Because he both builds on the insights of behavioral economists, showing relevance for pastoral ministry and Christian theology, and offers theological wisdom that deepens our understandings of human nature and communities in an era when social scientists and other "secular" disciplines are tempted by reductive or siloed accounts.

This book originated in part out of an encounter I had with Ken in the midst of a Doctor of Ministry seminar I was teaching. During the break, he came up to me and asked if I was aware of various experiments in behavioral economics and "game theory" that he thought would be relevant to our class.

He might have been surprised to discover that, in fact, I did have some familiarity with his interests. And in that brief conversation, a friendship was born. To be sure, it took some time for each of us to learn to trust that the other was serious about both sides of the conversation.

I assumed that Ken really was looking for a way to develop a paper, and perhaps a thesis, that would enable him to develop his interests with a minimum of theological research or engagement. And I suspect that Ken doubted that I really had read Axelrod, Ariely, Kahneman, and others—or that, if I had read them, I had thought about them deeply.

I agreed to supervise Ken's thesis for his Doctor of Ministry degree. I was surprised and delighted when he persuaded my Duke colleague Dan Ariely to serve as co-supervisor. Ken promised to work hard and develop some interesting arguments. It was a promise that he has exceeded by leaps and bounds, for which this stimulating and insightful book is testimony.

Ken's remarkable journey in developing the argument of his thesis, and then expanding his argument into this book, reveals both a gifted pastor and a deep and imaginative theological mind. Ken represents the life of a "reflective practitioner" at its best, for he takes both the reflection and the practice with the utmost seriousness.

As you read the book, you will learn about the challenges Ken had to address in order for Dan to believe that he was doing serious social-scientific research. Less visible in the book, though, but no less significant were my challenges to him to be sure he treated with equal seriousness classical Christian theology—and doctrines such as Christology, sin, holiness.

And so it was that he probed deeply into the thought of Calvin and Barth even as he was learning from Ariely and Kahneman, and designing his own experiments with those odd collections of people called "sessions" in Presbyterian churches. His playful evocation of Jesus' (and our own) "irrationality" may seem initially too clever by half, especially coming from a pastor in a Calvinist tradition known for its rationality (and at times, as a Wesleyan might note, its obsession with rationality).

Ken's emphasis, though, is on the limits of our rationality, not that we are never rational. In his gentle, humorous, and thoughtful approach, Ken returns us to a rich theological (and Calvinist) tradition that actually points us toward wisdom that is holistic precisely in the ways it points to the integration of our reason, limited though it is, with our emotions, perceptions, and actions.

As you read this book, I suspect you will discover as I did that you are learning a lot from Ken's insights and provocative ways of framing issues. You will discover a rich interweaving of Scripture with social-scientific studies, discussion of theological doctrines with humorous stories of congregational debates. And Ken will invite you to laugh with him, and occasionally at him, as you are drawn into the wondrous complexity of human life.

The tapestry that you hold, the book *The Irrational Jesus*, is a wonder to behold. As you pause to reflect and are stirred to argue with this or that point, as you chuckle at others' foibles and wonder about your own irrationality, I trust that you will be prompted also to reflect more deeply about God, about human beings, and about the purpose of the church and its ministries.

Ultimately, though, Ken and I both hope you will do more than reflect—we hope you will be inspired to live and lead differently, and more faithfully, in service to God in the midst of a fully human church, and a fully human world.

L. Gregory Jones
Executive Vice President and Provost
Baylor University

Acknowledgments

I have always assumed authors were being modest when they thanked those who contributed to their work. I had no idea. Never before have I been so aware that creation is only possible because of a dedicated, persistent, and lovingly critical community. Every idea presented here has been mulled over, picked apart, chewed on, and improved upon by incredible friends and colleagues to whom I am profoundly grateful.

Thanks to my Doctor of Ministry thesis supervisors, Greg Jones and Dan Ariely. Greg, you took a chance on a Presbyterian interested in working with the business school, of all places. You encouraged me to write, helped me every step of the way, and have been the best guide since Virgil told Dante to watch his step going into that Inferno place. Dan, you responded to an email from an unknown Divinity School student, made time to meet with me in Durham and in Portland, and relentlessly pushed my experimental thinking and statistical abilities. You expanded my vision of what is possible, and I have been only too happy to consider myself irrationally yours.

To my beautiful and brilliant Melissa Evers-Hood: you listened deeply, offered insightful criticism, held down the fort for me on more than one occasion, and all while rocking the world as Intel's Chrome goddess.

Jean and John Martin, aka Kirk and Spock: editing, illustrations, and typesetting tags. Oh my! The two of you have impacted this project more than anyone. You helped me organize and clarify, and every aspect of this book is better because of you. Is it time? Can we say, "Well, we're through with that?"

Huge thanks go to Kelly Gilmer at Duke's *Faith and Leadership* journal. You provided me the space to flesh out my initial thoughts on behavioral theology and game theory. You are a phenomenal editor, ask the best questions, and offer the kind of quiet leadership that changes lives.

I express appreciation to the Strategic Decisions Group for the use of their images. They brought clarity to my discussion of the decision quality chain and the appropriate amount of decision-making process. Many thanks also to Intel's Jim Driscoll, who connected me with the Stanford Strategic Decision and Risk Management program in the first place, making space for me in Decision Quality and Decision Analysis. Thanks also to Jordan Stephens and Amy Jaklich for making this crazy pastor feel at home surrounded by engineers.

Many thanks to Craig Dykstra, Dave Odom, Gretchen Ziegenhals, and everyone in the Duke Convocation of Leaders. You endured my endless references to cognitive bias and gameful thinking. If anyone could have put a stop to this project, it was you. Sure, I'm thankful, but the world wants to know how you sleep at night?

So many of you were kind enough to take the time to read early versions of this work. You discovered blind spots I missed, helped me see when I had missed the mark entirely, shared with me your own examples, and always offered me encouragement along the way. I'm particularly grateful to Paul Belz-Templeman, Sarah Moore-Nokes, and Cyndi Wunder. Paul, Katie's words continue to ring true: you never disappoint. You not only made this work stronger, but you have been a true friend along the way. Sarah, you gave me the best gift I mostly wanted: the unvarnished truth. And Cyndi, you helped me see and own my personal privilege, saving me from an epic blunder. I'm also thankful for the comments of Aric Clark, Pat Berger, Mark Evers, Annica Gage, and Ian Doescher.

Finally, I'm grateful for the good people of Cascades Presbytery, Tualatin Presbyterian Church, and in particular John Casebeer and the denizens of TPC's Adult Edge, our version of adult education hour. Cascades Presbytery taught me how to lead beyond the context of a single congregation. TPC gives me the freedom to try anything at least once. And Adult Edge endured repeated prisoner's dilemma games, decision quality chains, and more of my cognitive bias than anyone should have to suffer. You have all helped me become the predictably irrational pastor that I am.

About This Book

Just as biological life becomes more interesting and diverse when the edges of ecosystems meet, intellectual life crackles with energy and possibility when leaders from different disciplines collaborate. The recent emergence of behavioral economics, a fusion of classical economic theory with cognitive psychology, represents the best of what can happen when two fields collide. Classical economists offer sophisticated models of how people should behave according to rational self-interest. Behavioral economists question whether actual human beings really behave in such a rational way. Using an experimental approach, behavioral economists such as Dan Ariely (whom you will meet in the first section of this book) show that not only are we real-life human beings not entirely rational, but we are irrational in predictable ways. Behavioral economics does not undermine standard economic theory so much as adds to it, making it more accurate by predicting the behavior of fully human people.

As a pastor I see a similar dynamic in church leadership. On the one hand, pastors and theological educators cherish ideas about how Christians ought to behave. But, on the other hand, any fully human leader serving fully human churchgoers in an actual ministry setting knows that people (including leaders!) rarely behave the way leaders think they should. The disconnect between the ideas about church we learned in seminary and the reality in the pew is so great many new pastors feel as if they were prepared for a church that does not exist. This book attempts to better prepare leaders to understand the hidden, fully human forces driving our own leadership as well as the behavior of the people we serve—what I am calling a behavioral-theology approach to church leadership.

I will highlight a few points before we begin. First, we will be using the more narrow definition of rationality assumed by the standard economic model. Classical economists posit that we humans know our preferences and are able to rank these unmoving desires in order. We are able to coolly assess the market around us to accurately evaluate all the options that could meet our needs. And the rational human being will always act to maximize self-interest. That is, knowing our desires, we will always choose the path that is best at meeting our needs. I fully acknowledge this utilitarian understanding of rationality is not the only one out there. But it is so influential and so common in our congregations that I have adopted Dan Ariely's approach of simply accepting this definition as a given in order to more clearly point out how rarely fully human beings actually behave in such a rational and self-interested way. In this sense the term *irrational* is rhetorical. When I refer to Jesus and Paul as irrational, I am not saying they are mentally unbalanced or wildly unstable. Instead, I am arguing they are fully human, and as fully human beings they are as irrational as the rest of us when it comes to the standard economic understanding of rationality.

Second, the book is divided into three sections: the arc of the book begins with a more theoretical understanding of predictable irrationality in the life of Jesus; then moves through Paul's leadership as a mirror of an irrational, but effective, pattern of playing a prisoner's dilemma game; and concludes with the more concrete world of decision-making in the fully human church. While each section provides the foundation for the ones that follow, the first section highlights cognitive heuristics and biases, the second section introduces game theory and gameful thinking, and the third section centers on decision theory. Toward the end of each section, I have included a case study chapter to give readers a chance to practice their new knowledge. And, to provide a quick reference guide, the last chapter in each section is a ten-point glossary of terms.

Finally, between each of the three sections I have included a sermon that relates to the material covered. These sermons are in keeping with the practical, lived, experiential, enfleshed nature of behavioral theology. I will never forget a lesson from my undergraduate days at the University of Texas, where I completed a thesis on Luke-Acts and the magical tradition in the New Testament. When I presented my findings to a group of students, faculty, and friends, I was incredibly proud. I believed the work was original and fascinating. In hindsight I think it probably was fairly original . . . I now have my doubts about how fascinating it was.

When I concluded, I felt quite pleased with myself and asked if there were any questions. One woman, a seminary graduate, confronted me: "Does it preach?" I stared at her blankly. "This is all sort of interesting," she said, "but how in the world would you preach it?" I stammered and sputtered about as articulately as Hugh Grant in front of Andie McDowell in

Four Weddings and a Funeral. At the time I was angry with her for bringing up something that seemed beside the point. Today I realize that of all the questions asked of me that afternoon, hers was the most significant.

At the end of the day, if I can't communicate what I have to say clearly and in a way that connects with real-life people, then I probably need to spend more time until I can. Good preaching speaks to our minds and sings to our hearts, and behavioral theology tells us to keep working until we can do both. And just as it is important to preach to fully human beings, this turn from an academic understanding of theology to a more real-world behavioral theology applies to every aspect of church leadership.

SECTION ONE

The Irrational Jesus

1

We Can Be Taught!

I might have seen it coming. For the last eleven years I have served as pastor of a medium-size Presbyterian church just outside of Portland, Oregon. The church leans left (it is Oregon, after all), but the congregation is politically, socially, and theologically diverse. The community values both a sense of family and the freedom to think for themselves. It has been a perfect fit.

Long before the congregation's denomination, the Presbyterian Church (U.S.A.), voted to affirm openly gay and lesbian pastors and same-sex marriage, a small, progressive group of leaders in our church pressed for change. The congregation already embraced the few gay and lesbian folk who attended as part of the church family, but these leaders believed it was time to make the church's quiet welcome more vocal. For a year I worked with this small group to lead open discussions on the topics of homosexuality and the Scriptures, ordination, and gay marriage. We opened these meetings to all and announced them in worship, but the only people who showed up were mostly supportive.

Feeling emboldened by the lack of pushback, this core group believed the time was right to approach the session, the governing body of the church, with an action plan. The list was long. They wanted the session to publicly join a local or national network that affirmed lesbian, gay, bisexual, and transgender (LGBT) people and their families. The group requested that the pastor specifically address sexuality issues from the pulpit several times a year. They also wanted the session to craft a statement that made the congregation's practice of welcoming LGBT people loud and proud. There was more, but you get the idea.

I supported some of these moves, but at the same time I knew something this potentially controversial had to be a change led by the session and supported widely by the congregation. The session very much reflected the congregation. A few elders supported making most of these changes quickly. They agreed it was high time for the church to speak up. Most of the group felt warmly about the suggestions but harbored concerns about which actions would be best to take first. They also wondered how the whole congregation felt. A couple of members, while personally welcoming of LGBT people, were uncomfortable with the idea of singling any particular group out as welcome. By overtly welcoming LGBT people, they asked, were we *not* welcoming other marginalized groups? Weren't all people welcome? Optimistic at first about the session's ability to deal with this decision quickly and move on to the other business of the church, I realized resolution wasn't going to happen anytime soon. Any other leaders know this feeling?

After spending months in conversation, the session finally arrived at a decision they all supported without reservation. Opting to pick just one item from the list of recommendations, the session crafted a welcoming statement that would be included in the weekly bulletin, published in the newsletter, and posted on the church's website. While the session acknowledged this welcoming statement might seem like a timid first step to some, the elders saw it as an experimental start that could easily lead to bolder moves down the road. They felt good about hanging in there through hard conversations. They were proud of their work.

And so finally, after nearly a year of conversation among the elders, the pastor and session presented the welcoming statement to the congregation. At the time I actually felt as if we were offering a beautifully wrapped gift. Surely the progressives would be pleased their voice had an impact. The social conservatives would totally appreciate the moderation of the session in not going too far too fast. Surely, I thought, the congregation would laud our wise leadership.

As you can probably sense, the proposal fell like a sack of hammers. At first the congregation was silent. Then, as some in the session feared, a few voices began to wonder why one group was being singled out. Others began to grumble that this was the first they were hearing about it and that the session had kept them in the dark. The real excitement began when the talk turned personal. One said this whole conversation was about her and whether she and her partner were really welcome in the congregation or merely tolerated. In reaction another person angrily responded that it sounded to him as if, unless he agreed with this decision, maybe *he* wasn't really welcome. My mind suddenly flashed to a hapless Han Solo trapped in the trash compactor—I started to have a very bad feeling about this.

And the letters began to pour in. The letters revolved around the same theme: the congregation supported welcoming all people but believed this decision had been sprung upon them and might create unintended consequences. Of course, it could have been much worse. No one voiced hatred. No one quoted Scripture in their letters. After personally calling every single individual who sent a letter and mostly listening to folks vent, I could feel the emotional temperature lowering. We would survive this miscalculation. Sadly, however, given the uproar, the session and I agreed that for the time being the wisest course would be to acknowledge that "mistakes were made" and go back to square one. We would survive, but everyone—the progressive group who made the recommendations, the session, many in the congregation, and I—left the situation feeling as if we had lost.

While I did a great job leading the session in their discernment, I completely stumbled when it came to taking the full humanity of the congregation into account. As human beings made in God's image, we are a complicated mix of emotion and reason. We aren't bloodless machines that sift through data and logical arguments, calculating our way to conclusions. Data and arguments shape us, to be sure. But we are also emotional. Like God we are loving and prone to anger. The psalmist cries out in Psalm 13, "How long, O Lord?" Like God, it takes us time to process this complex mix of fact and feeling. I did a good job with the session, realizing they would need time for their hearts to line up with their heads. Yet, I treated the congregation like disembodied thinkers who would simply receive our report, see how much work we did, and logically realize that it was the best direction for all involved.

Something else I missed is what is known as a cognitive bias, a predictable blind spot we will spend more time understanding in the first section of this book. In the past fifty years cognitive psychologists have made tremendous advances in understanding how much our bodies shape our perception and thinking. One of the ways you know you are encountering a cognitive bias is when a person or group faces a similar situation but responds entirely differently due to some change in the framing or presentation of the challenge. When our congregation encountered a second controversial issue and experienced a different outcome, I realized a bias was at play. I knew the congregation prized their freedom to think for themselves. They have what today I call an authority bias. If the session makes a decision the congregation considers important and they are not involved in the process, the body will resist the decision even if individually members tend to agree with it.

How do I know? A year and a half after that disastrous congregational meeting the Sandy Hook Elementary tragedy rocked our nation. The news broke on the Friday before the third Sunday of Advent. Unusually early, I had already finished my sermon. I sat glued to NPR, wanting to tear myself away from the awful news but finding myself unable to. I knew the sermon I had written simply wouldn't do after the death of all those little children. I spoke plainly about what I considered a Gospel imperative for us as followers after the way of Jesus Christ to lift our voices for common-sense gun control legislation. You should know that in the West, even in Oregon, gun control conversations are easily more controversial and heated than questions of LGBT inclusion.

Two members of the congregation, Linda and Marshall, spurred in part by this sermon, requested time with our session. Well known and respected in our congregation, Marshall was a former Marine who was familiar with firearms, and Linda had served as a deacon for many years. Like the group pressing for a more visible LGBT welcome, they came with an action plan. Their key request was for the session to adopt an official position with regard to peacemaking and gun control.

I certainly understood the request. I obviously agreed with their view. And yet the Han Solo in me had that oh-so-familiar bad feeling, still bruised from the unexpected resistance to the welcoming statement. This time the session took just two months but arrived at a very different decision. We shared our appreciation with the couple for bringing this concern to us. We affirmed our support for their view. But rather than vote on some statement or resolution, we welcomed Linda and Marshall to assume more ownership of the issue. We invited them to make a presentation in worship and provided space to present educational materials and talk to those interested about their plans.

Linda and Marshall spoke to the congregation. They did a marvelous job of expressing their feelings, connecting peacemaking and gun control with the Gospel, and articulating their next steps. After worship all sorts of people approached their table—people who supported their position and people who disagreed. Eventually, I connected these two advocates with a larger state organization that led to a presentation at a meeting of the presbytery, our larger judicatory body.

Guess how many angry letters I received about their work. Zero. Not a single person was angered by what is arguably a more divisive issue within our congregation. They weren't angry for a lot of reasons, but the main reason is that the work was coming from trusted friends rather than being handed down to them by the powers that be. Because of the authority bias, if our session had crafted a statement that read exactly the same as Linda and Marshall's presentation, I'd still be answering letters and making phone calls.

We can be taught!

This is good news. We can be taught. We may not be able to change the fact that our bodies shape our thinking (and in some cases we wouldn't want to), but we can adjust for our blind spots and make better decisions. In the first section of this book we are going to learn more about what behavioral economist Dan Ariely calls our "predictable irrationality." We're going to discover how, in our full humanity, our bodies shape our thinking. We will see how mental shortcuts called cognitive heuristics and mental blind spots termed cognitive biases affect us even when (and perhaps especially when) we aren't aware of it. And we will explore how Jesus himself manifests this predictable irrationality, which helps us see that these blind spots aren't just a psychological word for sin but a wondrous, complicated aspect of how our God has made us.

2

"Irrationally Yours"

Just on the other side of the Mad Hatter Café and Whole Foods in Durham, North Carolina, lies a long row of red-brick, two-story buildings that used to comprise part of Erwin Mills, a textile factory opened by the Duke family in 1892. Today the former site of Erwin Mills houses a mix of tony apartments, retail shops, and the social science research offices of Duke University, including one fascinating office playfully named The Center for Advanced Hindsight. Inside you will find a brightly colored space filled with modern furniture, busy graduate students, and the offices of Dan Ariely, the James B. Duke professor of behavioral economics at Duke University.

Many people know Dan from his incredibly popular TED talks, regular *Wall Street Journal* column, and books such as his *New York Times* best-selling *Predictably Irrational*. Dan's obvious gifts include his ability to communicate complicated ideas in simple, humorous ways. What he is famous for in the less well-known field of behavioral economics is his incredible talent for thinking up creative experiments.

One of my personal favorites is an experiment he ran in the dorms of the Massachusetts Institute of Technology. Dan put a six-pack of cokes in the fridges of the common areas of the dorms. Then he sent a graduate student to check on the cokes every hour or so. In his humorous way Dan says he was trying to determine the half-life of cokes in an undergraduate dorm. Then, giving new meaning to the phrase "cold, hard cash," Dan repeated the experiment, but with a twist, substituting a plate of six one-dollar bills for the six-pack of cokes. At the time, one coke cost one dollar from the dorm vending machines. Given the exact equivalence of their value, rationally, the undergrads should filch the cash at the same rate as the cokes. But what do you suppose actually happened? While the cokes flew out of those fridges, the dollar bills were untouched. It felt OK to nab a coke or two without asking, but it felt more like stealing to pick up a dollar bill.

Another experiment with more direct relevance to the church is Ariely's matrix experiment, in which he observed rooms full of people taking a test of twenty math problems. The problems were not hard, but most people were unable to solve all of them in the time allowed. In the control group the students were asked to count up the problems they solved correctly and hand the test in to someone who would check their answers. They were paid for every correct answer. The second group was allowed to score their own sheets, destroy their sheets in a specially designed shredder that only *appeared* to destroy the evidence, and then collect their earnings. As you might expect, the group that was allowed to self-report and destroy the evidence reported getting more answers correct than they actually solved. As Dan puts it, "Most people cheat, but only by a little bit."[1]

The really interesting thing about the matrix study, and what made it so relevant to me, is that the groups were also tested with three conditions: a control group, a ten-books-from-high-school group, and a Ten-Commandments group. The group that was asked to write down ten books they read in high school behaved just like the control group. The control group solved 3.1 problems correctly on average. When the groups were allowed to cheat, the control and book groups reported solving 4.1 problems correctly. What about the group that wrote down the Ten Commandments before the test? Would this have any effect? Surprisingly, it did. The students who wrote down as many of the Ten Commandments as they could remember (personally, I would love to have seen those lists) reported solving 3 problems on average. In other studies Dan has shown that this religious priming promotes integrity, at least in the short term, as does having people sign honor codes.[2]

If this experimental sensibility came naturally to Dan, his gift for intuiting what the results might indicate about human nature was something of a learned skill. When Dan was in high school in Israel, he was part of a youth movement called *Hanoar Haoved*. For years they had been doing a ritual at night called *ktovet esh*, which means a fire inscription. During preparations for the ceremony a magnesium flare unexpectedly blew up

---

1. Ariely, *(Honest) Truth about Dishonesty*, 49.
2. Ariely, *Predictably Irrational*, 284.

next to Dan, and he suffered third degree burns over 70 percent of his body. His right arm was badly injured and causes him terrible pain to this day. He would spend his formative young adult years in the hospital.[3]

As he was healing from his burns, Dan noticed that the nurses would remove the bandages quickly, tearing them off and so causing terrible pain for the patients. He knew they were just doing their job, but the experimentalist in Dan—and no doubt the patient, too—wondered whether there was a better way. So, he devised an experiment in which nurses removed the bandages slowly from one group of patients and then compared the results with a control group where the nurses followed the standard protocol. The results were clear: when the nurses removed the bandages more slowly, patients reported experiencing much less pain. Dan presented his results to the whole burn unit staff—but then was baffled to see no changes in the nursing practice. More than a little angry, Dan wondered why the data was not bringing about change.

His favorite nurse, a woman named Etty, pointed out that he had forgotten something very important in his study. Etty explained that Dan was so focused on the patients he had forgotten to take the nurses into account. These nurses weren't robots you could just program. They were caring human beings who had feelings, too. Not only did it take a great deal more time to remove the bandages slowly, but more importantly the nurses experienced much more emotional distress watching their patients writhe in agony as they removed the bandages slowly. Even though the nurses realized it was painful to tear the bandages away quickly, it must have felt to them as if they were torturing the very people in their care when they removed the bandages slowly. The data, as convincing as it was, simply couldn't overpower the nurses' visceral, human feelings.[4] And thus Dan Ariely the behavioralist, concerned not merely with how people behave in theory according to the data but how we behave in real life, began to emerge.

Every note Dan sends ends the same way: irrationally yours. It's even the title of his most recent book, a collection of his popular *Wall Street Journal* columns. This puckish closing isn't accidental. Chances are if you have heard of Dan Ariely, you know about his seminal idea of predictable irrationality. Dan shines as one of the brightest lights in behavioral economics, a discipline that combines the insights of cognitive psychology with traditional economic theory. While viewed by most as an innovation, behavioral economists are quick to point out they aren't doing something new as much as restoring the psychological side of economics that was there from the

3. Shani, "What It Feels Like," subhead Daily Pain, paras. 6–10.

4. Ariely, introduction to *Predictably Irrational*.

beginning. Although he only mentions it once in *The Wealth of Nations*, Adam Smith is known for his notion of the "invisible hand," shorthand for the argument that society as a whole would be better off if individuals simply follow their rational self-interest. But *The Wealth of Nations* isn't the only book Adam Smith wrote. Smith also wrote *The Theory of Emotional Sentiments*, in which he lays out psychological motivations for human behavior every bit as brilliant as his view of rational self-interest.

I think it's fair to say, though, that Dan's brand of behavioral economics has a critical, corrective edge to it when it comes to the modern economic idea of rationality. When most of us talk about being rational, we mean that someone is thoughtful, reasoned, and sensible. When we think of people behaving irrationally, images of wild-eyed people acting erratically pop into our imagination. Dan gets this, but it isn't quite what he means when he refers to himself as being irrational.

When Dan talks about rational and irrational behavior, he's referring to an extremely influential but narrower definition of rationality that drives what behavioral economists refer to as the standard economic model. Rational people in the standard economic model are something like calculators with stomachs. First, they are perfectly self-interested. They care about themselves above all else. Second, they always strive to maximize utility, always preferring more value for the least amount of effort. And finally, they are capable of assessing all the options before them in order to maximize value for themselves far into the future. Behavioral economists Richard Thaler and Cass Sunstein refer to this self-interested, unemotional construct as an "econ," something like *Star Trek*'s Mr. Spock. In the view of behavioral economists, however, real-life human beings are the opposite of econs; we are far more affected by our emotional state and a host of other factors. Or, as Thaler and Sunstein put it, there's a lot more Homer Simpson in us than there is Mr. Spock.[5]

The rational view of human nature in the standard model maintains incredible influence in the world and in Christian congregations. Richard Thaler in his engaging history of behavioral economics, *Misbehaving*, cites what he calls the gauntlet facing every behavioral economist. The gauntlet is a series of typical objections hurled at aspiring behavioralists who have the temerity to question the standard economic establishment. The gauntlet mainly takes aim at the methods of behavioralists. Traditional economists develop normative models describing how people should behave. Behavioralists run studies using actual people to determine whether we do in fact

5. Thaler and Sunstein, *Nudge*, 22.

behave this way. Traditionalists attack these studies as too small, using insignificant incentives, and not adequately representing real life.[6]

While these rationalist objections are important and well thought out, my sense is that they mask a more personal animus against predictable irrationality. Many of us simply like to think of ourselves as rational people. *Others* may behave irrationally, perhaps, but we like to think of ourselves as knowing a good deal when we see one. People may not be able to articulate complicated economic theories; but if you have time to compare different items and possess a clear sense of your preferences, many of us want to believe that most of the time we will be marvelously adept, if not always aware, at pursuing paths that will achieve our best outcome. Fans of books like *Freakonomics* revel in how authors Steven D. Levitt and Stephen J. Dubner describe how rational self-interest can explain everything from cheating sumo wrestlers and crack cocaine dealers to how socioeconomic class largely determines what names parents choose for their children.[7] Yet, as intriguing as these findings are, Ariely and other behavioral economists argue perfect rationality is the exception rather than the norm. Most of the time we aren't remotely as rational as classical economists would like to believe. Moreover, our irrationality isn't random but systematic. We are, as Dan puts it, predictably irrational. Because of the way our brains and bodies are wired, there are predictable situations that shape how we see, think, feel, and make decisions.

To demonstrate, Dan accepts the lofty ideas economists posit about how rational people should behave and then creates studies to determine whether real human beings actually behave this way. This is an important point because many of us might rightly object to the narrow definition of rationality assumed by traditional economists. Theologian Sarah Coakley, for instance, argues for a more nuanced understanding of rationality that includes emotion and altruistic behavior. But the arguments she employs are incredibly complicated and require a greater understanding of philosophy than most people have. Dan's approach is to accept the standard economic model's definition of rationality and then show how we are all predictably irrational.

I agree with Dan's approach. Because I encountered Dan and his thinking after being a pastor for many years, I also sensed a correlation between his approach and my experience in the church. Theologians and pastors often behave like classical economists. We develop ideas, often biblically based ideas, about how people should behave. But then, of course, the reality of

---

6. Thaler, *Misbehaving*, 49.

7. Levitt and Dubner, *Freakonomics*, 201.

serving in actual churches is that people rarely behave as they *should*. Dan's response to this predictable irrationality is not to throw his hands up and say there is no hope. Rather, he advocates learning about our predictable irrationality so that we can avoid some of the more obvious traps that make it difficult to be the people we want to be and are called to be.

In a similar way, I wondered if by pairing the church's idealized notions of how people should behave with Dan's insights about full humanity we might ultimately find more fruitful ways of leading and caring for God's people. For me that is the bottom line: caring for God's people. In hindsight, I wonder if that is what made Dan so compelling to me. For Dan, devising studies and drawing conclusions is not merely interesting. He is not simply trying to make a point. He cares about people, and he wants institutions to pursue policies that are more humane.

One of the most significant contributions Dan makes is his insight that our irrationality isn't always a bad thing. There is, as the title of his second book implies, an upside to irrationality. This insight is particularly true when it comes to self-interest. The standard economic model assumes that we are fundamentally self-interested creatures and that this self-interest is a good thing. In theory, if individuals have freedom enough to pursue their own interests, the market will efficiently provide for individual and communal needs in the best possible way. In a spirited 1979 conversation on the *Phil Donahue Show*, Milton Friedman, the champion of the standard economic model, put it this way: "Is there some society you know that doesn't run on greed? You think Russia doesn't run on greed? You think China doesn't run on greed? . . . In the only cases in which the masses have escaped from the kind of grinding poverty you're talking about, the only cases in recorded history, are where they have had capitalism and largely free trade."[8] Friedman's derisive dismissal of the element of greed in capitalism is only a slightly more sophisticated version of Gordon Gekko's maxim "greed is good."

Friedman's ringing defense of capitalism sounds hollow today. The 2008 global financial collapse made it abundantly clear, even to noneconomists, that when investment banks go without regulations, bad things can happen. Not only did their greed hurt *them*, but they endangered the rest of us, too. Current inequality statistics belie Friedman's belief that capitalist nations such as America are morally superior because wealth trickles down to benefit the poor. Wealth inequality has skyrocketed in the decades since Friedman's interview, and not only in America; as Thomas Piketty notes in *Capital in the Twenty-First Century*, inequality is increasing on a global

8. Friedman, interview by Phil Donahue, 0:34/2:23.

scale: "If we look at the evolution of the shares of the various millionths of large fortunes in global wealth, we find increases by more than a factor of 3 in less than thirty years."[9] Even if this optimistic view of rational, selfish individuals all maximizing their utility to increase wealth for everyone were economically true, it could never be theologically sound for anyone following after the way of Jesus Christ, who consistently modeled radical self-giving, even to the point of death on a cross.

Here is precisely where Ariely shines. To Ariely, of course, we aren't perfectly rational creatures who selfishly pursue our own interests all the time. We're far more irrational than that, which is actually fantastic news. This irrational selflessness is what makes us our best selves. It is the basis for love and what drives us to give. Dan writes beautifully, "Sometimes we are fortunate in our irrational abilities because, among other things, they allow us to adapt to new environments, trust other people, enjoy expending effort, and love our kids."[10]

If it sounds as if I'm a fan of Ariely, I am. Not only is Dan a brilliant researcher and an incredibly engaging speaker, but his penchant for predictable irrationality might also explain why he's an unusually nice person on top of it all. Dan supervised the research side of my doctoral work, and about halfway through he sent me a pretty tough note—words along the lines of "you don't have enough data to make this acceptable for doctoral work yet." Fighting panic, I redoubled my efforts to gather more data. A couple of weeks later Dan emailed that he was coming to Portland to give a talk at Reed College and would be happy to meet with me to go over my work. If you've seen *Portlandia*, you know that keeping Portland weird is at the very core of Reed College, and it turned out to be a very strange rain-filled night indeed. Dan I were trying to meet, but it wasn't going well. The first coffee shop we tried closed early; the second was too full. But finally, finally we managed to connect in an unused conference room. Dan should have been preparing for his lecture. He should have been talking to a hundred people who are more significant and influential. Believe me, there was absolutely no rational self-interest in Dan's chasing after a wayward graduate student in the rainy dark of a Portland winter night just before giving a lecture. But that evening I was profoundly grateful for the unpredictably kind generosity of this evangelist for predictable irrationality.

9. Piketty, *Capital in the Twenty-First Century*, 435.

10. Ariely, *Upside of Irrationality*, Kindle locations 197–98.

3

We're of Two Minds

Two Systems, Elephant Riders, and Esau and Jacob

The core finding of cognitive psychology that informs behavioral economics is that we are, to some degree, strangers to ourselves. The "I" that I think of as myself is the "I" that thinks and reflects and makes decisions. But this "I" is not all of me. There is another "I," one that is emotional and reactive, that goes largely unnoticed. Psychologists Keith Stanovich and Richard West describe this dual cognitive system in terms of System 1, which is automatic and emotional, and System 2, which is reflective and logical.[1] These systems are numbered in terms of influence. It is imperative to understand, however counterintuitive it may be, that the system responsible for nearly all decision-making is not System 2, the "I" I think of as myself. The vast majority of decision-making occurs at the level of System 1, the automatic system that for the most part we're not even aware is there. Only situations that confuse System 1 get pushed up to the level of consciousness so System 2 can handle them.

To better understand System 1, Nobel laureate (and Dan Ariely's doctoral advisor) Daniel Kahneman gives the example of driving a car on a crowded highway at a high rate of speed. Let's put you behind the wheel and

---

1. Stanovich and West, "Individual Differences in Reasoning," 645–65.

see how you do. On one level your brain is processing an enormous amount of data: keeping track of where the car is in the lane, watching where other vehicles are in relation to it, and a million other details, all in constant flux. This is an incredible amount of data you are processing, but most of the time you aren't aware of all of it. No, your System 1 seamlessly keeps tabs on the world rushing by, freeing your reflective System 2 to hold a conversation with the person sitting in the passenger seat. Under normal conditions, all of those millions of perceptions and judgments just seem to take care of themselves. But what happens if a car suddenly pulls out ahead of you? Or what if without warning red brake lights begin filling the freeway? If you are chauffeuring me around, you had better stop talking and focus all your attention on the developing situation. When the world overwhelms your System 1, in other words, your reflective System 2 must rush to action, no longer able to keep chatting.

Another illustration: imagine a situation in which you are asked to perform a simple multiplication question in your head. Thanks to elementary times tables, most people are able to answer simple multiplication questions in their heads without much effort. You could probably listen to music or even have a simple conversation with someone while answering basic multiplication questions. But if challenged to find the product of twenty-four and forty-three in your head without using paper, unless you are Rain Man, you will feel the need to close your eyes and focus entirely on the problem at hand.[2] Again, the automatic System 1 is not up to this task and immediately calls on System 2 for help.

Once, during a sermon, I asked the congregation I serve to do this multiplication problem in their heads to help them feel the difference between the systems. I saw some people shake their heads and frown at me, some close their eyes, and some use their fingers as if they were multiplying in the air. To the chagrin of homiletics professors everywhere, after worship one woman walked up to me and handed me a piece of paper with the number 1,032 scratched on it. I looked at her with a puzzled expression. She explained with a smile that the question bugged her throughout the entire sermon and she just had to work it out. She had no idea what I said after that problem, but at least she figured out the math! Preachers like to believe the Holy Spirit can cover a multitude of sins, but that moment made me realize I should probably think very carefully before asking people to do math again in worship.

A third way to experience the difference between the two systems is to look at an image of a face showing some kind of expression. With some

2. Kahneman, *Thinking, Fast and Slow*, 23.

groups I show a picture of a small girl in a car seat with an incredibly expressive face. I ask people to take a moment and contemplate what this little girl is feeling. I've done this many times now, and the group almost always splits into two: half the people see the girl as angry, the other half see her as only playfully pretending to be angry. Rather than debate the actual emotional state of this toddler, however, I ask the groups how they know what she's feeling. They feel confident that they are reading the expression of the girl well, but how do they know? So far, I have yet to run into anyone like Cal Lightman from the TV show *Lie to Me* who consciously analyzes microexpressions with a numbered system to ferret out what someone is really feeling. Most people simply look at a face and their System 1 automatically reads the expression, so that you just somehow know whether a person is angry or playing like it. You don't contemplate the arch of the eyebrow in comparison with nose flare in any kind of conscious way. You just . . . know it.

Now, if you are scratching your head at the labels System 1 and System 2, have no fear. Another psychologist, Jonathan Haidt, comes to our rescue with a fantastic metaphor for understanding our dual nature. For Haidt the best way to think about our two brains is to imagine ourselves as tiny riders sitting on enormous elephants.[3] The elephant represents our automatic System 1, powerfully crashing through the rainforest, while the tiny rider on top represents the rational System 2 part of us. This metaphor is particularly helpful in understanding a second kind of problem that occurs between the two systems. In the previous examples we saw how System 1, now our elephant, makes most of our decisions but sometimes requires the help of the rider when confused. At other times we experience a system shift in the opposite direction—we move from being thoughtful and reflective to acting on impulse, allowing the elephant free rein.

It takes a great deal of energy for the rider to steer these powerful elephants of ours. Kahneman discovered this phenomenon when he was doing research on the connection between cognitive work and pupil dilation. Building on the insight of research connecting mental work with pupil dilation, Kahneman and a colleague set up a lab at the University of Michigan that must have looked like something out of *A Clockwork Orange*. They asked people to do mental math while observing their pupils with optometry equipment. (I can only hope they weren't playing "the Ludwig Van" while they conducted this experiment.) Kahneman made a crucial insight: the harder the rider works the more dilated the pupils become. Moreover, the rider tires easily. Kahneman measured what every tired student knows:

---

3. Haidt, *Righteous Mind*, Kindle locations 943–45.

mental work is extremely fatiguing. Kahneman observed subjects working on harder and harder problems until they would surrender. Their bodies were apparently unchanged, but their pupils would relax. Kahneman writes that sometimes, after seeing that their pupils had relaxed, he and his research partner would surprise the subjects by asking why they had stopped working. When they wondered how Kahneman knew, he would jokingly tell them, "We have a window into your soul."[4]

When the riders give up, the elephants take over. Psychologist Roy Baumeister at Florida State University has spent his professional career researching what happens when the rider gets tired and the elephant takes over. One of the most chilling examples comes from a study of an Israeli parole board. I would like to think that parole boards make judgments entirely based on the merits of each case. And no doubt each member of a parole board tries their best and most likely believes they do decide based on the facts. It turns out, however, that the most significant factor in whether you might be granted parole from an Israeli jail is the time of day your case is heard. After surveying more than one thousand cases, prisoners facing the board in the morning had a 70 percent chance of receiving parole, compared to just 10 percent for those who appeared late in the day.[5] Baumeister and others call this "decision fatigue"—and if it makes you question how rational and objective you are all the time, it should.

This picture of ourselves with our reason like a tiny rider on a giant elephant presents a challenge to the way we like to think of ourselves. It certainly challenges the assumptions traditional economists make about us as rational beings always maximizing our self-interest. Our ability to reason is still incredibly important. We can't make good decisions without it. But we must become more aware of how easily our rider will be led by the elephant rather than the other way around, especially when we are tired, faced with new or threatening situations, or under stress. This system shift happens so often and so seamlessly we frequently think we're acting on reason when we really aren't. Haidt suggests that much of the time, especially around emotional issues, our riders act more like presidential press secretaries, fashioning reasons after the fact to account for why our elephantine emotional selves feel and move the way they do.

This tendency on the part of our reasonable riders to shift control to our emotional elephants when we're tired leads to a third, more biblical image for these systems: seeing ourselves as Rebekah with Esau and Jacob struggling in her womb. We often tell the stories about Jacob and Esau

---

4. Kahneman, *Thinking, Fast and Slow*, 33.

5. Tierney, "Decision Fatigue," paras. 5–7.

fighting and reconciling as brothers, but I love this image of the two of them wrestling in their mother's womb before they're even born—it captures the dual cognition system perfectly: "The children struggled together within Rebekah; and she said, 'If it is to be this way, why do I live?' So she went to inquire of the LORD. And the LORD said to her, 'Two nations are in your womb, and two peoples born of you shall be divided; the one shall be stronger than the other, the elder shall serve the younger'" (Gen 25:22–23). At the literal level, of course, this story is about three distinct individuals: a mother carrying her two twins. When it comes to perceiving the world around us and making decisions, we are all Rebekah carrying an inner, emotional, elephantlike Esau and an inner, reflective, riderlike Jacob.

The story of the birthright makes the emotional elephant and thoughtful rider easy to identify in Esau and Jacob. To paraphrase the story, Jacob is hanging out, cooking up a mess of stew. Then Esau lumbers in, tired after working up an enormous appetite. "What's that?" he demands. "It smells amazing." "What, this?" says Jacob, with the slyest of grins. "I've gotta have me some of that. Give it to me now," Esau threatens. "Oh, you want it?" asks Jacob innocently. "Well . . . I'll tell you what. You trade me your birthright, and you can have the whole thing." "Done," agrees poor, impulsive Esau. And just like that Esau betrays his future to satisfy his present hunger. When our elephants take over, we simply will not make the best long-term choices.

In an experiment connecting willpower with food, subjects were divided into two groups and asked to memorize a set of numbers, walk down a hallway, and then record the number in another room as part of a brief interview. The experimenters promised to take care of their subjects, telling them they could have snacks when the experiment was over. If the subjects were feeling healthy, they could have a fruit salad. If they were feeling more indulgent, they could have a piece of chocolate cake.

The first group of subjects was given a two-digit number to remember. The second group of subjects was tasked with a seven-digit number. The experimenters didn't really care how well the subjects remembered the numbers. What they were actually interested in was whether the participants picked the salad or the cake. The first group, which only had to remember two numbers, chose fruit salad at about the same rate they picked the chocolate cake. But the second group, mentally working harder to remember a seven-digit number, overwhelmingly chose the chocolate cake. Just having to remember a longer number was enough to deplete their willpower!

Our reflective System 2, our inner Jacob, is the part of us that's able to delay gratification and make healthy choices, knowing that what tastes good at the time may not be what's best for us in the long run. Our automatic System 1, our inner Esau, is the part of us that is impulsive and wants what it wants regardless of long-term consequences. The surprising thing to me about this experiment is how little it takes to exhaust and deplete our Jacob. It takes so much energy for us to be rational, reflective, and focused on the long term—even trying to remember seven digits is enough to allow Esau to take over.

So now we have a better sense of how System 1 relates to System 2; we see how we are elephant riders and also Rebekahs with an Esau and Jacob struggling within us. Let's turn our attention to the host of other predictable irrationalities that shape how we perceive and think about the world. Before reading on, though, you may want to have a piece of cake. After reviewing that experiment, I'm hungry for chocolate.

4

Cognitive Heuristics

Sometimes the Shortcut Isn't the Fastest Way

The good news about our dual systems is that the concept works pretty well most of the time. Most of us are able to leave a great deal of the driving to the elephant, leaving our riders to think about whatever is on our mind. But as we've already seen, the less good news about this arrangement is that problems crop up between the two systems below the level of our awareness. Through pioneering experiments, psychologists Daniel Kahneman and his longtime partner, Amos Tversky, showed that human automatic systems rely on what they term heuristics in order to process enormous amounts of data quickly. They define a heuristic as a simple rule, or shortcut, employed by the automatic part of our brain to render a judgment regarding a perception.[1] These simple patterns of thinking allow the brain to work quickly, but they also lead to predictable errors. Tversky and Kahneman focus on three heuristics: the availability heuristic, the anchoring heuristic, and the representativeness heuristic. More recently others have added the affect heuristic as a fourth.

The availability heuristic refers to the way our inner Esau makes a judgment about how likely it is a certain event will take place.[2] Availability refers to the ease with which the brain can bring an event to mind. The more

1. Gilovich, Griffin, and Kahneman, *Heuristics and Biases*, Kindle locations 145–46.
2. Kahneman, *Thinking, Fast and Slow*, 129.

often an individual has heard of an event occurring or the more emotionally charged the event the more available it is to us and the more likely it is the brain will think of such events regardless of the actual numerical rates of incidence.

A few years back our family visited Hawaii for the first time. With three small children I thought it would be a fantastic idea to cram us into a tiny submarine and go for a tour. In case you are ever tempted to do this, feel free to email me, and I will set you straight. At one point the guide asked everyone in the group whether we were afraid of sharks. A few brave people including my wife raised their hands, and he commended them for their honesty. Then, the guide asked the group who was afraid of coconuts. Everyone laughed. A disturbing image of Tom Hanks on a deserted island entered my mind. Then, the guide proceeded to tell us that we should be far more concerned about coconuts than sharks because on average every year falling coconuts kill several times more people than do sharks. I didn't believe him at the time, but it turns out there is some evidence to support this.[3]

Still, knowing this information and processing it in System 2 will not help when you are snorkeling along a reef and encounter a great barracuda for the first time. When System 1 encounters a giant silver fish with jagged teeth and terrifying dead eyes, System 1, our elephant, our inner Esau, working through an availability heuristic, will instinctively recall frightening stories or a certain John Williams' score and feel a surge of adrenaline that a coconut will simply never produce.

The significance of the availability heuristic transcends snorkeling. This heuristic means that we will overestimate the risk of clear and present dangers that appeal to our most visceral emotions, and we will underestimate the risk posed by complicated threats that develop slowly. One of the great challenges of climate change is that even people who agree that rising carbon dioxide levels pose a serious threat will never feel an equivalent sense of fear. The availability heuristic makes it easy for people to believe intellectually a situation is threatening, but without the physical sensation of fear we miss the drive to act. Our elephants just aren't motivated enough.

This lack of urgency helps explain why the decline of the mainline denominations in North America, or even the death of a single congregation, can be so challenging. Several years ago a fire gutted a neighboring church during Lent. The whole neighborhood turned out for an impromptu Lenten service the church held in their parking lot to grieve what had happened. The churches in the surrounding area pitched in to help with space and other needs. The threat to the church was so immediate and so obvious. You

---

3. Barss, "Falling Coconuts," 990–91.

could see the charred sanctuary as you drove past, and it just compelled you to respond. But when a church or denomination ages or a few people begin opting for the sacraments of latte and biscotti at the local Starbucks, the threat is so slow and complex that leaders can know there is a problem but lack the drive to make the needed changes.

This disconnect is particularly painful in the current dynamic between larger churches, many of which are still flourishing, and smaller congregations struggling to pay their pastors and maintain their buildings. There are so many incredible resources in our thriving, larger congregations that many of their leaders and participants simply don't viscerally feel the urgency leaders do in more obviously threatened contexts. My first call in ministry was to start a new congregation just outside of Austin, Texas. Before we got underway I visited a major downtown church in Atlanta, Georgia, when I was in town for a wedding. I was introduced to one of the elders in the congregation as a pastor starting a new church. He told me he didn't mean to be offensive, but he didn't understand why anyone would want to do that. "Don't we have enough churches," he said, more a statement than a question. At the time I was offended. Now I understand why, from his vantage point inside that grand sanctuary, he really couldn't see the problem of an underserved Texas exurb. Those of us seeking to address denominational decline need to spend less time complaining about blissfully unaware people and more time figuring out how to skillfully present information to these friends in such a way that they feel as motivated as we do.

The second heuristic, the anchoring heuristic, helps us make quick estimates.[4] When asked to guess how high a building is, for example, most people start with something they know—the average height of a person, say—and then adjust off of this known anchor.[5] The anchor refers to the most available known number that seems plausible to the brain. Then, comparing the unknown number, the brain adjusts the guess up or down relative to the anchor. We do this when we're trying to place an event along a timeline. If you're trying to remember when something happened, you use the anchor of a well-known date. For instance, many people remember exactly where they were when John F. Kennedy was assassinated or when 9/11 occurred. Then they place the unknown event in relation to that known anchor. Did the unknown event happen before or after the anchor? How long before or after? As with the availability heuristic, the anchoring heuristic is great when it works. But also like the availability heuristic, sometimes the anchoring heuristic can lead us astray.

4. Ariely, *Predictably Irrational*, 27.
5. Kahneman, *Thinking, Fast and Slow*, 120.

The great challenge of the anchoring heuristic is the power the anchor has over our inner Esau. Rather than steering us in the right direction, an anchor can, as the word implies, weigh us down, preventing us from moving in the right direction. Dan Ariely ran an auction once in which students were first asked to write down the last two digits of their social security numbers on a piece of paper. Then, the students bid on different objects up for grabs. You wouldn't think that priming them only with the anchor of the last two digits would sway them much. Yet, the students who wrote down higher social security numbers valued items significantly higher than students with lower numbers.[6] While a cause for concern, the truly troubling problem is the students all protested that the higher number had no impact on their decision-making. So, not only are we influenced by something as insignificant as writing down a number, but when we are influenced, we aren't even aware of it. Indeed, our sense of being rational and in control is so central to us we become defensive and offended when anyone suggests otherwise. (Dan offers some comfort if you are now wondering if you've been overpaying for everything your whole life. Have no fear. Priming effects like these are very short lived. Unless you are constantly writing down your social security number, you are probably safe.)

When I present this information to groups, at the very start I hand out a small slip of paper to each participant. I ask all participants the same question—the population of the Philippines. Given most folks I speak with live in North America and rarely, if ever, travel to that part of the world, I'm confident that hardly anyone knows the answer. What the group doesn't realize is they are split into two groups—half primed with the fact that Australia has a population of 23 million, the other half with the fact that Indonesia has a population of 247 million. The important thing here isn't the population of the Philippines—a whopping 100 million as of 2014—but the influence the anchor has on each group. To date groups primed with Indonesia estimate the population more than twice as high than groups primed with Australia. Anchors make a huge difference in how we see the world.

Anchors really help to explain why sometimes we have such a hard time communicating in the church. I remember when I was considering attending Princeton Theological Seminary. When I visited, I asked students if the seminary was more theologically liberal or conservative. About half the people I asked rolled their eyes and said it was way too conservative. The other half said it was freakishly liberal. At the time I didn't know what to make of this. Today, I'd say the communities these students called home gave a tremendous anchoring power to their perceptions. If you came out of

6. Ariely, *Predictably Irrational*, 30–31.

a conservative evangelical background, you were horrified that Old Testament professors were teaching that given the lack of archaeological evidence the walls of Jericho probably didn't fall quite as depicted in the famous story. (In one of my classes a young man was so angry about what he saw as a biblical attack that all he could do was hold up his Bible and tap it while repeating, "But this is the Bible! This is the Bible!") My liberal friends actually looked at that same example and were horrified to be going to school with an honest-to-God Bible thumper. The context out of which we come largely determines how we judge what we see. The anchoring heuristic reminds us "facts" are never just facts.

The anchoring heuristic explains why merely teaching our congregations about generational theory will never cut it. The church I serve, for example, is very much a tale of two cities, depending on whom you ask. The boomer cohort that gave birth to this community in 1983 is aging, but in comparison to many other mainline churches our community has a healthy mix of different generations. At least that's how some see it. If you spend most of your time around boomers or seniors, your contemporaries anchor your experience. In my neck of the woods when you go from the senior center to the church, you think, "My word, there are children here. This is great!" But my cohort, Generation X, and the younger Millennials see an awful lot of white hair. One young woman said to me once, "Can I ask you a personal question?" Her grim tone of voice made my heart race a little: "Um, I guess?" "Doesn't your church seem . . . really *old* to you?" Relieved, I laughed and realized our anchors caused us to see the exact same place with very different eyes. So it isn't enough to learn about other generations and their tendencies. We have to absorb the difficult truth that when we gather together across generations, we are all looking at the same places, but we won't actually see the same thing. Repeating our perceptions more slowly and more loudly won't help.

The representativeness heuristic is probably the most familiar of the three. With the representativeness heuristic our System 1 divides the world into categories and then makes decisions regarding how well an individual or event fits into that category. Normal people refer to this as stereotyping; and while there is often some truth in stereotypes, most of us know better than to trust these assumptions. Kahneman runs a thought experiment asking people how likely it is a well-dressed stranger on a subway reading the *New York Times* holds a PhD. Because our inner Esau is processing so much information quickly, he views either/or questions as being equally likely. All our poor Esau can do is compare this imaginary person on the train with preset categories to decide how likely it is that he or she fits into the PhD box. Given the attire and the fact that the person is reading the *New York*

Times, both consistent with the PhD category, Kahneman finds that most people wildly overestimate how likely it is that the person holds a PhD.[7] As with all heuristics, the gut decision, the one that feels right, is very likely the one that is wrong.

In the church I see the representativeness heuristic most when it comes to choosing congregational leaders. For six years I served on the Commission on Ministry in the Presbytery of the Cascades. In English this means I worked with churches to call their pastors and cared for them during times of conflict. One of the things that surprised me the most was what pastor nominating committees valued. Pastors tend to care about worship and theology. A lot. I suspect pastors have this inclination growing up, and then seminary pushes it to the limit. But people who serve on these pastor nominating committees are teachers, nurses, lawyers, and businesspeople— much less interested in theology and the nuances of worship. They cared very much whether they could sense the Holy Spirit's presence in the life of a potential pastor, and some of their most important questions centered around how likely a potential candidate would be to accept a call and fit in with their church culture. To gauge whether a candidate would be a good match they used the representativeness heuristic. Did this person have family in the area? They believed people with family in the area would be most likely to accept. Did this person seem like the kind of pastors they've known in the past? People who looked and sounded like other pastors were easy to accept.

At first the pastor in me recoiled at this nontheological attitude. (What? It didn't matter whether this candidate was a Barthian or a Tillichian? Barbarians!) But these committees knew that their congregations, seeing through the lens of the representativeness heuristic, would largely decide whether or not to give a new pastor a chance long before the candidate could expound on sanctification and justification. Over time I began to appreciate some of the wisdom in these concerns about culture and whether a candidate had family in the area. Although, regarding gender and race, the representativeness heuristic makes it difficult for racially homogeneous churches used to white men with beards to see women and people of color as potential pastors.

In fact, I would say the representativeness heuristic probably carries the most danger in regard to taking a chance on someone who doesn't fit the profile. One of the strongest biblical themes about vocation is how God is always going around lifting up the unlikeliest of people. God blesses an old couple, Abraham and Sarah, to become a blessing to the world. God selects

7. Kahneman, *Thinking, Fast and Slow*, 151.

the scrawny shepherd David over his older brothers: "But the LORD said to Samuel, . . . the LORD does not see as mortals see; they look on the outward appearance, but the LORD looks on the heart" (1 Sam 16:7). Jesus picked fearful disciples too often concerned with their own greatness. They fell asleep on him, betrayed him, and left him abandoned on the cross—hardly A-team material at first glance.

The representativeness heuristic is what continues to lead congregations to say they desire radical change and then call the same safe, usual suspects as pastors. These committees can't always articulate exactly why they believe a given candidate is the one whom God is calling; they just know this pastor feels right. It's why judicatory bodies keep saying it's a new day and they can't continue to do business as usual but end up tapping the same folks who have been around forever. As one wise member once said to me in his Tennessee accent, adding an extra syllable to my first name, "Kay-en, the same people doing the same things are gonna get the same results. We gotta mix it up!" I say all this not to deride our congregations or our judicatory bodies. They face extraordinarily challenging difficulties today, and in many cases leaders are really trying hard to find new faces. The representativeness heuristic, however, means trying hard isn't enough. It requires conscious effort to seek out candidates who may not always look like pastors have in the past but may bring exactly the qualities needed for this new season.

Finally, we have the affect heuristic. Affect here refers to emotion. Whether we are mad, sad, glad, or afraid (the only four emotions we were allowed to discuss when I endured the peculiar joy of Clinical Pastoral Education) influences how we think and evaluate information. Intense emotional states can have an enormous impact on human cognition. While this idea may seem like common sense, what the affect heuristic adds to our understanding is how little knowledge we have of our motives when we move from one emotional state to another or of the impact this shifting can have on our decision-making. Experimental evidence demonstrates what behavioralists refer to as an "empathy gap"—not only do we make different decisions when placed in highly emotionally charged situations, but we can't predict or sometimes even recall these decisions when in a less emotional state.

For example, in a study with phenomenal value for moral decision-making and public health, Dan Ariely asked young men a series of questions regarding sexual decision-making: questions about condom use and whether participants would consider having sex with someone they do not know well. The men answered these questions first on a computer in an office. There was nothing interesting about the setup. Other than the questions, Ariely and his peers created the coldest state they could. Then, in

another setting the men were asked to masturbate while looking at sexu-
alized images and answer the same questions.[8] (The board that approves
human research at Dan's graduate school, the Massachusetts Institute of
Technology, blanched at this experiment. Dan had to go all the way to the
University of California, Berkeley before he received permission to run the
study. I'll let you decide what that says about the two institutions.)

Not surprisingly, the men were far less risk averse in the hot state.
Who couldn't guess that? What was absolutely shocking about the study,
though, was the response of the participants later when they viewed their
answers recorded in that hot state. The young men expressed surprise at
their responses. Some of the men even angrily denied that they could have
answered some of the questions in the way they did. It was as if the men in
one state simply could not understand the person they became in another.[9]
It was like Dr. Jekyll waking in the morning with no memory of Mr. Hyde's
troubling behavior just the night before.

Anyone who has been a pastor or worked with human beings for any
period of time has encountered the affect heuristic. When strongly moved
about a concern, a person may seem to become someone else entirely. A
normally calm and kind person can become downright vicious when discussing something deeply threatening such as race, sexuality, or economic
justice. I certainly have experienced emotionally charged moments in which
I have not been my best self. In those times I might have marshaled logical-
sounding arguments and quoted theologians and the Scriptures, but given
the affect heuristic I can admit in hindsight there was very little rational
thought happening.

The affect heuristic is why it is so crucial in heated situations for leaders to know when not to make a decision and to create space for prayer and
silence. These practices are easy to say but hard to do. When emotions run
high and create anxiety, leaders often just want to make a decision quickly
to avoid the crucible of conflict. Especially when decision-makers believe
that the organization may miss an opportunity by not making a quick decision, they can feel pressure to reach an immediate resolution. In *Wait*, legal
scholar Frank Partnoy notes that although humans crave the speed of fast
decision-making, our bodies are not geared to make complicated decisions
quickly. Human brains, according to Partnoy, are good at making some fast
decisions. Because humans evolved on the African savannah, the human
brain is expert at deciding instantaneously whether a lion is going to attack;

8. Ariely, *Predictably Irrational*, 121.

9. Ibid., 127.

these same brains are poor at making quick decisions when it comes to complicated, interrelated social situations.[10]

Some well-known leaders are famous for taking their time to make decisions. Warren Buffett spends a great deal of time studying companies that interest him but hardly ever makes trades, humorously describing his philosophy this way: "Lethargy bordering on sloth remains the cornerstone of our investment style."[11] This unusually deliberative style has helped him avoid major catastrophes like the dot-com implosion and anything related to subprime mortgage-backed securities. Former president of USC and author of *The Contrarian's Guide to Leadership* Steve Sample lives by two rules when it comes to decisions: "1. Never make a decision yourself that can reasonably be delegated to a lieutenant. 2. Never make a decision today that can reasonably be put off to tomorrow."[12] Sample claims many people who want to appear decisive and engaged just start wading into complicated situations, making decisions before they really understand what is going on.

The good news for the church is that what is contrarian wisdom in Sample's sphere falls smack dab in our wheelhouse. Yale Divinity School professor Christopher Beeley, in *Leading God's People*, urges church leaders to remember that the most practical disciplines they can observe are not staying constantly busy and making fast decisions but attending to personal holiness, prayer, and the study of the Scriptures, all of which slow down the decision-making process. Beeley credits Gregory of Nyssa with this metaphor for grace-filled (as opposed to spiritually empty) church leaders: "What does it matter how magnificent the aqueduct is for those who are thirsty, if there is no water in it? What the church needs is fresh spring water, even if it flows through a wooden pipe."[13]

In every case, and perhaps especially when they feel behind and pressured to vote, it is leaders' most important responsibility to remain prayerful and reflective, slow to render judgments and quick to recognize that God's ways are not always immediately clear. Leaders should not view the time that deliberative bodies take to pray and read the Scriptures together as tangential to the work of the body; often this spiritual work plays the very practical role of giving bodies the room they need to mitigate the impact of the affect heuristic.

---

10. Partnoy, *Wait*, 68.
11. Buffett, "Chairman's Letter," subhead Marketable Securities, para. 2.
12. Sample, *Contrarian's Guide to Leadership*, 71–72.
13. Beeley, *Leading God's People*, 29.

5

Cognitive Biases
Our Blind Spots

*B*ias is a loaded word. None of us like to think of ourselves as biased. But given what you now know about heuristics, you may have the sinking feeling that all of us are more biased than we imagine. Many different kinds of bias exist, but not all of them are examples of cognitive bias. First, we will look at two common kinds of bias—motivational bias and racial (or group) bias—and understand how they differ from cognitive bias. Then, we'll walk through several cognitive biases and see how they relate to church leadership.

Motivational bias means we respond to incentives. When you are choosing a financial advisor, for instance, a wise friend might tell you it is prudent to pick someone who doesn't receive a commission on the products they sell. We know that even the nicest salesperson, especially if they are in a financial bind, might exaggerate the merits of a product that generates the highest commission. The saying *caveat emptor*, let the buyer beware, has been around since Roman times, and I imagine it's older than that. Motivational bias is relatively easy to deal with because of how easy it is to spot. We understand rational self-interest and can counter this bias easily by avoiding conflicts of interest. The great thing about motivational bias is that it is situational. It isn't something built into us, as it were, but only related to our situation. Change the situation, erase the bias.

Another kind of bias that comes up often is bias toward a particular group of people based on some attribute they share—like race. All of us walk around perceiving the world through the largely unconscious filters of race and gender bias. I was particularly struck by the polling done after the events of Ferguson, Missouri, in 2014. In a poll reported in the *New York Times*, 62 percent of blacks believed Officer Darren Wilson was at fault in the shooting death of Michael Brown in comparison with only 22 percent of whites.[1] One of the deep challenges of racial bias is that two groups of people can see the same images and examine the same evidence but arrive at opposing conclusions, as if seeing something completely different. Often when we are confused or uncertain, we just try to collect more information in the hope that a clearer picture will emerge. This kind of bias means that more information will only reinforce the original view.

If you are a skeptic who believes you are somehow immune from such bias, I urge you to go online and participate in Project Implicit, a joint effort by researchers at Harvard, the University of Washington, and the University of Virginia. Project Implicit offers implicit association tests to determine how strongly you associate certain groups with positive or negative identity. The great thing about Project Implicit is how many tests they offer. If you wind up with little bias toward people based on their skin tone, not to worry. You can test yourself with regard to women in the workplace or Muslims or body size. It may be unsettling to discover you show preference for one group over another, but the belief behind the test is that knowing this bias can help us question our judgments in helpful ways.

While more challenging than motivational bias, the kinds of bias the implicit association test examines are largely learned behaviors. There is truth to the Rodgers and Hammerstein song "You've Got to Be Carefully Taught" that before we're seven or eight we have to be taught to hate. And learned behavior can be unlearned. People who show bias toward one group of people can, over time, unlearn this behavior and become more neutral. The incredible changes regarding attitudes toward homosexuality are a case in point. While bias obviously continues to exist, no one can deny profound changes have taken place in cultural receptivity toward gay and lesbian people in the last forty years. Biases toward groups can change. Like motivational bias, group bias is not some kind of fundamental aspect of our nature.

But unlike motivational bias and group bias, cognitive biases are blind spots that are hardwired into us. We can adjust for these blind spots, but we

1. Wines, "Reaction to Ferguson Decision," para. 5.

can't get rid of them. In theological terms, God created us with cognitive biases. The best way to understand cognitive biases is to use a visual analogy. All the way back in 1889 sociologist Franz Carl Müller-Lyer created an optical illusion using a set of stylized arrows. While the lines were all the same length, Müller-Lyer could make the lines appear longer or shorter simply by changing the orientation of the arrows on the ends, which pointed either toward or away from the center. Our inner Jacob, our System 2, understands that the lines are all the same length. The arrows connected to the ends of the lines, on the other hand, always sway our inner Esau, our System 1. No matter how long you stare at this illusion your reflective inner Jacob will just never be able to persuade your inner Esau. Even when we know something intellectually, our bodies may remain unconvinced—in this case the lines will always appear to be different lengths.

Cognitive biases are like these lines and arrows: blind spots that are always with us because of how the two parts of our cognition system communicate with one another. While we can't change the fact that we have these biases, we can account for them and make adjustments accordingly. But the best we can hope for by learning about these biases and adjusting for them is to be wrong less often. The lists of cognitive biases is voluminous and continues to grow, but four rise to the top in terms of their impact and relevance for church leaders. In this chapter we will look at confirmation bias, loss aversion bias, status quo bias, and optimism bias.

Confirmation bias is the habit of noticing information that affirms the beliefs people already hold and discounts information that challenges them. In *Decisive*, Chip and Dan Heath cite a study of smokers done back in the 1960s. Smokers were far more likely to express interest in reading stories in the newspaper headlined "Smoking Does Not Lead to Lung Cancer" than they were stories headlined "Smoking Leads to Lung Cancer."[2] Nonsmokers were willing to hear both sides, but smokers protected themselves by avoiding stories that would be challenging, even painful, to read. The truly concerning aspect of confirmation bias is that the smokers in the study thought of themselves as entirely rational. After all, they could cite scientific studies to support their view. They did have seemingly confirming factual evidence. But just as walking out onto a snow cornice gives us an illusion of safety, confirmation bias makes us feel as if we're on solid ground even when there's nothing but a long way down beneath our feet.

Thanks to cable news, the Internet, and confirmation bias, now it is easier than ever for us to surround ourselves with multiple voices offering the same opinion, giving us the happy illusion of being well informed. Dan

2. Heath and Heath, *Decisive*, Kindle locations 185–87.

Lovallo, a professor and researcher of decision-making, states, "Confirmation bias is probably the single biggest problem . . . because even the most sophisticated people get it wrong. People go out and they're collecting the data, and they don't realize they're cooking the books."[3]

Without using the language of confirmation bias, in his essay "Biblical Authority" Walter Brueggemann describes the mechanism of confirmation bias that afflicts us when we approach theological and biblical reflection:

> We are seldom aware of or honest about the ways in which our work is shot through with distorting vested interests. But it is so, whether we know it or not. There is no interpretation of scripture (nor of anything else) that is unaffected by the passions, convictions and perceptions of the interpreter. Ideology is the self-deceiving practice of taking a part for the whole, of taking "my truth" for the truth, of palming off the particular as a universal. It is so already in the text of scripture itself, as current scholarship makes clear, because the spirit-given text is given us by and through human authors. It is so because spirit-filled interpretation is given us by and through bodied authors who must make their way in the world—and in making our way, we humans do not see so clearly or love so dearly or follow so nearly as we might imagine.[4]

Our preconceptions color what we notice in the Scriptures and in the theological tradition. Only aware of what we see and blind to what we're overlooking, it is all too easy to believe that our theological position is reasoned and grounded while an opposing perspective is merely emotional and based on nothing more than wishful fantasy.

At least two elements are required for leaders to reduce the effects of confirmation bias: they must accept that confirmation bias afflicts them even when they are not aware of it, and they need to seek out voices who will raise objections to proposed decisions. Congregational leaders may have an advantage over business leaders when it comes to accepting that they are affected by confirmation bias. When faced with discerning God's will for their congregation, leaders formed by a biblical faith should believe to some degree that God's ways are not always their ways. Steeping themselves in the scriptural tradition can help leaders accept that even ideas about which they feel strongly may not be exactly what God, prompting through the Holy Spirit, desires for their congregation. Even the best idea any leader can articulate will not exhaust God's plan for a people.

3. Ibid., Kindle locations 194–96.
4. Brueggemann, "Biblical Authority," 18.

And yet, as much as congregational leaders may agree that they cannot perfectly articulate God's plan, which should allow for some room to push on and question any and all proposals, another factor of congregational life makes this room for examination perhaps more difficult than it is in the business world. In a volunteer organization few people show up to meetings to experience emotional discomfort, a discomfort that many experience both in giving and in receiving criticism. Because of the challenging nature of pushing against the confirmation bias, the development of an institutional practice to push against it seems even more important.

One practice that checks confirmation bias can even be traced back to the church itself: the role of a formal devil's advocate. Up until the papacy of Pope John Paul II the Roman Catholic Church acknowledged the importance of the devil's advocate, a leader whose role was to bring to light disconfirming evidence in the canonization process. It is easy to see why the church would need to institutionalize such a role. Human beings on their own find it difficult to speak against people many view as saints. However, when it is an individual's role to promote the faith (from *Promotor Fidei*, the official title of this office) by playing a critical and questioning role, the office takes the personal conflict away. It is no surprise that since this role was abolished, the number of saints canonized by the church has soared.[5] While it's possible people became suddenly more holy in the twentieth century, call me a skeptic. Leadership teams in the church would be wise when considering major decisions to appoint one or two people on the board to play the role of promoters of the faith and, whether they personally agree or disagree with a possibility, bring to light as much strategic thinking and data as possible that would show why an idea may not be good for the institution.

The second major cognitive bias we need to understand is loss aversion bias. Loss aversion, simply put, refers to the greater pain we feel over losing something relative to the positive feelings we experience in gaining it.[6] In other words, it really hurts to lose stuff. Through experimentation theorists demonstrate that the pain of losing something is double the experience of gaining the same thing.[7] Given that a perfectly rational person should value equivalent gain and loss equally, loss aversion bias helps us understand why people hold on to underperforming investments, why we stay in bad relationships, and why change is so hard. Anecdotally, every pastor knows by experience how much easier it is to start something new at a congregation than it is to shut a program down. Almost all congregations,

---

5. Heath and Heath, *Decisive*, Kindle location 1494.

6. Ariely, *Upside of Irrationality*, Kindle locations 423–24.

7. Kahneman, Knetsch, and Thaler, "Anomalies," 200.

vulnerable to loss avoidance and reluctant to change, prefer starting a new ministry to ending a cherished tradition even though only a few seem to care about it any longer.

Indeed, congregations may be the *most sensitive* organizations to loss aversion. Even when they agree with a decision resulting in good changes, church participants may still feel some pain because every change represents difference, which means loss. In *Open Secrets* Richard Lischer painfully and beautifully describes the education he received in the first parish he served when he attempted to remove the American flag from the sanctuary. He writes, "I should have known not to try to remove the American flag from the chancel. To me, the national flag represented an intrusion into the sacred space of the congregation, an obvious symbol of civil religion."[8] Predictably, the young pastor met a brick wall in the form of a resistant congregation. Unpredictably, Lischer was gifted with the realization that his understanding of what the flag symbolized was neither the only understanding possible nor even, perhaps, the deepest understanding. An older parishioner, Don Semanns, clarified the issue by simply telling a story about receiving the news of his uncle's death during World War I. The motion was tabled, and Lischer came to a realization: "The flag, as it turned out, did not represent civil religion or any other abstraction, not, at least, for my congregation. It simply told a story that everyone wanted to remember but found too sorrowful to repeat."[9] At first Lischer was speaking only to the tiny elephant riders of the congregation by making intellectual, theological points about the flag. Semanns helped Lischer understand the elephants underneath the riders who were emotionally invested in the story associated with the flag.

It is true, of course, that loss and change are a part of life. Sometimes a leader can't escape this fact. But too often we rely on truisms about change to avoid the hard work of thinking through creative alternatives. A leader who can find ways to avoid triggering the loss aversion bias can escape major headaches. I am grateful to Professor James F. Kay of Princeton Theological Seminary, who passed along a helpful suggestion for a gender-inclusive baptismal formula consistent with the tradition. He recommended to our class that pastors avoid the common solution of substituting Creator, Redeemer, and Sustainer for Father, Son, and Holy Spirit. Not only is this substitution theologically problematic, as the identity of the one God becomes merely three different job descriptions, but it also creates needless loss by removing the familiar and meaningful language of God as Father. Rather, Kay suggested, consider this formula: "I baptize you in the name of God the

8. Lischer, *Open Secrets*, 89.
9. Ibid., 90.

Father, Son, and Holy Spirit. One God: Mother of us all." While maternal language may not fly in every congregation, I have never received negative feedback when using this added language. Finding ways to add rather than take away language has helped the congregations I serve to be more faithful and more inclusive.

A third bias, status quo bias, describes our tendency to accept default settings around us. When we are pressed for time or encountering a complicated new setting, we are especially at risk for accepting options as they are presented. Status quo bias can create massive challenges involving incredibly important choices like organ donation and retirement savings. Indeed, when it comes to organ donation, status quo bias is quite literally a matter of life and death. The United Kingdom and the Netherlands have organ donation rates of only 17.7 percent and 27.5 percent, respectively, while Belgium and France boast rates of 98 percent and 99.91 percent. While many put forth cultural or religious explanations, the truth is that countries with low organ donation rates require drivers to opt in to organ donation at the Department of Motor Vehicles (DMV).[10] The default choice is non-donation. However, in the countries where the DMV default is set to donation, countries see nearly 100 percent rates of participation.

Cass Sunstein and Richard Thaler lamented a similar problem at the University of Chicago where they teach. Every year in November, when the open enrollment period began, university employees made decisions about health insurance and retirement. Every year the default setting went back to zero. Even if they had been participating in the 401(k) plan, every November their choice reverted to nonparticipation; they had to consciously choose to opt in each year. The effects were predictably abysmal. Many busy professionals assumed they were saving for their future when in fact they were not. Thanks to Sunstein and Thaler, who presented this information to the administrative officers of the University of Chicago, the institution changed its policy.[11] Now, rather than resetting to zero, the choice made the previous year is the default setting for the next plan year. Employees are always free to opt out, but now it is nonparticipation that requires an active choice.

Status quo bias plays a powerful, hidden role in the life of every congregation. If individuals are particularly prone to accept defaults when they are emotionally vulnerable and encountering complicated situations that are new to them, churches are almost perfectly designed for status quo bias. Many people who show up on Sunday, particularly those who are there for

10. Johnson and Goldstein, "Do Defaults Save Lives?," 1338.

11. Thaler and Sunstein, *Nudge*, 13.

the first time, already feel uncomfortable in a new environment and possess little sense for the complicated theological and polity considerations that have gone into shaping how individual congregations practice worship, what rules govern church membership, and how the church makes decisions. Pastors need to watch out for status quo bias even more when they care for people at the crucial moments of life: baptisms, weddings, and funerals.

I remember well when one of the pillars of the congregation died suddenly. The family was shocked and grieving when the hospital staff gently informed them that they needed to make a decision about what to do with the body. And they needed to make the decision by the end of the day. This family had never experienced losing anyone close to them before. The hospital staff gave them a list of funeral homes, but the family members just stared at it. They didn't know the wishes of their family member and had never heard of any of these funeral homes. They relied on me as their pastor to lead them. After offering them my personal experience with several of the funeral homes, they landed on one. Later we met with the director, who was lovely but was also running a business. The information she handed them offered the most expensive option first. Knowing what you know about the anchoring heuristic, you understand how powerful the first number you see can be. The family members were all extremely uncomfortable talking about the prices of these options. One of them said at one point that he didn't want to feel like he was shopping for a car. These are the very moments when we are most likely to be swayed by status quo bias and choose the default—whatever is offered first. It is imperative at such moments for pastors to suggest a course of action—in this case, asking the funeral director to step out of the room so that the family can think or have time to call other funeral homes to make sure they are getting a price that's fair. Most families in the midst of life crises are so fragile; they absolutely need someone who cares about them to make sure they aren't allowing status quo bias to lead them in directions that seem right at the time but that they will regret later.

A fourth important bias for leaders to know about is the optimism bias. Ironically, despite all the evidence of human limitation, the optimism bias—the sense that *others* might be biased, but *we* are not—is strong in us. Sunstein and Thaler humorously remark that when it comes to judging one's own performance, we are all from Lake Wobegon: we see ourselves as above average.[12] In one study, 90 percent of drivers believed they were above average in their driving abilities, and in another study at a large college 94

12. Ibid., 32.

percent of professors believed they were above average teachers, stretching the meaning of average far beyond the breaking point.[13]

The optimism bias carries an important message to decision-makers in two ways. First, the optimism bias stands as a warning to decision-makers not to trust in rosy feelings regarding plans and decisions. Decision-makers should anticipate that even when they feel a strong intuitive sense that they are right, there may be no good reason for this internal sense of well-being. In his famous expert study, management and psychology professor Philip Tetlock found that when experts expressed 100 percent confidence in an opinion, they turned out to be wrong 23 percent of the time. It is one thing to be wrong when you do not feel certain about an answer, but to feel absolutely certain you are right and still be wrong nearly one out of four times is humbling indeed.

A second side to the optimism bias has to do with messaging. Leaders are not the only people affected by the optimism bias. The people whom leaders serve also believe their judgment to be above average. Leaders who fail to exercise caution when challenging the optimism bias will suffer the consequences. Jimmy Carter's 1979 address to the American people, popularly referred to as the malaise speech, offers leaders a grim warning in this regard. People often respond to negativity by tuning the message (and the messenger) out.

On a more positive note leaders who frame messaging in light of the optimism bias will communicate their ideas with great effectiveness. Psychologist Robert Cialdini led a study in the Petrified Forest National Park to determine the most effective signage for reducing the incidence of people removing petrified wood from the park.[14] The study compared the effectiveness of signs that emphasized a negative message versus a positive one. Negative signs expressed how poor behavior had deleterious effects on the park; positive signs emphasized how individual compliance made a difference. Cialdini theorized that the positive messaging would be more effective, and his hypothesis proved correct.

Church leaders should think twice before attempting to shame congregations into action through negative messaging; it is likely that they may achieve exactly the opposite of what they intend. How many times have you witnessed a speaker get up and tell a congregation that no one has signed up to help with the children's program or not enough people have volunteered to help with the mission trip? The leader who is familiar with optimism bias understands that a negative speaker is unwittingly telling the

13. Ibid.

14. Kallgren, Reno, and Cialdini, "Focus Theory of Normative Conduct," 1002.

whole congregation that no one else has signed up for those things so they shouldn't either. Showcasing people who have had great experiences and can speak from their passion is far more likely to generate interest. Even if they know a ministry opportunity may be difficult and time-consuming, people will participate if they think that the result will be positive and that others will be walking with them.

Finally, framing bias, more commonly known as framing effects, refers to the fact that how a choice is presented to an individual can significantly impact what an individual chooses. Amos Tversky and Daniel Kahneman tested the framing effect by asking two groups of doctors to make a choice regarding a hypothetical medical procedure. The information they used with both groups was numerically equivalent, but they framed the question for the first group using a survival frame and for the second group using a mortality frame. The choice for both groups of doctors was the same: surgery or radiation. Tversky and Kahneman told the first group that of 100 people having surgery 90 lived through the postoperative period, 68 were alive at the end of the first year, and 34 were alive at the end of five years. Of 100 people having radiation therapy all lived through the treatment, 77 were alive at the end of one year, and 22 were alive at the end of five years.

In the mortality frame group the numerical information was exactly the same, but Tversky and Kahneman inverted the numbers to describe how many patients died. So, of 100 patients having surgery, 10 died in the postoperative period, 32 were dead at the end of the first year, and 66 were dead after five years. The numbers were equally reversed for the radiation choice in the mortality frame. The data shared was exactly the same. Rationally, the doctors should make similar decisions about treatment under both conditions. But focusing on the number of those who lived versus those who died made an enormous difference; doctors presented with the mortality frame preferred radiation, the more risk-averse choice, to surgery far more often.[15]

Leaders intuitively know that how we frame decisions makes an enormous difference in terms of how deliberative bodies and congregations choose. On the one hand, knowing more about framing can help leaders cast information about decisions in the best possible light. All deliberative bodies, for instance, want to be the best stewards of congregational money. Folks want to save money, but at the same time they want to avoid being cheap. When our congregation purchased an automated external defibrillator a few years ago, our parish nurse came to me with a machine she highly recommended. My guidance to her was to give our deliberative body, in our polity called a session, at least one good but more expensive option and

15. Tversky and Kahneman, "Rational Choice," S254.

one viable but less expensive option. Although it was possible our session would vote for one of the less preferable machines, framing the decision with the parish nurse's choice in the middle put the model she believed was the strongest fit for the congregation in the best possible light.

On the other hand, it should go without saying that leaders should never use framing effects to manipulate deliberative bodies toward poor choices. Henry Kissinger remembers using what amounts to a manipulative technique by giving President Richard Nixon three policy choices: nuclear war, continuing with the present policy (Kissinger's preferred choice), and surrender.[16] Such framing constitutes fake options that don't serve the body well. Leaders who consistently use framing to manipulate will create counterproductive ill will in the long run.

These biases represent just the tip of the iceberg. Given the prevalence of cognitive biases in our human lives, the Christian leader has to wonder about Jesus. For those who follow after the way of Jesus, everything hangs on how we understand him. Traditionally, Christians have proclaimed Jesus to be fully divine and fully human—yet also perfect. Was Jesus somehow immune from these cognitive biases, or in his humanity did Jesus experience these limitations, too?

---

16. Heath and Heath, *Decisive*, Kindle location 939.

6

The Irrational Jesus Lives

Do we really believe Jesus is fully human? And if we do, what do we mean by fully human? Even though here and there I hear people acknowledge Jesus' full humanity, most of the time in the church when we talk about Jesus we are long on his divinity and very short indeed on his humanity. And when we do talk about his humanity, it's through such a stained-glass lens the picture we see feels about as real as a Hollywood action hero. This is a problem. When we overemphasize Jesus' divinity, we betray the surprising and radical orthodox claim that Christ is mysteriously fully human and fully divine, which is indeed a problem for those who care about tradition and our connection with our grandmothers and grandfathers in the faith. And when we don't have language to describe Jesus' humanity, we wind up making tortured interpretations of the Scriptures in the attempt to explain away Jesus' less heroic moments.

I believe in a predictably irrational Jesus. By describing Jesus as predictably irrational, I'm arguing that the evangelists offer portraits of Jesus honest enough to show the presence of powerful emotion, a limited ability to foresee the future, physical limitation, and a remarkable lack of self-interest. I'm not saying Jesus is entirely unhinged. But in his full humanity, Jesus is limited by time and place and by imperfect information, and he experiences the same heuristic shortcuts and predictable blind spots as the rest of us. An irrational Jesus may sound like bad news, but it isn't. While Jesus is as constrained by his humanity as we are, it isn't all negative. In line with

Dan Ariely's view of irrationality as having an upside, I will show that the same irrational humanity that causes Jesus to make mistakes and regrettable statements is the same irrational humanity that generates his compassion and hunger for justice.

To give us a clear outline of where we're headed, irrationality in Jesus' life falls into four major categories: the presence of strong emotion in Jesus' life, the limited knowledge Jesus possesses, the mistakes Jesus makes in the Gospels, and the adaptive behaviors Jesus employs that are consistent with the actions behavioral theorists would expect of humans subject to cognitive limitations. The self-emptying that marks the teachings of Jesus and his sacrificial death and joyous resurrection merit their own discussion in the next chapter.

Jesus was an emotional guy. Remember our friend the affect heuristic? According to the affect heuristic, strong emotions not only shape how we think about the world, but these emotions even color the facts we see in the first place. To revisit the language of Sunstein and Thaler, Jesus is nothing like a cool, Mr. Spockesque econ gliding through Palestine untouched by the world around him. In two of the Gospels, Matthew and John, Jesus starts out in ministry deeply shaped by strong feeling. In Matthew, following Jesus' baptism, the Holy Spirit hurls him into the wilderness to be tested by Satan. While Mark simply acknowledges this account and Luke portrays Jesus in a more rational and philosophical mode, Matthew shows Jesus forcefully denouncing the devil after the third temptation—the temptation to rule all the kingdoms of the world: "Away with you, Satan! for it is written, 'Worship the Lord your God, and serve only him'" (4:10). While the reader has no access to Jesus' tone and volume, it is hard not to feel a sense of anger and passion in Jesus' words.

Even better evidence for Jesus' anger comes from the Gospel of John. While the cleansing of the temple occurs toward the end of the synoptic accounts, after Jesus has entered Jerusalem, the writer of John's Gospel places the cleansing of the temple at the beginning of Jesus' ministry. In John 2 Jesus makes a whip of cords to forcefully expel those exchanging idolatrous Roman coinage for acceptable Hebrew currency. However long it took him to weave this cord Jesus' anger only grew more intense. John shows Jesus turning over tables and denouncing the sellers of doves for making his Father's house into a marketplace. The disciples remark on Jesus' zeal, a word connoting powerful emotion indeed. A man who turns over tables and chases people out with a whip is an emotional man.

Strong emotion does not just mark the beginning of Jesus' ministry, but constantly colors it. The most famous example of Jesus' emotion is also the shortest; it is the verse every child volunteers to memorize because of its brevity: "Jesus began to weep" (John 11:35). But this short verse is just the tip of the iceberg. Several times different evangelists write that Jesus is filled with pity or is moved by pity. In Matthew 9:36, when Jesus looks at the crowds gathering around him, he sees they are like sheep without a shepherd and is moved by pity for them. Later in Matthew, Jesus heals two blind men: "Moved with compassion, Jesus touched their eyes" (20:34). Here the Greek is vital for understanding the emotional power behind these verses. The word for "moved by pity" is *splagchnizomai*, a visceral, Homeric word meaning that Jesus was literally moved in his "inward parts or entrails."[1] We still use terms like "gut feeling" to describe the deep connection between our bodies and feelings. When Jesus sees these men, he isn't having some disembodied thought about how nice it would be to help them. Something inside of him demands that he respond.

We see even more evidence for strong emotion toward the end of Jesus' life. While Luke and John mute the affect in the suffering and crucifixion narratives, Matthew and Mark both describe Christ as suffering agony in the garden of Gethsemane. Matthew describes Jesus as being "grieved and agitated" (26:37) and depicts him going back and forth with God over his impending death. Matthew's Jesus even sounds like a behavioral theorist when he says to the disciples, "The spirit indeed is willing, but the flesh is weak" (26:41). On the cross Jesus cries out, "My God, my God, why have you forsaken me?" (Matt 27:46). One commentator argues that because Jesus was quoting Psalm 22, which ends as a call to trust the Lord, his cry of dereliction was not tortured but hopeful.[2] But given the strong presence of emotion throughout Jesus' life, this interpretation seems strained at best. The Jesus we see in the Gospels is not a man with total equanimity breezing through ministry but a passionately emotional man given to deep compassion, blistering anger, and sorrowful tears.

A second fundamental component of Jesus' irrationality is his lack of perfect knowledge. With perfect knowledge rational agents can sort through every option to make the best possible decision, but, as behavioralists note, actual humans simply do not have access to all the information they need, and even if they did would not be able to process it perfectly due to their cognitive limitations. Jesus, as a fully human person, manifests this imperfect knowledge in two ways: first, in being limited by the particularity of enculturation; and second, in making mistakes, which a plain reading of the text shows. It is evident through what he does not say that Jesus was indelibly shaped by the times in which he lived: Jesus' humanity was bound

1. Bauer, *Greek-English Lexicon*, 763.
2. Marcus, *Way of the* Lord, 177–82.

by particularity; he lived in a particular time and a particular place. Second, the Gospels leave a record of Jesus openly, if rarely, admitting to lack of knowledge; we will look at these instances of limited knowledge in conjunction with the mistakes Jesus makes.

Jesus was a man of his time; he was shaped by the history, geography, language, and culture of first-century Palestine. What the writers of the Reformed Confession of 1967 say of the evangelists is true also of Jesus: he was "conditioned by the language, thought forms, and . . . views of life, history, and the cosmos which were then current."[3] Many attempts to understand the first-century Jesus suffer from projecting the worldview of the author, leading to the famous observation made by nineteenth-century theologian George Tyrrell that the search for the historical Jesus amounts to little but scholars staring into a deep well only to find their own reflection.[4] However, contemporary New Testament scholars have given far more attention to the ways in which Jesus' context shaped him. Amy-Jill Levine writes, "Jesus of Nazareth dressed like a Jew, prayed like a Jew (and most likely in Aramaic), instructed other Jews on how best to live according to the commandments given by God to Moses, taught like a Jew, argued like a Jew with other Jews, and died like thousands of other Jews on a Roman cross."[5] More specifically, Luke Timothy Johnson asserts that the Jewish apocalyptic worldview of the first century profoundly shaped Jesus.[6] Notably, E. P. Sanders (among others) has written extensively that the way to understand Jesus best is to place him within the first-century worldview: Jesus articulated and believed in cosmic dualism as well as an apocalypse, or revelatory moment, that would usher in an imminent end to the age in which he was living.[7] This apocalyptic conceptual framework thoroughly marked and shaped Jesus' humanity.

Is this enculturation limiting? To the extent that Jesus in his humanity could think of and speak of the world only in the thought forms and language of his day, this enculturation is, by definition, limiting. To paraphrase writer Derek Sivers' clever story: enculturation is like one fish asking another fish, "How's the water?" and the second saying, "Water? What's water?"[8] Jesus, at least in his humanity, was bound as all human beings are by particularity. Jesus didn't walk around somehow above the times; he was a real human being who lived in a certain place at a certain time. This par-

---

3. "Confession of 1967," 9.29.

4. Tyrrell, *Christianity at the Crossroads*, 44.

5. Levine, *Misunderstood Jew*, 51.

6. Johnson, *Writings of New Testament*, 48.

7. Sanders, *Historical Figure of Jesus*, 95.

8. Sivers, "Fish Don't Know," para. 2.

ticularity, this time and place, shaped Jesus as it does us all. Anyone with an ounce of self-awareness today knows that growing up in a privileged North American context compared to growing up in a postcolonial, post-genocide Rwanda, for instance, changes how we hear and understand the Scriptures and the world around us. One context isn't necessarily better or worse than the other, but they are different. It's time we acknowledge that the time and place in which Jesus grew up shaped him in profound ways.

Even more radical than a Jesus shaped by the culture of his time are the moments when Jesus appears, by a plain reading of the text, to make mistakes. Again, it is what we would expect of a fully human, predictably irrational person, but many of us stop short when it comes to Jesus. But in at least two clear instances Jesus admits to not possessing perfect knowledge. The author of Mark describes a woman who pushes through the crowd to touch the hem of Jesus' garment, believing that by doing so she will be healed. As so often is the case in Mark, something happens immediately. Mark writes that power flows from Jesus, resulting in the woman's healing. What is interesting in this discussion is that Jesus is unaware of exactly what happens. Sensing that power has left him, Jesus scans the crowd; he is unsure who it is that came forward. "Who touched my clothes?" he asks the disciples. The disciples, depicted by Mark as not especially bright, are no help to Jesus. "You see the crowd pressing in on you," they protest. "How can you say, 'Who touched me?'" (Mark 5:25–34).

You might say that this example seems small and picky. And I agree that Jesus' knowledge of what happens to him minute by minute may not seem that important. Perhaps, you might say, it's more significant that Jesus has perfect knowledge of truly significant events. Well, few things could be more important, especially to a man with an apocalyptic eschatology, than knowledge regarding the coming of the kingdom. However, in both Mark's little apocalypse and in Matthew's Gospel, Jesus confesses to his disciples that he does not know exactly when the Son of Man will come: "But about that day or hour no one knows, neither the angels in heaven, nor the Son, but only the Father" (Mark 13:32). Jesus does not tell the disciples that he possesses this information but has chosen not to share it with them. Jesus says the Son simply does not know when this time will take place. In his full humanity even Jesus himself is not entirely clear about the plan. He just doesn't know.

Another well-known mistake Jesus makes is his claim that the mustard seed is the smallest of seeds. Clever plant lovers jump out of their chairs to point out that mustard seeds are not, in fact, the most diminutive seeds in the world. Apologists, anxious to defend Jesus, point out that Jesus was telling a parable rather than giving a lecture in botany.[9] Other Jesus defenders cite first-century sources to confirm that mustard seeds were proverbially believed to be the smallest, suggesting that while Jesus himself may have known the truth, he was speaking in a way his limited contemporaries would understand.[10] Seeing Jesus as fully human, shaped by all the forces that impact us, helps us avoid such exegetical contortions that really seem pretty unimportant to most people outside of the church. A behavioral Christology, a way of understanding Jesus influenced by behavioral theory, can admit that Jesus, in his humanity, was indeed limited in his knowledge of botany and then move on untroubled, able to focus more on the meaning of the parable than on the question of Jesus' mistake.

But mistakes occur that we cannot attribute to Jesus' human knowledge simply being bound by his time. In Mark 2:24 the Pharisees accuse Jesus of breaking Sabbath laws when he and his disciples eat grain they picked along a field as they traveled. Jesus, likening himself to David, reminds his interlocutors that the great king himself went into the temple and ate the loaves of offering when Abiathar was high priest. The only problem with this defense is that Abiathar was not high priest when David ransacked the temple for the Hebrew equivalent of the communion bread. In 1 Samuel 21:1 we learn that David took the bread when Ahimilech, Abiathar's father, was priest rather than Abiathar, who does not appear for another chapter. Doh! Is it possible that the author of Mark made an error, or that a translation error occurred, or that through the years a sleepy monk failed to transcribe this text accurately? All of these explanations are possible, although there is no evidence of a transmission error in the manuscript tradition. The simpler possibility is that Jesus, in his humanity, made a small factual error. It is possible that Jesus, like all human beings, committed a slip of the tongue. While unsettling at first to those who overemphasize Jesus' divinity, this interpretation does not impinge on Christ's divinity and is certainly more elegant than having to conjure up a tired monk when no evidence of a manuscript transmission error exists.

Jesus is not merely prone to relatively insignificant slips of the tongue either. In Mark 8:22–26 Jesus encounters a blind man in Bethsaida. Applying saliva to the man's eyes and laying his hands on him, Jesus asks the man if he can see. The man replies that he is able to see people but that they look like walking trees. Staring at the man intently, Jesus lays his hands on the

9. Longman and Garland, *Expositor's Bible Commentary*, 762.
10. Black, *Mark*, 127.

man's eyes a second time. This second effort does the trick, and the man is able to see normally again. Interpreters have struggled with this partial healing since the first century. Some argue that Jesus healed the man partially on purpose as a symbolic gesture to indicate how the disciples see and understand only in part.[11] Or it is possible that the double healing refers to the two epochs commonly envisioned in apocalyptic dualism.[12] But again, how much more elegant is it to acknowledge that in his humanity Jesus became tired, thirsty, and sometimes made a mistake even in something as important as his healing ministry? Understanding that Jesus makes mistakes does not diminish his divinity; minor errors like this partial healing only underscore his humanity. What kind of real humanity could Jesus have were he not prone, as all human beings are, to error?

Even greater than a slip of the tongue and more damaging than a two-part healing is Jesus' excruciating encounter with the Syrophoenician woman. A deeply troubling text for lectionary preachers who must face this Scripture at least once every three years, few pericopes in the New Testament inspire more defensiveness and indignation than Jesus' conversation with the Syrophoenician woman. While Jesus is seeking some peace and quiet in Tyre, a local woman with a suffering daughter discovers Jesus and requests his help. Jesus delivers this chilling response: "Let the children be fed first, for it is not fair to take the children's food and throw it to the dogs" (Mark 7:27). Referring to the children of Israel and the Gentiles, Jesus tells the woman that he is interested in helping Jews first. It is only possible to understand "dogs" as a slur aimed at Gentiles.

The interpretive gymnastics inspired by this ignominious moment testify to the anxiety a fully human Jesus provokes. One of the more daring interpretations is that Jesus was not actually saying anything harsh to the woman at all. These folks point out the word Jesus uses for dogs here is *tois kunariois*, the diminutive form of dog. In this reading Jesus is not calling her or other Gentiles dogs but something more like little puppies.[13] In this interpretation Jesus is really just using a literal pet name for the woman, which should be heard by the reading community as endearing. William Barclay hypothesized that Jesus was playing with the woman, using a jesting tone, and smiling to let her know he was not intending his words with cruel intent.[14] Others attempt to salvage Jesus by arguing that while what he says

---

11. Marcus, *Mark 8–16*, 597.

12. Ibid., 600.

13. Iersel, *Mark*, 249–50.

14. Barclay, *Gospel of Mark*, 179.

is cruel, he only means it to test the woman.[15] While this interpretation at least acknowledges the harsh tone used by Jesus, scholars such as David Lose point out that Jesus' statement doesn't sound like a test.[16] Rather, it seems his statement was a thoughtless remark offered without reflection— something all human beings are prone to doing (especially when discovered while hiding out on sabbatical).

The better reading is that Jesus in his full humanity makes a thought- less statement. Perhaps due to the strong short-term emotion of being both- ered while lying low, Jesus speaks rashly and angrily. Perhaps because of the representativeness heuristic, Jesus falsely assumes this Gentile woman was not intellectually or emotionally worth his time. Perhaps it is simply because Jesus is exhausted. Remember those Israeli clemency hearings and what happened to the judgment of the parole board as the day wore on? When we're tired, we're simply not our best selves—and that goes for Jesus, too.

Whatever the reason, the woman surprises Jesus and the reader by giving back as good as she gets. Called an unworthy dog, the Syrophoeni- cian woman spits back, "Sir, even the dogs under the table eat the children's crumbs" (Mark 7:28). The woman deftly accepts the label of dog given to her by Jesus, pointing out that the dogs in his analogy are still fed. Realizing himself bested, what else can Jesus do but respond, "For saying that you may go—the demon has left your daughter" (7:29). At this point one can sense Barclay might have been right about Jesus smiling; it was just that Barclay was wrong about why and when Jesus smiled. One can imagine a knowing smile crossing Jesus' face as he responds to this woman's brilliant riposte, a generous acknowledgment of his mistake.

Peter Hawkins of Yale notes the full humanity of Jesus on display in this passage: "There is one occasion, however, that stands out among these human moments—an occasion when we see him learn something new and, as a result, become someone different; as recorded by Mark as well as Mat- thew, Jesus is brought up short by an unexpected truth. Not only does he change his mind, but does so in a breathtaking 180-degree turn. Most as- tonishing of all, it is a pagan woman who makes him do it."[17] While initially it may be difficult to accept that Jesus in his full humanity is capable of weak moments, ultimately it makes for a more spartan exegesis with a strong abil- ity to preserve the plain sense meaning of the text.

Not only does a behavioral lens shed light on the powerful way emo- tion affects Jesus, the limited knowledge he possesses, and the mistakes he

15. Iverson, Gentiles in Mark, 48–54.

16. Lose, "Mark 7:24–30," paras. 9–12.

17. Hawkins, "Dogging Jesus," 18.

seems to make now and again in the Gospels, but a behavioral perspective also shows that patterns Jesus employs resonate with the guidance behavioral theorists offer regarding effective ways to cope with the blind spots that come with human cognition. One of the easiest patterns to note in Jesus' life includes his constant habit of retreat: finding solitary places to pray, seeking the wilderness places, and just putting distance between himself and those depending on him. A vast amount has been written regarding the spiritual wisdom in this pattern of time with, and time apart from, ministry. Less well studied, however, is the cognitive necessity of getting distance from emotionally charged situations.

In their book *Decisive* Chip and Dan Heath offer a behavioral framework for decision-making that we'll learn more about in the third section. When it comes to making a choice, the Heaths lift up the problem of short-term emotion:

> Perhaps our worst enemy in resolving these conflicts is short-term emotion, which can be an unreliable adviser. When people share the worst decisions they've made in life, they are often recalling choices made in the grip of visceral emotions: anger, lust, anxiety, or greed. Our lives would be very different if we had a dozen undo buttons to use in the aftermath of these choices. But we are not slaves to our emotions. Visceral emotion fades. That's why the folk wisdom advises that when we've got an important decision to make, we should sleep on it. It's sound advice, and we should take it to heart. For many decisions, though, sleep isn't enough. We need strategy.[18]

One of the most powerful strategies the Heaths recommend is simply putting distance, physical and emotional distance, between people and a difficult choice environment. This distance allows human beings to move from a more emotionally labile hot state, associated with the automatic system, to a cooler state associated with the reflective system. In other words, distance and alone time do not just allow Jesus *time* to gather his thoughts, as if all he needed were time to rationally assess his plan; they allow him the *space* in which reflective thought is actually possible. Without space, Jesus, like all human beings, would be acting on automatic; and as already discussed regarding the Syrophoenician woman, even Jesus is capable of a thoughtless moment when acting on impulse.

I realize it's troubling for many of us to think about Jesus making mistakes and not knowing everything. As a pastor, when I have presented this material and preached it, I have faced pushback from people as they grapple

18. Heath and Heath, *Decisive,* Kindle locations 2488–93.

with these new ideas and the difficult Scriptures we've touched on here. But if Jesus isn't human, and human in the same way we are, then all is lost. Only a fully human Jesus can heal and redeem a fully human people. And for those who worry that lifting up Jesus' humanity automatically means we have to abandon a high Christology, one that emphasizes the centrality of his crucifixion and resurrection, they need not fear. In Jesus' crucifixion and resurrection we find some of the most compelling evidence for his irrational, full humanity. But this is so significant a topic, it requires its own chapter.

7

The Irrational Jesus Dies
. . . and Lives Again

Right around lunchtime on January 2, 2007, Wesley Autrey was standing on the subway platform at the 137th Street and City College station with his two young daughters. A student, Cameron Hollopeter, was also standing there waiting for the train. Suddenly, Hollopeter went into convulsions; he was experiencing a seizure. Autrey dropped the hands of his daughters to join two other women in providing aid to the young man. Fearing for Hollopeter's airway, Autrey used a pen to keep the young man's jaw open. When the seizure subsided, Hollopeter thanked everyone for their help and stood up, but he was unsteady on his feet and fell onto the tracks as a train hurtled toward them. Autrey did the unthinkable: leaving his daughters behind, he leapt onto the tracks. Unable to revive the young man and with no time to pick him up and carry him off, Autrey placed his body on top of Hollopeter's and pushed him into a drainage trench between the tracks as the train rumbled over them closely enough that grease from the train marked Autrey's hat. While Autrey, who was familiar with the subway tracks from his work in construction, dismissed his actions as something anyone would do, the world rightly lifted him up as a hero.

To lay down one's life on behalf of another is the very definition of heroic behavior. Remember that from the perspective of the standard economic model of rationality, such selflessness is also the epitome of irrational behavior. In this chapter we will take a closer look at Jesus' life and teachings, examining to what extent selfless, irrational altruism marks what Jesus does and says. We'll gaze at the drama of the crucifixion and ponder whether it was a calculated choice or an irrational, passionate act. And finally, we will consider how the various resurrection narratives help or hinder the image of Jesus as fully human.

In terms of his life and teachings Jesus' irrational selflessness takes our breath away. The very essence of Jesus' life and teachings stands in direct opposition to the utility maximization of the standard economic model. Jesus lived, as Dietrich Bonhoeffer put it, as the man "for others."[1] The most consistent feature of Jesus' itinerant ministry in the region of Galilee was the crowds that massed around him seeking healing. Almost without exception Jesus gave himself to these others, no matter their state of ritual cleanliness or whether it was the Sabbath. Crossing lines of religion, race, and gender, Jesus constantly poured himself out. He healed pagan demoniacs and taught women, saying of Mary that she "has chosen the better part, which will not be taken away from her" (Luke 10:42). This self-giving behavior is what many Christians hold most dear about Jesus.

This self-emptying, what theologians refer to as *kenosis* (from the Greek word for emptying that Paul uses to describe Christ taking the form of a slave in Philippians 2) also pervades Jesus' teachings. What could be less rational, according to the standard economic model, than Jesus' description of the landowner in the parable of the laborers in Matthew 20:1–16? The kingdom of heaven is like a landowner who goes out and hires laborers. Some of these laborers are hired in the morning, some later in the day, and some at the very end, and yet they are all paid the same wage. Enraged, they demand that the landowner pay them fairly. The landowner tells them not to compare themselves to one another and to be happy with what they have been given. To be sure, Jesus' primary point here is theological and not economic: he is emphasizing the grace of God and perhaps making room for latecomers to faith, saying it does not matter when someone comes to faith, just that they come to faith. But one cannot help being astonished at Jesus asking his followers to imagine a world driven not by standard rationality, fair pay for a fair day's work, but a world driven by grace and generosity. This thought experiment is as radical today as it was when it was first uttered.

And what about the entirety of Luke 15? Accused of spending time with all the wrong people, Jesus asks the Pharisees and scribes, "Which one of you, having a hundred sheep and losing one of them, does not leave the ninety-nine in the wilderness and go after the one that is lost until he finds it?" (15:4). Jesus' point in this parable is the joy God experiences over

---

1. Bonhoeffer, *Letters from Prison*, 381.

the lost being found, but the instrumental rationalists have to be scratching their heads in response, thinking to themselves that no rational person would leave ninety-nine sheep to go after one. According to the standard economic model, a rational person would just chalk it up to a frustrating but acceptable loss, a kind of flock depletion. As if seeing they were not getting it, Jesus continues with the parable of the coins, switching the metaphor from animals to money.

And finally, Jesus offers the absolutely stunning parable of the prodigal son, perhaps the finest articulation of grace ever offered. A man with two sons faces rejection from the younger, who asks his father for his inheritance and runs off on a spending spree that leaves him at rock bottom. Coming up with a clever apology to offer his father, the boy is shocked to find his father standing at the edge of the horizon with a robe in one hand and a ring in the other. Before the boy can utter his self-interested apology, the father has wrapped the boy in his arms and called for the party to begin. The elder brother, a rationalist from the standard economic model through and through, bristles at this absurd behavior, saying, "Listen! For all these years I have been working like a slave for you, and I have never disobeyed your command; yet you have never given me even a young goat so that I might celebrate with my friends. But when this son of yours came back, who has devoured your property with prostitutes, you killed the fatted calf for him!" (Luke 15:29–30). The elder brother, a figure with whom many of us sympathize, wants to earn his father's love in a rational world in which a fair amount of love is given in exchange for a fair amount of obedience. At such calculations, however, the predictably irrational Jesus can only laugh.

As important as Jesus' life and teachings are, in the Christian tradition his sacrificial death and resurrection are central. To Anselm, in this mystery of sacrificial death and resurrection we have the answer to why God became human. In Jürgen Moltmann's view of Jesus' crucifixion we discover the crucified God. In Karl Barth's Christology we see the judge judged in our place. Jesus' sacrificial death and joyous resurrection offer nothing less than a hinge around which our understanding of his whole life turns. But how should we understand Jesus' sacrifice? Is it the calculated action of a man who knew his preferences and chose to lay down his life on our behalf? Is it an irrational act of human altruism grounded in love?

The fundamental underpinning of the standard economic model of rationality is that after sorting through their options and calculating the most advantageous choice for them, rational actors will choose the path that maximizes their self-interest. They will choose what is best for them. While on the surface it would seem you could scarcely identify something less in your immediate self-interest than being put to death, rationalists point out it isn't so simple. Rationalist choice subscribers hold that we can't really judge someone's desires as rational or irrational. They say we can really only judge the rationality of a choice by whether or not an individual goes after their goal in an efficient way. Steven Brams, a game theorist who has written an interesting book on game theory and the Old Testament (about which we'll learn more in the second section), argues that a person who wants to commit suicide simply has a goal. Suicide, he grimly maintains, isn't rational or irrational. The person choosing suicide is rational, he argues, if they choose a means that is likely to be successful and irrational if they don't.[2] From this rationalist choice perspective, Jesus isn't necessarily irrational in choosing to lay down his life on behalf of others. Indeed, in following the path toward crucifixion, so this argument goes, Jesus is simply achieving his own desire. What appears to be altruism is really masked self-interest.

Many evolutionary biologists are quick to lend their support to this view, particularly with regard to seemingly altruistic behavior. Sacrificial behavior posed a particular problem to evolutionary biologists who believed Darwin's theory of evolution mandated a fierce competition in the sometimes violent natural world. If competition for resources and reproduction is so fierce, people wondered, then why are there so many observable acts of apparent altruism in the animal kingdom?

Evolutionary biologists such as Maynard Smith, W. D. Hamilton, and George Price rushed in to solve the problem. Using algebraic formulae these biologists claimed to show that seeming acts of altruism in the animal kingdom, including the human animal kingdom, boil down to relationships. The more closely two people are related, for instance, the more likely they are to sacrifice for one another. According to this kinship theory, though a father would jump into dangerous waters to save just one of his children, the same man would take the same risk only if there were *two* nephews or *four* cousins. Why? Because to an evolutionary biologist animals only care about what's in it for them. They only care about passing on their genetic material. Genetically, a child carries on your DNA and represents a one-to-one match. But a nephew or niece is only worth half, so it takes two. And like the old raisin bran commercial that said it would take four bowls of Kellogg's to equal one bowl of Total, it would take four cousins, since they represent only a quarter of your genetic material. So, to George Price altruism isn't altruism at all. It's merely self-interest disguised in the evolutionary imperative to pass along our genes. In a fascinating, sad turn of events Price was

2. Brams, interview by Austin Allen, quest. 2, paras. 1–5.

so troubled by his conclusions that he wound up converting to Christianity toward the end of his life, giving away his possessions to the poor, and ultimately taking his own life in the midst of poverty. It was almost as if Price died trying to prove himself wrong.[3]

The standard economic argument that Jesus' sacrifice is rational in the sense that Jesus maximizes his self-interest by efficiently carrying out his goal of sacrifice is interesting. There is certainly a scriptural tradition of Jesus predicting his own death and setting his face toward Jerusalem. Some New Testament scholars argue this emphasis on the passion predictions is a later creation of the church, but there is not clear agreement. However, we can allow for Jesus to acknowledge and even predict his death without saying he has some kind of macabre preference for death. Especially given the powerful emotions swaying back and forth in the garden of Gethsemane when Jesus is imminently facing this path, it seems clear that Jesus' preferences are unresolved at best. Listen to Matthew's description of the tug of war inside Jesus' mind: "And going a little farther, he threw himself down on the ground and prayed, 'My Father, if it is possible, let this cup pass from me; yet not what I want but what you want'" (26:39). That he sweats blood, asks the disciples to sit vigil with him, and berates them for falling asleep all indicate an extremely human picture of an emotional man struggling with an excruciatingly painful decision. We do not see a cold, calculating Jesus marching determinedly through his final moments on his way toward a clear preference.

And what about the evolutionary biologists? There's no such thing as altruism to folks like George Price. Sacrifice is merely a mechanism for ensuring your genes will endure, which is, in genetic determinism, the definition of self-interest. But do you remember Wesley Autrey's story? Wesley Autrey willingly risked his life on behalf of a man unrelated to him and dropped the hands of his daughters. Autrey and Hollopeter couldn't have been more different. Hollopeter was a student, Autrey a blue-collar worker; Hollopeter was white, Autrey African-American. There is simply no genetic calculus by which this risk makes sense. And it's the same for Jesus. Jesus dies on behalf of the whole world, sacrificing himself for others, most of whom are entirely unrelated to him in any ordinary sense of children, nephews, or cousins.

Moreover, the Apostle Paul shows awareness of this quid pro quo thinking and rules it out. In Romans, Paul writes that, rarely, some may be willing to lay down their lives for a truly righteous person. In other words, in the case of one who is really *worth* it, Paul sees that such sacrifice could

3. Harman, *Price of Altruism*, Kindle locations 5900–01.

make sense. But what makes Jesus' sacrifice so remarkable, such a gift, is that there was nothing in our action to merit this kind of sacrifice: "God proves his love for us in that while we still were sinners Christ died for us" (Rom 5:8). Jesus dies for people unrelated to him who weren't even worth it in the first place. Dying on the cross is a wonderfully, horrifically, beautifully, emotionally, fully human, irrational act. There is no calculus you can fit this mystery into by which you could somehow get to the bottom of it and figure it out.

So, if the crucifixion is Jesus' fully human willingness to pour himself out on behalf of others, do we see only his divinity on display in the resurrection or is there something fully human here, too? Although it may sound strange to those who haven't read through the resurrection narratives recently, they bend over backward to showcase Jesus' full humanity. First, I'll offer a word about the resurrection in general, and then we'll survey some of those stories.

So, first a word about the resurrection: if sacrifice is difficult to comprehend, the resurrection is impossible. The resurrection of Jesus Christ is a mystery that eludes any and every attempt at explanation. We can enter into mystery, but we can't get to the bottom of it. That said, I want to offer a word of friendship to those who struggle with even the basic concept of resurrection. I have cared for so many of you who grew up in churches or families where you were taught that the resurrection is simply a fact you must accept and that questioning this fact is tantamount to questioning God. Today, I can personally affirm my trust in Jesus Christ and in his resurrection, but at the same time I can also question it and welcome those who wonder if this just isn't some ancient superstition that has no place in a postmodern world.

On a personal note I will share that I have the unusual (some might say dubious) distinction of being converted to the faith in part by the work of people such as John Dominic Crossan and the late Marcus Borg. For those who aren't familiar with their work, they are longtime fellows of the Jesus Seminar, a group dedicated to searching for the historical Jesus. Many people told me the Jesus Seminar was more likely to convert a person *out* of the faith than into it, which just made them all the more interesting to me. Borg and Crossan exhaustively question seemingly every aspect of the New Testament—Borg doubts whether Jesus said half the words attributed to him in the Gospels, and Crossan writes that it is plausible that Jesus wasn't resurrected and that his body was probably eaten by dogs.[4] Believe it or not, they, along with fantastic pastors and friends and family, converted me to the faith by showing me the church doesn't have to be a place where

4. Crossan, *Jesus*, 127.

you check your brain at the door. Today, I believe in resurrection because it is something I have seen and lived, but I will always treasure and defend the questions of the Borgs and Crossans. If you are someone who isn't sure whether you can accept some stale doctrine because some authority figure says you must, don't worry—neither am I. I would rather invite you to meet me in what Karl Barth calls the "strange new world" of the Bible. Especially when it comes to the resurrection and Jesus' full humanity, the Bible is a strange place indeed.

The biblical understanding of resurrection is a foreign concept to most of the mainline North American Protestants with whom I spend my time. When most of the faithful churchgoing people I care for share their vision of the afterlife, they sound far more like Greek pagans than Jewish Christians. They talk mostly about being a disembodied spirit far removed from the aches and pains they know only too well in their present, embodied form. When I teach about the embodied, fully human nature of resurrection that some first-century Jews (including Jesus himself) believed, normally the first reaction is disbelief. A close second is revulsion. And yet, whether we're studying the strange vision of Ezekiel 37 in which the bones of Israel shake, rattle, and roll with new flesh and sinews or we're looking at the night of the living dead in Matthew 28 where tombs open and the formerly dead are walking around, you can't help noticing the very bodily humanity of the resurrection.

On a side note the recent cultural fascination with zombies can add a whole new twist to the conversation. When my youngest daughter was four I took her to the Rose City Comic Con in Portland. At one point a woman convincingly wrapped up as a zombie limped by. A friend of ours was trying to get my four-year-old's attention for a picture, but she wasn't having it. The zombie had her attention. My little one wasn't afraid, exactly, but she was keeping a very close eye on this creature's progress. Later, that Easter I wound up having the strangest conversation with her and my then seven-year-old daughter about their view that Jesus was a zombie due mainly to the bodily resurrection.

"But . . . he's not a zombie," I offered.

"He died, didn't he?"

"Uh . . . yeah."

"And he came back to life, right?"

"Um . . . yeah."

"So, he's a zombie," they both concluded.

"But he's not," I said defensively.

"How is he not? He was dead. Then he's walking around again. That's a zombie."

"Ugh. But he's just *not* . . . I mean, he's . . . It's time for bed."

If you have a better explanation for children under eight, I'm all ears. The part of the story they totally nailed is that Jesus dies and comes back in the flesh. While Mark's Gospel famously ends with the women fleeing the tomb in fear and no resurrection appearance, Duke Divinity School New Testament professor Joel Marcus makes a compelling argument that Mark's audience assumes the resurrection. He suggests Mark leaves the resurrection out as a rhetorical gesture that now invites the reader to ask herself how she will respond.[5] In that sense the reading community is called to become the resurrection response.

In Matthew we've already discussed how the bodies of the dead rose up in response to Jesus' resurrection. Luke's witness is even more detailed. The disciples assume the resurrected Christ is a ghost at first. Jesus responds, "Why are you frightened, and why do doubts arise in your hearts? Look at my hands and feet; see that it is I myself. Touch me and see; for a ghost does not have flesh and bones as you see that I have" (24:38–39). And just to drive the point home, he then eats a piece of broiled fish. In John's witness Jesus invites Thomas to touch the nail wounds and place his hand in the side where Jesus had been pierced (20:27). Later, when Jesus appears to Peter and the others as they are fishing, Jesus helps them bring in an enormous catch and eats fish and bread with them. When they eat, they know it is Jesus (21:12).

By going over these resurrection appearances in the Gospel narratives, I'm not trying to argue that you can read your way into faith, although that has been known to happen on occasion. I'm merely saying that whether you already believe in the resurrection or you question it, what is beyond a doubt is that in the Gospels themselves, the resurrected Jesus isn't a disembodied spirit. In the narratives again and again Jesus is flesh and bone. He is hungry. He eats. He presents his body to be felt and touched. Jesus, even the resurrected Jesus, is human—a fully, wondrously, predictably irrational human.

5. Marcus, *Mark 8–16*, 1096.

8

But Isn't Bias Just Sin?

But aren't we really talking about sin? Don't these limiting heuristics and biases outlined by cognitive theory simply describe human sinfulness with great scientific precision? Since bias so often leads to mistakes, risk management in fields as diverse as engineering and medicine utilizes the study of heuristics and biases to prevent error, a word whose Latin root is connected to sin. And long before Descartes penned *cogito ergo sum*, Augustine, who developed the concept of original sin, wrote, "Si enim fallor, sum," meaning, "If I err, I am."[1] Augustine's use of *fallor*, etymologically related to words like *fallible* and *fallacious*, seems to connect human nature with error and sin. So, if I have convincingly shown that Jesus' own humanity reflects the same heuristics and biases that shape the rest of us, am I saying, in direct opposition to Augustine and the entire Christian tradition, that Jesus himself is not without sin?

When I first started studying heuristics and biases, I initially thought this was an intriguing connection between social science and sin. But after a great deal of reflection, I conclude that the cognitive limits behavioral science describes aren't sin but instead point to our full humanity. In the same way that you don't feel bad about yourself for the fact that you need to use mirrors when you drive a car to compensate for your visual blind spots, behavioral science provides us with cognitive mirrors, if you will, to help us compensate for our cognitive blind spots. You don't think of limited

1. Augustine, *City of God*, XI, 26.

peripheral vision as sin, do you? Of course not. You recognize that God made you with limitations. Theologians call this finitude. And finitude, or limitation, is not sin. In fact, quite the opposite is true. At least one classical tradition holds that one of the chief ways to understand sin is to see it as the hubris, or pride, *not* to accept our limitations. So, with this definition in mind let's take a look at how the Scriptures define sin in a multitude of ways, and let's see how two major theologians, John Calvin and Karl Barth, think of sin in relationship to Jesus and his predictably irrational humanity.

Scripturally, deciding whether bias points to sin or full humanity is not easy to answer. Holy Scripture, particularly the Old Testament, contains a rich and complex vocabulary of sin. *The New Interpreter's Dictionary of the Bible* includes this list of common terms used for sinful behavior in the Old Testament: *khatta'th*, missing the mark; *pasha'*, transgression; *'awon*, iniquity; *meri*, rebellion; and *ra'*, evil.[2]

While the notion of *khatta'th* as missing the mark might seem in keeping with equating bias to sin, the vast majority of the terms for sin in the Old Testament refer not to human error per se but to unjust, broken relationships and false religion. The prophets in particular reserve their harshest condemnations for a nation and individuals breaking covenant with God by their treatment of the poor. Isaiah, using a broad range of language for sin, laments the *pasha'* (transgression), *khatta'th* (missing the mark), and *'awon* (iniquity) of the people as seen particularly in their oppression of the poor and in the corruption of justice. While the prophets also include hard words for covenant infidelity, Leviticus places the accent on sin as breaking covenant with God in the form of religious violation. Leviticus offers an extended account of the sacrifices to be offered for *khatta'th* (missing the mark). While there is certainly a component of social justice to be found in the Levitical conception of sin, especially justice for the stranger, the greater emphasis in Leviticus falls on sin as a violation of religious law: becoming unclean through contact with a dead body, or by the eating of blood, or by other acts leading to religious pollution.[3] A more thorough analysis of the Old Testament would certainly add greater nuance to the Hebrew understanding of sin, but the conception of sin as lack of human perfect reason or will is almost wholly absent.

More challenging is the understanding of sin in the New Testament. To begin with, the vocabulary for sin is narrower, with only three possibilities: *kakia*, wickedness; *anomia*, lawlessness; and, the most prevalent, *hamartia*,

2. Attridge, "Sin, Sinners," 263.
3. Ibid., 267.

which also means to miss the mark.[4] Again, as we saw with *khatta'th* in the Old Testament, this sense of sin as mistake and error certainly seems consistent with cognitive bias. The difference between the Old Testament and New Testament contexts is that *hamartia* dominates the New Testament vocabulary for sin in a way that *khatta'th* does not in the Old Testament. As in the Old Testament examples, the use of the word *hamartia* in context will offer the best sense of whether the New Testament links sin with bias. Especially because of its prevalence in the New Testament, understanding the use in context is crucial.

The meaning of *hamartia* as Jesus uses it pairs well with the connotation of sin in the prophets. Jesus refers to sin both in a social and a religious context. In terms of a social critique Jesus, like the prophets, reserves harsh words for the sins of the elite. Sounding like the prophet in Ezekiel 34 complaining that the priests of his day were like shepherds feasting on their sheep, Jesus goes after the scribes and the Pharisees with righteous anger. In Matthew 23 Jesus lays out the many sins of the Pharisees: laying heavy burdens on those in their care, loving the appearance of being holy without actually being holy, confusing unimportant matters with weighty matters, and neglecting justice and mercy. Memorably, in Matthew 23 Jesus also refers to the Pharisees as whitewashed tombs that look good on the outside but that are full of dead men's bones. What is important to note is that while the Pharisees are in some sense making mistakes, what Jesus is criticizing is not their imperfect reason or will but their unfair treatment of those in their care. Jesus is not saying that they aren't thinking clearly but that they aren't loving well.

In a religious context, while Jesus certainly challenges the Levitical understanding of cleanliness on many occasions, he still links sin with illness and the religious establishment of the day. Jesus often links sin with illness and the forgiveness of sin with healing and, in many of these instances, directs the recipient of healing to go and show himself to the priests. Even in John's Gospel when Jesus heals the man born blind from birth in chapter 9 and argues that the man was not born blind due to sin, he still links the man's healing to a religious epiphany of demonstrating Jesus as the Christ. While the concept of sin in the life and work of Jesus is more complicated than what can be presented here, it is enough to point out that when Jesus uses the term *hamartia*, there is no sense that the mark being missed is imperfect reason or will.

In the letters of the Apostle Paul, however, the picture of sin in the New Testament shifts. While Paul joins with other Hellenistic moralists of the era

4. Ibid., 275.

in sometimes simply generating lists of "do's" and sinful "don'ts," Paul also offers a more sophisticated theological understanding of sin. Particularly in Romans, Paul expands the sense of sin from a social or religious violation to something closer to a state of being. Paul argues that sin is a fundamental weakness of human nature, inherited through Adam, in which we can know the good but are unable to do it. What could be more poignant than Paul's description of the sinful human condition: "I can will what is right, but I cannot do it. For I do not do the good I want, but the evil I do not want is what I do. Now if I do what I do not want, it is no longer I that do it, but sin that dwells within me" (Rom 7:18–20).

In this context Paul's sense of sin sounds a bit more like our cognitive blind spots. While the majority of the biblical witness does not view sin as a human condition that impairs human reason and will, Paul makes it sound as if imperfect human reason and will might be the condition of sin itself. Yale Divinity School professor Harold Attridge writes that in Paul's understanding of sin, "the fundamental character of human nature, 'the flesh' . . . is beset by the force of passionate desire that overcomes the rational recognition of what is right."[5] This interpretation sounds as if forces such as the affect heuristic—when emotions keep us from seeing and following our best course—signify a deeper, sinful, broken state. To make sense of Paul's understanding of sin we will need more help. John Calvin and Karl Barth both grapple with sin, will, humanity, and the humanity and divinity of Jesus and will help us find a way forward.

First, we'll start with Calvin. John Calvin was an amazing guy. Or, at the very least, I will say he is better than most people probably think. Born in the Picardy region of France, Calvin soon left the champagne-growing vines of his homeland for an education in Paris. Breathing in the radical humanism of his day, Calvin got swept up in an ill-behaved Protestant crowd and wound up becoming one of the most influential leaders of the Reformation, establishing a Protestant center in Geneva, Switzerland.

While he was a serious man, I do defend Calvin from the widespread belief that he was someone who couldn't enjoy himself or allow others to enjoy themselves either. As part of his terms of call Calvin enjoyed two hundred and fifty gallons of wine.[6] Surely he shared some of the bounty, but still, that's a lot of wine. And when Calvin went after prominent socialites like the Perrin family for partying too heartily, it was in the context of his caring for hundreds of French refugees who were just scraping by. It's not that Calvin

---

5. Ibid., 277.

6. Kee et. al., *Christianity*, 291.

couldn't enjoy a party as much as he didn't believe it was right for some to have so much while others' children went hungry.

Amazingly, in spite of all this dorm-room hall monitoring, Calvin did have time to write theology. In his theology he shows himself to be an astute psychologist, sounding like a behavioralist before there were behavioralists: "For if it is considered disgraceful for us not to know all that pertains to the business of human life, even more detestable is our ignorance of ourselves, by which, when making decisions in necessary matters, we miserably deceive and even blind ourselves!"[7] Moreover, before any psychologist came up with the term *optimism bias*, Calvin had already observed that this behavior is endemic to humanity: "There is, indeed, nothing that man's nature seeks more eagerly than to be flattered. Accordingly, when his nature becomes aware that its gifts are highly esteemed, it tends to be unduly credulous about them. It is thus no wonder that the majority of men have erred so perniciously in this respect. For since blind self-love is innate in all mortals, they are most freely persuaded that nothing inheres in themselves that deserves to be considered hateful."[8] Five hundred years before Sunstein and Thaler wryly pointed out how we all tend to think of ourselves as above average, Calvin already recognized how hard it is for us to see ourselves as anything less than wonderful. This isn't worm theology (a piously low view of humanity), by the way. This is just realism.

But Calvin faces a problem. What about Jesus? If Jesus is fully human, and Calvin most certainly believes he is, surely Jesus isn't plagued by these problems, is he? Is Calvin's Jesus prone to such weakness and delusion? Absolutely not. Calvin is explicitly worried about this:

> For if man's soul be from the essence of God through derivation, it will follow that God's nature is subject not only to change and passions, but also to ignorance, wicked desires, infirmity, and all manner of vices. Nothing is more inconstant than man. Contrary motions stir up and variously distract his soul. Repeatedly he is led astray by ignorance. He yields, overcome by the slightest temptation. We know his mind to be a sink and lurking place for every sort of filth. All these things one must attribute to God's nature, if we understand the soul to be from God's essence. . . . Who would not shudder at this monstrous thing?[9]

Calvin's solution? Theologians use the word *anthropology* to talk about human nature. Calvin's anthropology relies on viewing people as perfect

7. Calvin, *Institutes*, II.i.1.
8. Ibid., II.i.2.
9. Ibid., I.xv.5.

before the Fall and subject to bias after our exit from Eden: "We cannot have a clear and complete knowledge of God unless it is accompanied by a corresponding knowledge of ourselves. This knowledge of ourselves is twofold: namely, to know what we were like when we were first created and what our condition became after the fall of Adam."[10] In Adam, Calvin argues that reason and will were intact. Calvin exceeds even the philosophers and the poets in his exultation of human capacity in this first condition. In this sense Calvin argues that *originally* humanity did not suffer from limiting heuristics and predictable blind spots generated by biases, while at the same time observing that in his day gross irrationality abounded.

And in this way Calvin can on the one hand argue that Jesus is fully human and on the other hand defend him from what Calvin detested as the flawed sinfulness of humanity. For Calvin, Jesus wasn't merely perfect in doing justice, loving kindness, and walking humbly with God; Jesus was perfect in thought, perception, and . . . well, everything. Before the Fall, humanity possessed perfect reason, but now, after the Fall, we're lamentably riddled with blind spots. And Christians shouldn't just accept this predictable irrationality, as Dan Ariely proposes. Calvin would suggest that we should strive for sanctification through spiritual disciplines.

But what kind of full humanity is this? How on earth can Jesus sympathize with us in every way if, when it comes down to it, he fundamentally experiences and perceives the world in a different way? To me, Calvin turns Jesus into a kind of superman, and I stand 100 percent with Edna Mode from *The Incredibles* in saying, "No capes!" The Jesus that Calvin and so many in the church believe in is more like one of Professor Xavier's mutant X-Men straight out of the Marvel universe. They can save the world through the force of their actions but not through their being. But if salvation through Jesus Christ entails that he assume *our* flesh and become God Emmanuel, God *with* us, then a mutant X-Man Jesus will not do.

Enter Karl Barth. Barth is something of a theological hero for me. Steeped in the German liberal tradition, he basically performed a theology reboot that redeemed Protestantism after the professors he admired failed to speak out against the rise of the German war machine prior to World War II. Simply put, Barth believed church leaders were making God into an idol fashioned in their own likeness. Human reason had become the measure of all things. Barth worked to radically invert this elevation of human reason such that church leaders had to acknowledge before anything else that God is God and we are not. This fierce determination to follow after God no

10. Ibid., I.xv.1.

matter what gave Barth the courage to be one of the few brave pastors and theologians in Germany to oppose Hitler's rise to power.

Not only does Barth make a stand against Hitler, but he also manages to update Calvin's anthropology. While Calvin's two-state solution may solve Calvin's dilemma over whether God could take flesh without fully assuming the fallen human condition, it comes at the cost of God's freedom and Christ's full humanity. Barth's respectful critique of Calvin's anthropology outlines a God freely capable of assuming humanness in all its brokenness merely because God is God and delineates a fully human Jesus in whom God and humanity become partners. Barth's emphasis on the divine initiative and his acknowledgment that limitation is not sin frees behavioral theology to understand cognitive systems, heuristics, and biases not as sin but as the finitude, the limitation, of full humanity. Barth offers a pathway to see that while human finitude is not sin, how humans respond to this finitude may well be.

First, for those who know Barth well, I completely acknowledge that Barth may initially seem like an unusual choice for a theology seeking to relate the Christian tradition to social science as I am doing here. It is Barth who describes the entirety of nineteenth-century theology as "religionistic, anthropocentric, and in this sense humanistic. . . . To think about God meant to think in a scarcely veiled fashion about man."[11] Wolf Krötke is correct in writing, "For Barth, in fact, means that if we want to know who and what the human being is, we are not in the first place to look to ourselves. Nor are we to begin with what the empirical sciences say about the human being; nor are we to orient ourselves to the phenomena of human existence past and present in an attempt to interpret the experiences which are there expressed."[12]

To be sure, Barth himself would have had little if any interest in what behavioral theory has to say about humanity, at least as a *primary* source of constructing a theological anthropology. However, the word *primary* is key. While Barth's theology itself is not behavioral in any sense of the term, his critique of Calvin coupled with his understanding of what he calls "the humanity of God" open a pathway in which the church can primarily understand human nature, or anthropology, as stemming from God's desire to be with and for humanity. Then, secondarily, the church can freely turn to social science for additional insight into the particularity of the human experience.

11. Barth, *Humanity of God*, 39.
12. Krötke, "Karl Barth's Anthropology," 159.

While brimming over with respect for Calvin, Barth offers an explicit correction to Calvin's understanding of Christ and human nature. Barth's main challenge to Calvin's anthropology is Calvin's starting point: he starts his investigation of anthropology with humanity. While starting with humans to understand humanity seems like a sensible beginning, Barth attacks this approach again and again, insisting that the only starting place for theological anthropology is with God in Jesus Christ: "The ontological determination of humanity is grounded in the fact that one man among all others is the man Jesus. So long as we select any other starting point for our study, we shall reach only the phenomena of the human."[13] Calvin's anthropological starting point is human beings: specifically the dual nature of humanity pre- and post-Fall. By changing the starting point, Barth opens up octaves of possibility closed to Calvin.

When Jesus Christ is the starting point in understanding humanity, then the good news of grace is the ultimate frame as opposed to the judgment of the Fall. In this grace and because of God's divine freedom, Barth doesn't see the essential conflict between some idealized divine perfection and human limitation that Calvin did. Because God is God to Barth, God can freely assume humanity without in any way compromising God's nature, which is love and freedom: "God's deity is thus no prison in which He can exist only in and for Himself. It is rather His freedom to be in and for Himself but also with and for us, to assert but also to sacrifice Himself, to be wholly exalted but also completely humble, not only almighty but also almighty mercy, not only Lord but also servant, not only judge but also Himself the judged, not only man's eternal king but also his brother in time. And all that without in the slightest forfeiting His deity!"[14] While Calvin works anxiously to protect God's divinity from human corruption, Barth confidently asserts our limitations represent no threat to God's divinity.

Moreover, because of this divine freedom, just as there is no conflict between God and humanity, there is also no conflict between Christ's divinity and his full humanity. While Calvin offers a vision of Jesus so perfect in reason and will as to be scarcely recognizable as a human being, Jesus Christ in Barth's view is fully human in every way:

> Is it not true that in Jesus Christ, as He is attested in the Holy
> Scripture, genuine deity includes in itself genuine humanity?
> There is the father who cares for his lost son, the king who does
> the same for his insolvent debtor, the Samaritan who takes pity
> on the one who fell among robbers and in his thoroughgoing

13. Barth, *Church Dogmatics*, 3/2:132.
14. Barth, *Humanity of God*, 49.

act of compassion cares for him in a fashion as unexpected as it is liberal. And this is the act of compassion to which all these parables as parables of the Kingdom of heaven refer. The very One who speaks in these parables takes to His heart the weakness and the perversity, the helplessness and the misery, of the human race surrounding Him. He does not despise men, but in an inconceivable manner esteems them highly just as they are, takes them into His heart and sets Himself in their place.[15]

Barth is also careful to point out that God's assumption of full humanity is not only in keeping with God's majesty, but it maintains the authentic nature of humanity. Describing what happens in baptism when the baptized dies to self and rises in Christ, Barth views the new creature as "not engulfed and covered as by a divine landslide or swept away as by a divine flood."[16]

What is sin, then, for Barth? In his characterization of sin Barth veers further still from Calvin. For Barth sin is not a lack of perfect reason, understanding, and will exhibited by a second, post-Fall humanity. For Barth, as for Augustine, sin is nothingness, an ontological impossibility. Wolf Krötke expands on Barth's position as follows: "Over against this, everything sinful in human being is without meaning or ground. It cannot be derived either from God's determination of the human or from God's conduct toward the human. It has no ground whatsoever. It is absurd. That is why it does not belong in an anthropology that deals with God's elected, ontologically good creature."[17] For Barth, then, sin is not a lack of human perfection compared to the light of Jesus Christ or some kind of imagined pre-Fall existence. Sin is the human freedom to respond to God's desire for partnership, the divine "Yes," with a sad, meaningless "no." This "no" is meaningless because the human "no" can never negate God's divine "Yes," which provides the very ground of human existence.

Sin is also hubris to Barth. Whereas Christ emptied himself, taking the form of a slave, human sin rejects this freely chosen limitation; humans choose instead a false, Promethean understanding of freedom. God's freedom in Jesus Christ is the freedom to love; and because of this freedom to love, Jesus Christ freely accepts the limitations and finitude of human creatureliness. Human sin as hubris rejects the very idea of limitation, wanting to assert itself against every possible line. Barth's devastating critique against humanity's desire to elevate itself without the help of God is right in line with the human pretense of objectivity. Sin, then, from a behavioral

15. Ibid., 51.
16. Barth, *Church Dogmatics*, 4/4:163.
17. Krötke, "Karl Barth's Anthropology," 165.

perspective, is not cognitive limitation but pretending one is somehow immune or can outwit heuristics and biases.

Ultimately, Barth's theological anthropology offers such a contrast to Calvin's understanding that Barth could only lament, if somewhat humorously, Calvin's half measures: "It is when we look at Jesus Christ that we know decisively that God's deity does not exclude, but includes His *humanity*. Would that Calvin had energetically pushed ahead on this point in his Christology, his doctrine of God, his teaching about predestination, and then logically also in his ethics! His Geneva would then not have become such a gloomy affair. His letters would then not have contained so much bitterness."[18] Barth's correction to Calvin's unduly complicated two-state vision of humanity that links sin with human imperfection frees behavioral theology from having to understand heuristics and biases as sin.

In a Barthian anthropology the human being finds primary expression in the meeting between the divine and the human in the person of Jesus Christ. God in God's freedom elects to partner with humanity in the person of Jesus Christ, and this partnership impinges neither on God's majesty nor on the creatureliness of genuine humanity. Unlike Calvin's Christ, who is fully God and only vaguely recognizable as a human being, Barth's Christ is fully God and fully human. Barth frees us to understand the heuristics and biases described by behavioral theorists not as broken aspects of human sinfulness but as facets of our full humanity.

Thus, when we view Paul's frustration that the good we want to do we don't do through the lens of Barth, it isn't about perfection in reason. It's about perfection in love. For Barth, when Paul writes in First Corinthians that for now we see through a mirror dimly but then we will see face to face, it doesn't mean our cognitive blind spots will somehow disappear when we meet God. It means that God's love is more powerful than whatever limitations we bring.

And so what about our own cognitive heuristics and biases? Are behavioralists really saying we just have to accept a little sin and make the best of it? Absolutely not. By saying we have to account for full humanity, Ariely is simply stating that leaders have to be thoughtful about how we process and present information. Sin isn't the fact that humans are limited and biased. Sin looks like people believing they are somehow without bias or are capable by mere awareness of bias of making themselves rational. Sin is the arrogance of assuming *others* may be irrational, but *we*, certainly, are not.

18. Barth, *Humanity of God*, 49.

9

Practical Docetism, Theologicons, and Fully Human Leaders

So now we've learned about cognitive heuristics and biases, our two minds, and the predictable irrationality of Jesus. And we've waded through a lengthy argument about why all this predictable irrationality is not sin. Now it's time to look at how behavioral theology plays out in the practical world of churches today.

In case you don't spend a great deal of time around seminaries, one of the enduring topics of conversation is how awful it is that so many local congregations are driven more by cultural accommodation than by good theology. Take the perennial issue of Christmas carols during Advent. Conversations go something like this: "It's Advent, for goodness sake. Don't they know that in the pews? We aren't of the world. We are called to be distinct." Of course, what better way to show how different we are than to make a whole bunch of people drone "Let All Mortal Flesh Keep Silence" when they want to sing "Away in a Manger"?

Now don't get me wrong. I love Advent and look forward to singing "Let All Mortal Flesh Keep Silence" at least once every season. I'm certainly not saying we should give into requests for "Grandma Got Run Over by a Reindeer." (Don't laugh—someone once asked for that. I *think* they were joking?) What I am suggesting is that something unhelpful happens in seminary when theologically minded people gather together and imagine what *ought* to be happening in the church, without a great deal of appreciation for what's *actually* taking place. I left seminary something of an Advent fanatic myself, but as a pastor of fully human people from all sorts of different backgrounds I've learned to mellow on such issues over the years. But this softening took some time. I spent years being rigid and feeling responsible for upholding all I had been taught in seminary. At one point I remember a stalwart member coming up to me after worship on the Third Sunday of Advent just enraged. She got right in my face and yelled, "Even the malls know it's Christmas! Why. Don't. You?" I was tempted to explain to her that it would be a very cold day in a certain place before I looked to the malls as my liturgical guide. Mercifully, I exercised my somewhat limited verbal filter and responded with quiet words and an understanding look.

That moment did give me pause to wonder if the project of changing minds was something I wanted to continue—because changing minds was a significant message I received in my training. We were steeped in the theological and liturgical traditions, and then charged to go back into the church and hold the line against what many of my professors perceived to be the barbarians at the gate. And our job, largely, was to somehow convince people, some of whom have never heard of Advent, that they are supposed to wait for Christmas even as the world around them is decked out in red and green. Or if it isn't Advent, it is other theological traditions and practices we are supposed to defend. We are supposed to tell influential members that no, we can't baptize their out-of-town grandchildren because there's this thing called the *Book of Order* that they've never heard of. Again, as with Advent, I'm a good Presbyterian and agree that baptism is an act of the community, and you can't ask a congregation to make promises they can't keep. But often the difficulty of these conversations and the legitimate feelings of these members aren't given enough attention.

As I mentioned earlier, this gap between the neat, tidy theological theories about what was supposed to be happening in churches and the reality pastors face on the ground is what initially spurred my interest in behavioral economics. The behavioral economics critique represents a shift in anthropology that occurred as researchers grew increasingly aware that their neglect of full humanity jeopardized the validity of their predictive models. This gap between theory and practice is a story the church knows all about. It isn't something new to us.

In one of the earliest misunderstandings surrounding Jesus Christ, the second-century bishop Serapion grew concerned about something he called Docetism after learning that the reading of the Gospel of Peter was causing troubles in the Church at Rhossos.[1] There's a talking cross in the Gospel that probably raised a few eyebrows, but what concerned Serapion most was the fact that the Gospel of Peter states that Jesus on the cross "was silent as having no pain."[2] Docetism, from the Greek *dokeo*, meaning "to seem," claims Jesus was not truly human but only appeared to be human. This belief appeals to believers then and now. What could be better than to get rid of the messiness and weakness of the flesh? But this temptation to lift up Christ's spirit and mind and deny his humanity was ruled out by the church at Nicaea in 325. Without the fleshy-ness of Christ, the humanity of Christ, the fundamental connection between God and humanity through the God-man Jesus Christ is lost. As Gregory of Nazianzus put it, "For that which he has not assumed he has not healed; but that which is united to his Godhead is also saved."[3] In other words, if Jesus does not assume the whole of our humanity, he cannot save our whole selves.

Yet for all of our history with Docetism, the church today suffers at times from a kind of practical Docetism, to borrow and modify a concept from Duke Divinity School professors Ken Carder and Laceye Warner. This practical Docetism is most evident in the way the church trains leaders. Carder and Warner in *Grace to Lead* lament the habit of church leaders who slip into a kind of practical atheism when planning for the future, wrongly thinking that the future of the church depends on human strategic thinking alone rather than the outpouring love of the triune God.[4] While their point is well taken that faithful ecclesial leaders must ground their decision-making in the love and grace of God, a behavioral theology would add that faithful leaders also need to make decisions in light of an adequate theological anthropology encompassing our full humanity. Without an adequate theological anthropology, church leaders, like classical economists, unreflectively ascribe greater rationality to church leaders and church members than behavioral theorists have demonstrated is present.

Rather than the econs of Sunstein and Thaler, though, practical Docetism assumes what I call "theologicons": idealized, entirely rational church leaders and members unswayed by emotion, unaffected by behavioral blind spots, and able to renew their minds without serious attention to their brains or bodies. Such thinking (and the training founded on it) may be not merely unhelpful but professionally damaging to those called to lead. Michael and

1. Arendzen, "Docetae," para. 1.
2. Brown, *Gospel of Peter*, 10b.
3. Hardy, *Christology of Later Fathers*, 218.
4. Carder and Warner, *Grace to Lead*, 11.

Deborah Jinkins sense this: "Over a combined experience of almost forty years of leadership and study of nonprofit organizations, . . . we have become convinced that many of the things that leaders in these institutions are taught in professional schools may actually work against their effective leadership and that their highest ideals may compound the problem."[5] They could have been describing me when I wouldn't even consider people's feelings about Christmas carols in Advent.

I am not alone. Many church leaders articulate what feels like a disconnect between academic theology and the practice of ministry. Seminarians often complain that academic training is not practical enough, while scholars rightly respond that faithful ministry today is more complicated than any set of practical techniques could possibly address. A behavioral perspective suggests that both sides in this debate have a point. In order to take into account a more complicated anthropology, behavioral econometric models grew more rigorous than classical economics. In other words, rather than simplifying or watering down rigor, behavioral economics became more rigorous even as it helped economics as a discipline become more practical.

In the same way a behavioral theology holds that theological training needs to continue to be as theologically rigorous as possible with no decrease in the amount of time seminarians spend learning church history, systematic theology, ancient languages, and biblical interpretation. The reflective rider, the inner Jacob, must be trained as well as possible. But a behavioral theology would add to this rigorous study a more complicated understanding of our full humanity, taking into account how cognitive limitations can affect both teacher and student alike. Behavioral theologians and pastors know we have to sing to the elephants and inner Esaus, too. Behavioral theology will be just as interested in what is actually happening on the ground, in real churches and in the lives of real people, as it is with articulating what should be taking place. Behavioral leaders will want to know what is possible on the ground as much as much as they want to know what is ideal. Because of this practical interest, church leaders have much to learn from game theory and behavioral game theory, which we will tackle in the next section.

---

5. Jinkins and Jinkins, *Character of Leadership*, 1.

10

Let's Get Real

Here's a chance now to put your learning to work. The following is a mostly true story with certain details changed. Read the story first. Next, take some time to write down your thoughts about what behavioral forces might be at play in the narrative. Then read my analysis and compare. As I mentioned in the "We Can Be Taught!" chapter, I love to learn, and I encourage you to share your insights and thoughts about these stories with me by way of the book's website: www.irrationaljesus.com.

One church I know, like so many other mainline congregations, has seen better days. With more than five hundred members in its heyday, only about seventy remain on the books. The demographics of the town around the church have dramatically changed. As the white population aged and declined, a young, vibrant Hispanic population moved in and continues to grow, along with an increasing Vietnamese and Korean population. This church, like so many others, not only missed these demographic waves but laments them, feeling like a tiny island in a sea of change.

Into this mix entered a young pastor I'll call Alex. (Alex is based on several real stories of pastors I have known and admired.) Alex was a brilliant, spiritually gifted, intense man with a quiet but passionate faith. He was not only incredibly intelligent and an astute interpreter of the Scriptures and the theological tradition, but he also knew what it was to work with his hands, having worked blue-collar jobs before he became a pastor. Given the blue-collar background of many in the congregation, these shared roots were an important connection. They trusted and respected Alex as a leader. While he was more socially progressive than the average member of his congregation, pushing a progressive agenda was not his interest—transforming tired, lukewarm mainline church members into spiritually vital disciples of Christ was.

Even though the church had experienced significant loss in the past, there were some hopeful signs. More recently membership and giving had stabilized. Given all the retirees, there was also a lot going on in the congregation for a church of its size. Along with a slew of fellowship groups and study groups, the church boasted a beautiful community garden. The garden wasn't just used by the church members, but was an honest-to-goodness community garden. They were able to donate a huge amount of food to the local food pantry and felt really good about it. Many in the congregation were feeling really hopeful when Alex came along that with some stable leadership they would be able to make further inroads into the community and maybe begin to pull out of their negative spiral.

Unfortunately, Alex wasn't very excited about the garden and dismissed most of the groups that met as just social. Alex believed his job was to turn this place from a rotary club with a cross on the wall to an authentic church. Moreover, he decided that change needed to happen sooner rather than later.

I was surprised when the congregation accepted Alex's first major change—celebrating the Lord's Supper weekly rather than monthly—so easily. Influenced by the liturgical renewal movement, Alex held an extremely high view of the sacraments. Some members of the church pushed back, saying that celebrating the sacraments on a weekly basis would take away the "specialness" of the moment. Alex responded that a husband who stopped telling his wife he loved her because he was worried about diminishing levels of specialness probably wouldn't be married for long. This analogy was a hard argument to refute, and the congregation didn't fight it; but, Alex admitted, they probably weren't too excited about it either. Perhaps not wanting to look the gift horse of acceptance in the mouth, Alex made the decision not to give too much information or teaching about the reasons behind this change. He wanted to let the experience speak for itself. He was disappointed, then, when after months of observance many people still said they didn't really know why they had to celebrate communion so often and liked the monthly schedule better. They weren't angry about it, Alex would say. They just didn't seem to get it.

While this communion resistance was frustrating to him, the real trouble came after the next major change. The people he served were mostly nice, decent folks. They lived responsible lives. Yet worship seemed little more to them than a time to gather socially. They told him they prayed, but he never really saw them do it and didn't know quite what prayer meant to them. And they would agree that Scripture was, of course, important— but few, if any, seemed to read the Bible devotionally or at any time other than Sunday morning worship. Alex was embarrassed that the members he served had so little facility with the Bible. In fact, they almost seemed proud of their unfamiliarity with Scripture. One of the things that bugged him the most was that his congregation seemed to revel in telling him the sermons they loved best were short on Scripture and long on personal anecdotes.

So Alex decided they were going to take the year and read through the Bible together. And they weren't going to jump around, either. Nope. Given the congregation's woebegone state, Alex determined they would read every book in order, from Genesis to Revelation. And he conveyed this edict with the attitude of "we will do this and you will like it!" As with weekly communion, the congregation mostly went along with Alex's plan, but they surely weren't liking it. They bogged down in the genealogies. They were baffled and bored by the rules in Leviticus. No shrimp and grits? Really? They were critical of the constant failings on the part of Israel. Worst of all for Alex was they didn't like how God behaved. They found God fickle and capricious. The congregation went into the study not really sure they wanted to know more about the Bible; they finished the study confident they did not. Alex entered into the study not sure he was called to pastor that congregation; he finished the study confident he was not. In the end Alex left the ministry, embarking on another graduate degree and career altogether. He often said he felt prepared to lead a church that didn't really exist.

In the North American church this story (and others like it) is playing out again and again. It's hard to lead a church or a faith-based institution. Really hard. And the changing context means it will only get harder. Leaders receive excellent training in biblical interpretation, theology, church history, and pastoral care. And they should. More than ever leaders need to be able to think theologically and read and interpret the Scriptures with sophistication. But it's not enough for them to be "masters" of divinity; leaders need to learn more about humanity at the same time. They need to move from considering how the people in their care *ought* to behave (according to their theological training) to considering how they *actually* behave in real life, and understand why.

Take a moment and think about everything you have learned about our two minds and the cognitive heuristics and biases that operate below the surface of our awareness. Think about what forces might have been present in the congregation. Consider the changes that Alex made and how he went about making them. Were they good changes, all things considered?

Were these changes instituted in such a way that fully human people could follow them easily? Take a few minutes and write down what you think before moving on to what I think.

The most powerful behavioral force present that just imbues the entire setting is loss aversion bias. Alex didn't come into a neutral setting. He walked into a community who remembered better days and felt sad and guilty at the decline of the institution on their watch. Many pastors, annoyed with this reality, privately express frustration and even anger at times. In public they will be polite and professional, but with one another they vent and wonder why these people can't just let it go and move on. Of course, if people could with the push of a button just get on with life, they would. But people don't. And loss is extremely painful. It makes us risk averse, unwilling to try new things. Even when we are aware that we are being affected by loss aversion we may not be able to bring ourselves to be excited about change. Then we feel doubly bad because we're stuck and we know we're stuck.

On the positive side of the ledger Alex was smart to seize on changes that added to the congregation's life rather than subtracting from it. Sometimes people roll their eyes at us when we remain in painful relationships or stay mired in a job we despise, but what they don't understand is how powerful and pervasive the pain of loss is. When we are already experiencing loss, any additional thing that is removed compounds our distress. Even if the latest thing taken away is something we don't even care about, it can feel excruciating.

A woman at a church I once served became surprisingly angry with me at one point over a ficus tree. I had never really noticed this ficus tree, but apparently she believed that its proper home was a corner of the sanctuary. Well, things got moved around quite a bit at this church, and someone at some point moved the tree out near the entrance. Then it was moved into our administrative office. When the tree failed to thrive, she came in and yelled at me. Then she doused the sucker with the most pungent fish oil I have ever smelled. There were moments during the summer when I had to step out of the office to breathe. My initial reaction was anger. How stupid or crazy could this person be to get so upset over a ridiculous tree? Talk about fighting over the carpet color!

When I was whining about this incident to another member who had been there for a long time, he asked me if I knew how that tree came to be at the church. Nope, I said. I didn't. On the day the church celebrated the memorial for the woman's husband, she brought that tree into the church as a gift. It was his and he loved it. All of a sudden I understood. We weren't fighting over a tree. Whether she knew it or not, when she looked at that tree, she felt connected to her husband. And when that tree was moved and started to fail, it was as if she were losing him all over again. Loss aversion is so powerful; but when we are in the grip of it, we will not be aware of it.

So, I give Alex strong marks for choosing changes that didn't take anything more away from the people he was serving. Adding communion and adding a Bible study may not have been things the people there cared very much about, but at least he didn't try to remove something that was sacred to them. I do question the pace of change, though. I appreciate the sense of urgency Alex felt—many young leaders feel the same—but he could have moved more slowly, especially in a setting where things were already trending in a more stable direction. I've heard all sorts of rules for how many changes a leader can make in a certain time frame. I suspect these rules vary from one context to another. But leaders at least need to be thoughtful about the temperature of their congregation and know when to back off. A good change implemented at the wrong time will still be viewed as bad change.

Alex might have tapped into the congregation's optimism bias more when it came to the community garden. Alex looked at the huge and productive community garden as mere social work. Because people weren't making explicit theological connections, Alex wasn't very interested in their work. But, of course, he could have spent a huge amount of time helping his members make better connections between the garden and the importance of food in the Scriptures and of caring for the poor. By investing in something that was already going well, Alex would have encountered more passion. And all the fellowship and study groups should have been a signal to him that even if people weren't always discussing the Bible or praying together, they liked each other enough to meet. This kind of positive energy doesn't exist in every church. Rather than overlooking these gatherings as merely social, spending some time with them and just listening might have given Alex valuable insight into some of the themes these people cared about the most.

The community garden also seems promising because of the representativeness heuristic. Alex had a working-class background. The congregation loved that the new pastor shared their blue-collar roots. They were used to recent seminarians from more privileged backgrounds with big words and soft hands. Because of the representativeness heuristic, when they looked at Alex they saw themselves. The representativeness heuristic may sometimes fall into stereotyping, but in this case the stereotype was true. Alex was a hard worker, skilled with his hands. Working in the garden alongside his congregation would have strengthened the relationship he already had based on the congregation's assumption that he was one of them.

While I think the community garden might have been a fruitful place to start, I still say the changes Alex picked were solid because they were adding to and not subtracting from an environment already feeling loss. The greatest opportunities for growth in this story aren't the changes themselves but the way in which Alex implemented them. When he implemented these changes, Alex connected to only one cognitive system of the congregation instead of both. When he instituted weekly communion without teaching about it, he was hoping the power of communion would so affect the emotional elephants that their reflective riders would just somehow understand why they were doing it. But his tactic didn't work. The people didn't resist weekly communion, but they didn't embrace it either. In this case it would have been helpful for Alex to clearly explain to the reflective, conscious riders why weekly communion was important to him, which might have created the conditions under which the congregation's emotional elephants would have been more receptive.

The opposite happened with the Bible study. Alex was so frustrated with the lack of their biblical knowledge that he just wanted to throw these people into the deep waters of Leviticus until they swam. He wanted their reflective riders to plow through and somehow become as excited about the Bible as he was. He didn't care that their emotional elephants might balk at endless genealogies and a fickle and capricious God. If Alex wanted them to love Scripture, a better approach might have been to start with more familiar books like the Gospels. He could have eased their elephants into the Bible and then allowed their riders to tackle the harder, darker passages down the road. Whenever anyone tells me they want to "read the whole Bible," I suggest they start with the Gospels and give themselves grace upon grace when they get stuck.

Unfortunately, the story of Alex isn't unique. Thousands of pastors have walked in his shoes; they enter ordained ministry with high hopes only to leave it with dashed expectations—broken down by a humanity they were never taught to expect. Church leaders will always need a deep theology and a profound understanding of Holy Scripture. But more than ever leaders today also need to understand how full humanity shapes their own thinking as well as those in their care.

11

Ten Behavioral Concepts, Heuristics, and Biases to Know

1. **Behavioral Theology**: Behavioral theology follows the same interdisciplinary path as behavioral economics, training church leaders to ask not only how people should behave theologically but also attending to how actual human beings are likely to behave. Behavioral theology restores the balance between Christ's full divinity and full humanity. Notably, behavioral theology lifts up cognitive bias not as sin but as a way of describing the limitations of our created humanity. We sin not by being biased but by failing to humbly accept and adjust for being biased.

2. **Availability Heuristic**: Information that we have gained through recent occurrences or through emotionally charged or frightening circumstances will be more available to us and easier to notice and recall. This heuristic will cause us to overestimate the frequency and risk of vivid events and underestimate the frequency and risk of less noticeable phenomena.

3. **Anchoring Heuristic**: When we judge something unknown to us, we use an anchor, or reference point, and then intuitively adjust from that point. Sometimes the anchors we use are arbitrary and can lead us astray.

4. **Representativeness Heuristic**: Using this heuristic, we evaluate individuals based on how well they seem to conform to our idea of the larger class in which we believe they fit. As with all stereotyping behavior, sometimes our sense of how similar an individual is to a larger group is right, but often our assumptions are wrong.

5. **Affect Heuristic**: Affect, or emotion, changes the way we perceive the world. When we are angry and tired, we think and make decisions differently than when we are calm and rested.

6. **Confirmation Bias**: We seek out and privilege information that supports the beliefs we already have. We ignore or invalidate evidence that challenges our beliefs.

7. **Loss Aversion**: We prefer avoiding loss more than we prefer gaining something. In many studies loss feels roughly twice as painful to us as gain.

8. **Status Quo Bias**: We tend to accept the default decisions given to us by others. This tendency is especially true when we find ourselves busy, pressed for time, or facing a new situation.

9. **Optimism Bias**: We tend to be overconfident of our abilities and like to think well of ourselves. We warm to people who encourage us and avoid or ignore people who question us.

10. **Framing Effects**: The way a question is posed substantively alters the way we respond. In conjunction with loss aversion, framing effects can be intense. Framing a decision around loss will make us more risk averse than posing the same decision around gain.

Interlude

THE CONGREGATION WITH TWO BRAINS

Sermon given at Tualatin Presbyterian Church, Palm Sunday, March 24, 2013

Luke 19:28–40: After he had said this, he went on ahead, going up to Jerusalem.

When he had come near Bethphage and Bethany, at the place called the Mount of Olives, he sent two of the disciples, saying, "Go into the village ahead of you, and as you enter it you will find tied there a colt that has never been ridden. Untie it and bring it here. If anyone asks you, 'Why are you untying it?' just say this, 'The Lord needs it.'" So those who were sent departed and found it as he had told them. As they were untying the colt, its owners asked them, "Why are you untying the colt?" They said, "The Lord needs it." Then they brought it to Jesus; and after throwing their cloaks on the colt, they set Jesus on it. As he rode along, people kept spreading their cloaks on the road. As he was now approaching the path down from the Mount of Olives, the whole multitude of the disciples began to praise God joyfully with a loud voice for all the deeds of power that they had seen, saying, "Blessed is the king who comes in the name of the Lord! Peace in heaven, and glory in the highest heaven!" Some of the Pharisees in the crowd said to him, "Teacher, order your disciples to stop." He answered, "I tell you, if these were silent, the stones would shout out."

Luke 23:13–25: Pilate then called together the chief priests, the leaders, and the people, and said to them, "You brought me this man as one who was perverting the people; and here I have examined him in your presence and have not found this man guilty of any of your charges against him. Neither has Herod, for he sent him back to us. Indeed, he has done nothing to deserve death. I will therefore have him flogged and release him."

Then they all shouted out together, "Away with this fellow! Release Barabbas for us!" (This was a man who had been put in prison for an insurrection that had taken place in the city, and for murder.) Pilate, wanting to release Jesus, addressed them again; but they kept shouting, "Crucify, crucify him!" A third time he said to them, "Why, what evil has he done? I have found in him no ground for the sentence of death; I will therefore have him flogged and then release him." But they kept urgently demanding with loud shouts that he should be crucified; and their voices prevailed. So Pilate gave his verdict that their demand should be granted. He released the man they asked for, the one who had been put in prison for insurrection and murder, and he handed Jesus over as they wished.

In 1996 the great state of Minnesota decided to run a little experiment with their tax system. They were trying to figure out how to increase the number of people paying their taxes. They selected thousands of people at random and sent four different messages. One message recounted all the good things taxes paid for—education, police, roads, etc. You wouldn't want to deprive people of all those good things, right? The second letter threatened people, enumerating the risks of noncompliance. Still others were told about a new office dedicated to helping people with their tax questions, with the phone number included. A fourth letter simply told people how many other Minnesotans were paying their taxes. (Believe it or not, just over 90 percent of Minnesotans were paying their taxes at that time.) So, one letter talked about the positive benefits of taxes, another talked about the ramifications of not paying taxes, a third letter gave them access to help with tax questions, and a fourth told them how many other people were already doing their tax duty.

Of all of these letters only one had any effect. But the effect was considerable.[1]

While you ponder which one of the letters was helpful—and how annoying it is for me not to give you the answer right now—I'll give you another puzzle. One that hits us every year about this time. Why on earth are the crowds so excited about Jesus on Palm Sunday only to cry out for his crucifixion a mere five days later? How is it that we go from "Hosanna!" today to "Crucify him!" by Good Friday?

1. Thaler and Sunstein, *Nudge*, 66.

Because that's what happens this week. On Palm Sunday Jesus enters Jerusalem like a Roman general—with people screaming Hosanna (save us!) and throwing palms and blankets down before him. But then, by the end of the week, this crowd completely turns. They cry out for Jesus Barabbas to be released, but Jesus of Nazareth—the Jesus whom they cheered on Palm Sunday, the Jesus who healed their wounds, the Jesus who fed them, and the Jesus who opened Scripture to them? For this Jesus of Nazareth they cry, "Crucify!"

How does this happen? And what does it mean for us?

So, a little psychology. In the last few years I've been doing a ton of thinking about thinking. (It hurts my brain just to say that.) I've been learning a great deal about how our minds experience and process the world. What most folks think is that there are two levels of processing going on in our brains all the time. Psychologists call these two levels of thinking System 1 and System 2, but fortunately others have come up with more descriptive terms such as automatic thinking and reflective thinking.

System 1, our automatic thinking, is going on all the time. Automatic thinking happens without us really knowing it. Every face you see—when you look at it, you instantly know whether this person is having a normal day or if they're upset. You don't really think about this, you just know it. When you drive your car, you process thousands and thousands of pieces of information, but you do it so seamlessly that when things are going OK, you can also listen to music or have a conversation. As long as things are going as you expect, your automatic brain can handle it.

Now System 2, our reflective thinking, is what you are aware of when you realize you are thinking. Reflective thinking happens when automatic thinking runs into something too complicated or surprising to handle. For instance, suppose someone hands you a math problem like twenty-four times forty-three. You can do this. It's not a hard problem. But, especially if you were going to do it in your head, most normal people would have to really think about it. You couldn't be having other conversations. You probably couldn't listen to music with lyrics or maybe any music at all. It would take a great deal of focus and concentration. This is reflective thinking. Most of the things we're really proud of in the world—our organizations, our architecture—are the fruits of reflective thinking.

Now, here's the interesting thing: when we think about ourselves, we tend to identify ourselves with this reflective thinking part of us. This is the part we have control over. This is the part of us we're aware of. But you know what? According to all the people who study this stuff, this reflective thinking is only about 1 percent of who we are. One percent. Most of us, they say—99 percent of us—is this automatic thinker, meaning we go through our day reacting and responding to the world at a level well below our level of awareness.

Psychologist Jonathan Haidt says we're like a rider sitting atop an animal; we're like a tiny reflective rider sitting atop an enormous elephant running around on automatic. Yes, we feel like we're in control; we feel like we're moving the animal in the direction we want it to go. But the reality? When we're busy or tired, or when we're in an emotionally overwhelming situation, the reality is our automatic system is the one making decisions for us. And this would be fine, except our automatic system is particularly prone to making predictable mistakes, called biases.

One of the most powerful biases we have is the desire to follow the herd. You may have heard of the famous experiments done by Solomon Asch back in the fifties. Asch was trying to figure out what happened in Nazi Germany—how all of these good, moral people could go along with the Holocaust. He would invite groups of people into a room to look at a row of lines. The lines were all the same length. What people didn't know is that only one person in the room was actually the subject of the experiment. Everyone else in the room was a confederate of Asch. So everyone in the room was asked which of the lines was the longest. All the confederates had been trained to point to one of the lines and say emphatically this line was obviously longer than the rest. The question is, what would the real person, the study subject, say? Over and over and over again, normal people—people whose eyes were working perfectly well—went along with the group. The more they looked at the line, the more they convinced themselves that the group was right. After all, how could all these people around them be wrong?

So, given the Asch results, maybe you've figured out which of the four experiments worked in Minnesota. The first group was told about all the good things their taxes would do, the second group was warned about what would happen if they didn't file, the third group was offered help, and the fourth group was told how many of their friends were filing. And in the case of Minnesota a huge majority of people were already filing. Now, personally, I would have thought hearing about all the good things taxes were doing would have helped. But it didn't. Nothing increased compliance except for the last letter—the one telling people that all their friends were doing it. The herd nudged them.

Now, nudging people to pay their taxes? This is a good thing. But we aren't always nudged in good ways.

It just took a few people at first, crying out for Jesus Barabbas—a few of his friends, no doubt. But Jesus' disciples, who led the crowd on Palm Sunday, were scared; they were nowhere to be seen. Even Peter, even the best of them.

That girl says to Peter, "I can hear by your accent you're a Galilean. You're one of his disciples, aren't you?"

"What, me? That's crazy," says Peter.

She insists, "You were with him, weren't you?"

"You're mistaken," says Peter.

"Come on," she presses. "Admit it."

"I tell you—I don't know the man!" he shouts in frustration.

And that's all it takes. It takes just a few people to turn a blind eye, a few people to keep silent. Jesus' friends didn't show, but Barabbas' friends did. And his few friends shouting turned into a group. And the group soon turned into a crowd. Pretty soon people who really didn't care much about either of these guys knew whom to shout for—because everyone else was shouting for Barabbas. There were so many of them. And they sounded so sure. Surely so many people couldn't be wrong?

The memory of Jesus on his donkey had already faded. And the elephants of the crowd were all stampeding in one direction. This is how we get from Palm Sunday to Good Friday.

This is how we get Enron. This is how we get Abu Ghraib. This is how we get the Steubenville, Ohio, rape case. The media focused in on the perpetrators and the girl, but to me the real tragedy of Steubenville was the dozens of kids, good kids, who saw what was happening, who saw a sixteen-year-old girl stumbling around, incapacitated. And instead of helping her, instead of calling a caring adult or even the police, they turned a blind eye. Worse, they snapped pictures. A memento to laugh about later. And shame on many in the media who focused on how the girl shouldn't have had so much to drink. Find me someone who has never done anything foolish in high school or in life that they wish they could take back—poor decisions never justify criminal violation.

Now maybe this sounds like bad news. Ninety-nine percent of us is on automatic pilot—easily swayed by events and pushed around by life? But listen to this. New researchers have redone the Asch experiment. Only they've added to it. They've redone it so that some of the confederates in the room don't go along with the group. They wondered: maybe if it wasn't the whole group in total agreement, the real person might trust themselves a little more. And they were right. They started with ten confederates who disagreed with the group and saw a huge change. They bumped it down to five rebel voices and still saw a huge change. They went all the way down to one. What if just *one* person in an entire crowd had the guts to say, "Yeah . . . I see it a little bit differently." Even when just one confederate went against the group, the real study participants were far more likely to go against the crowd.

And that's what this entire week is about. We follow Jesus into Holy Week—and one of the most remarkable things about him is no matter what is happening, he remains true. When he's at table with the disciples, he tells them goodbye and that whenever they break this bread and drink from this cup to remember him. He serves everyone at the table. Even Judas. And later that night, when Judas betrays him and leads the Romans into the garden? Jesus kisses him and tells his friends to put their swords away—to live by the sword is to die by the sword. Even at his lowest point—when he's tempted to run and when he begs God to take this cup—Jesus says, "And yet thy will be done, not mine." When they strip him and beat him, he does not waver. When they tell him to come down off his cross—to jump down off that cross and stop loving us—he stays. He chooses love. He always chooses love.

No matter what happened, no matter how great the crowd—Jesus always stood his ground and remained true. And that's why more than two thousand years later we're still here, gathered around the flames of this ancient story, telling it and retelling it and retelling it again, until we live it, until he lives through us.

Sometimes it only takes one person to have the courage to say how they feel, to raise their voice. One person. And it can make all the difference. Will it be you? Amen.

SECTION TWO

The Irrational Paul

12

Let the Games Begin!

Several years ago I had the opportunity to visit Israel. I marveled at the freshwater pool Herod built into the Mediterranean just to show that he could. I survived a terrifying ride up Mount Tabor to visit the Church of the Transfiguration. (My favorite thing about that church? While Jesus smacks Peter down for suggesting they build "booths" for Moses and Elijah, there are now two small, booth-like rooms dedicated to the dynamic duo. It took centuries, but Peter finally got his way.) Our group sailed on a magical, sunlit morning on the Galilee. We remembered our baptisms in the company of several terrifyingly large nutria in the River Jordan. We floated in the Dead Sea, ascended to Masada, and caught our first glimpse of Jerusalem, the "city of peace," next to young Israeli soldiers equipped with fully automatic weapons.

It was an incredible trip. But of all the wonders I saw, the thing that made the greatest impression on me was something most pilgrims could walk right by. Along the Via Dolorosa, the path Jesus walked on the way to his crucifixion, if you slip into the Sisters of Zion convent and watch where you are stepping, you will find a circular pattern of boxes etched into the stone floor. It looks like a crude gameboard. According to our tour guide, and also documented by author of *The Holy Land* Jerome Murphy-O'Connor, a gameboard is exactly what it is.[1]

The site is near where many believe the Antonia, the fortress housing Roman soldiers, stood. Our guide asked if any of us knew what it was like

---

1. Murphy-O'Connor, *Holy Land*, Kindle locations 695–97.

to be a soldier. Answering his own question, he said it's hours and hours of boredom punctuated by seconds of terror. To pass the time soldiers try to find ways to keep themselves entertained. Today they might smoke or play cards. In the first century Roman soldiers played a dice game known as the *basileus*, or king, game.

Basileus was a dice game, most likely played with sheeps' knuckles. Two soldiers would set up two game pieces known as kings. Depending on the roll of the dice, the soldiers would use staves to push their game pieces along the winding pathway. When one game piece finally made it to the center, they would declare the piece king and decorate it with a robe and crown.

Sound familiar?

It's intriguing to imagine that the soldiers guarding Jesus became tired of playing the *basileus* game with little game pieces and decided to play with the life-size figure of Jesus instead: "They stripped him and put a scarlet robe on him, and after twisting some thorns into a crown, they put it on his head. They put a reed in his right hand and knelt before him and mocked him, saying, 'Hail, King of the Jews!' They spat on him, and took the reed and struck him on the head. After mocking him, they stripped him of the robe and put his own clothes on him. Then they led him away to crucify him" (Matt 27:28–31).

It might have been a game the soldiers were playing, but there was nothing amusing about it. This game was deadly serious. And for the believer, it's revelatory, too. It's a game that reveals who Jesus really is. The soldiers believe they are mocking Jesus by crowning him as *basileus*, as king, but the person of faith sees a deeper truth—Jesus, Lord of lords and King of kings—hiding underneath.

Anyone who has ever been truly involved in a game knows this serious and revelatory side of games. All those watching the Americans play the Soviets during the 1980 Winter Olympics knew in the deepest part of themselves that it was never "just a game." When against all odds the Americans won the contest, now known as the "Miracle on Ice," some of the toughest men in the world openly wept, and the crowds in the stands spontaneously burst into "God Bless America." Or when Nelson Mandela supported South Africa's all-white rugby team and shook hands with team captain Francois Pienaar after their World Cup victory in 1995, everyone knew it wasn't *merely* a game. Their handshake was the most visible symbol of racial reconciliation South Africa had ever seen. Games often uncover unknown strength and determination and possess the power to bring strangers into community.

So, let the games begin!

13

Getting to Know Game Theory

Imagine you are a brilliant Harvard MBA student. You've made it. Your future's so bright you have to wear designer shades. One day you're sitting in class when your professor, Max Bazerman, whips out a crisp twenty-dollar bill and invites you to play a game. Intrigued? The rules of the game, Bazerman tells you, are simple. There are only three. The first rule is that whoever offers the highest bid in one-dollar increments will pay their bid and walk away with Andrew Jackson. Rule number two is that whoever offers the second highest bid will also have to pony up their bid amount. The third rule is that players may not collude. Both players have to play for themselves and avoid making side agreements.

What could be better? It's a simple game with easy rules, and at the end of it someone will walk away with lunch money. The bidding starts. Someone offers to pay one dollar. Who wouldn't? One dollar in exchange for twenty? Yes, please. So, you offer two. It's still an amazing deal. The bidding continues until you get up to nineteen dollars. You aren't thrilled about this, but you aren't upset either. At nineteen dollars the twenty-dollar bill isn't really such a great deal. But at least you aren't losing money. Then, the other bidder offers up an even trade: he offers twenty dollars. First you smile, thinking he made a poor bid. Then you frown. You realize that if you don't offer a higher bid, you're going to lose. Not only will you lose the twenty-dollar bill, but you will lose the nineteen dollars you already bid. Nineteen dollars for what? For the right to look like an idiot in front of all

91

your friends. So even though you know it doesn't really make sense, you offer a bid of twenty-one dollars. The other bidder, feeling that same sinking sensation, looks at you with a sour frown and keeps on raising the bid.

This strange scenario isn't fictional. Professor Bazerman plays this dollar auction game with every entering Harvard MBA class. So far the highest take was $407 with combined bids of $204 and $203, and in ten years Bazerman has donated quite a bit of money to charity.[1] A lot of these bright, young people, the so-called smartest guys in the room, would ultimately go on to run investment banks and hedge funds partly responsible for the 2008 global financial collapse. Even very intelligent people can become enmeshed in games they can win and still very much lose at the same time. Game theory, the study of strategic decision-making in conflicted situations, holds that the key to understanding human behavior lies in understanding the game one is playing. This maxim is true when people know they are playing a game. It is especially true when they don't.

Princeton's John von Neumann and Oskar Morgenstern developed the outline of game theory in 1944. Morgenstern, an economist, lent the economic frame to game theory, but it was von Neumann who put game theory on the map. A Hungarian-born mathematician, von Neumann was something of a cross between Mozart and Mr. Wizard. A *wunderkind*, he grew up joking with his father in classical Greek and showing off his talents when guests came over for dinner. He would memorize a column in a telephone book, and a guest would quiz the boy on names and numbers.[2] Von Neumann would go on to participate in the Manhattan Project, the push to develop the hydrogen bomb, and is considered a pioneer in computer science.

Von Neumann was also quite the *bon vivant*, throwing wild parties and pulling practical jokes on friends. Von Neumann laughed at how he once took an unsuspecting Albert Einstein to the train station at Princeton Junction and put him on the train heading south to Philadelphia rather than north to New York where Einstein was headed. (I'm not sure how much of a knee-slapper that is, but I suppose there aren't that many people who could say they put one over on Einstein.)

Game theory initially related only to economic behavior. In the years since von Neumann and Morgenstern developed the concept, game theory has grown in application to concerns as diverse as evolutionary biology, race relations, and even which way a professional soccer goalie should lean during a penalty kick. I will begin by outlining the fundamental components

1. Brafman and Brafman, *Sway*, 30–32. See also the note on 188–89.

2. Poundstone, *Prisoner's Dilemma*, 12.

of game theory: I will define what a game is; examine the importance of players; look at what strategy means in game theory, in contrast with how most of us think of strategy; and finally, explore payoffs.

A game in game theory is really a specialized term of art. To a game theorist a game is a social situation in which at least two people find themselves in conflict, and the actions of one player affect the outcome for the other player.[3] What's important about this definition is that game theory is essentially about people in community. Solitaire is most definitely a game in the minds of most people, but solitaire fails to qualify as a game for the purposes of game theory. A game must involve at least two people, and often games involve entire communities.

Games can also be zero or positive sum. Zero-sum games produce winners and losers—one player's gain comes at the expense of another player's loss. I've found that many people who have negative feelings about games, especially around games in the world of sports, carry painful memories of losing. Given what we know about loss aversion, it's little wonder that many would rather avoid games than get stuck in a losing situation. But zero-sum games aren't the only kinds of scenarios game theorists study; they certainly aren't the most common. The most common kind of game is a positive-sum game, a game in which multiple players can triumph together.

Andy Crouch, executive editor of *Christianity Today*, offers the most beautiful example of a positive-sum game in *Playing God*. He relates that at the age of forty-one he decided to try learning how to play the cello. Each time he took a lesson from his teacher, he became a slightly better player—yet his teacher's skill suffered not at all. The teaching game they were experiencing was positive sum: both players could flourish.[4] One of the most important skills leaders can hone is the ability to identify bad games that create losers and transform them into positive games that build up the body.

This communal definition of a game and the acknowledgment of conflict are important for church leaders. The children's rhyme about the church, the steeple, and the people is right on. The church is the body of Christ, Paul reminds us. Individuals constitute different members of Christ's body, and it takes all of us together to make the whole. No one is a Christian alone; we are always Christians together. Another reason game theory is important in a church setting is that it recognizes the element of conflict. And as every leader knows, wherever two or more Christians are gathered, not only is Jesus present but conflict is, too. And conflict, in game theory,

3. Harrington, *Games, Strategies*, 2.
4. Crouch, *Playing God*, 41.

isn't always a bad thing. Conflict can be productive. Conflict is simply what happens when different people come together with varied wants and needs.

Next, the most obvious feature of a game in game theory is the players. To understand a game well, you have to be able to identify all the players involved. Unfortunately, this is easier said than done. Think back to the first story I shared about how our congregation rebelled when leaders presented a plan to more openly welcome the LGBT community. Remember, I did a great job working with our session, the church's governing body. We met for months, sometimes spending hours in prayer and study and conversation. It was easy to identify the importance of the session members as players in this game. But I almost entirely ignored the other players, the members of the whole congregation. I was so focused on finding common ground among my decision-makers, and so pleased we finally found that ground, that I forgot it would probably take the congregation at least as long as the session to arrive at the same place.

Wise leadership bodies will take extra time to consider those who don't have a voice in shaping the decision but still may be affected by it. Leadership bodies can easily move too quickly when they sense alignment among the obvious players, the decision-makers, but fail to take into account the possible responses of those impacted by the decision who, especially if angered, may become very active players indeed.

In 2014 the Presbyterian Mission Agency revealed a new advertising direction for the 2015 special offerings. Hoping to draw positive attention to the worldwide problem of access to clean water, the campaign relied on a number of promotional ads, one of which showed a young Asian girl with the caption: "Needs Help with her Drinking Problem."[5] The campaign certainly drew attention, but not the kind leaders were hoping for. Pastors and leaders who weren't part of the decision-making body took to social media to protest what they perceived as a campaign that would likely increase racial stereotyping rather than focus attention on clean water. The uproar caused by these forgotten players became so intense the campaign was shelved at what must have been an extraordinary cost.[6] My guess is the Presbyterian Mission Agency will probably try to solicit more feedback from all those affected by advertising campaigns in the future.

After making sure we take time to understand the role of all the players, especially those on the margins of our awareness, game theorists encourage us to explicate the strategy of the game. As with the specialized meaning of the term *game*, *strategy* also means something unique in game theory. For

5. Scanlon, "Special Offerings Campaign," para. 3.

6. Locke, Statement from Special Offerings, paras. 1–5.

most church leaders, when we talk about strategy we mean a single plan to achieve a goal. For instance, the church I serve wanted to hire a staff person to oversee our family ministry program in 2008. We've already mentioned 2008 and what a lousy year it was for the world financially. So, our first plan, which we thought of as a strategy, was to ask the congregation for more money during the annual stewardship drive; that plan failed. Undeterred, we came up with a different plan. We had a little over $300,000 left on our mortgage, and we realized the interest payments came close to the amount we needed to pay a staff person. So we embarked on a plan to retire the debt. This was a great plan in that it appealed to fiscal conservatives who liked the idea of being debt-free as well as those who supported family ministry. We used the terms *plan* and *strategy* synonymously, but in game theory a strategy is something far more comprehensive.

In game theory a strategy is a map that includes all the players, all the possible decisions, and all the imaginable outcomes of these various decisions.[7] There are two ways game theorists depict these strategies. They use the strategic form, also termed the normal form, to represent simple, simultaneous games by creating a matrix. In a very powerful, elegant way a strategic form can show all the players and their outcomes depending on the different paths they take. In later chapters we will use this form to illustrate the chicken game and the prisoner's dilemma.

Game theorists use the extensive form of a game, also known as a game tree, for sequential games as well as more complicated games. A game tree depicts decision nodes in ever-increasing branches of complexity. Counter-intuitively, game theorists teach us to read a game tree backward by starting with the outcome, then moving through all the decisions until we reach the first decision. This is kind of like Fred Craddock's advice in his *Thirteen Ways to End a Sermon* to start with the ending first.

What's so important about this more robust understanding of strategy is that it helps us think through all the possible decisions and outcomes we might face before they happen. Anticipating what might happen and thinking through our response ahead of time is the very definition of good planning. To begin to tie this section on game theory to the first section on predictable irrationality, advanced planning is part of what helps us keep decision-making more in the realm of our inner Jacob than our inner Esau. Surprise triggers our automatic system, prone as it is to predictable irrationality. It is incredibly difficult to think well when our bodies are flushed with alarm caused by the unexpected.

7. Harrington, *Games, Strategies*, 34.

That campaign we embarked on to retire our debt and hire a new staff person? We did it. We asked a small circle of contributors to give $15,000 over the course of three years. We collected about half the money we needed for the campaign from this small circle and then went public, enlisting the support of the whole congregation. And in three years we paid off our debt and celebrated at our congregational meeting. For part of the celebration I created a symbolic mortgage that I lit on fire. It was a good idea. It would have been a great idea had I bothered to think through the ramifications of lighting a piece of paper on fire in our sanctuary—had I explicated a strategy! After setting fire to the symbolic mortgage, I realized very quickly that I didn't know what I was going to do with this burning paper. The paten that holds the communion bread was on the Lord's Table, but I didn't feel right about putting it in that. The sanctuary has a beautiful baptismal font made from Turkish alabaster, but it welcomes you into worship and was on the far side of the congregation from me. Finally, as my fingers started to burn, I panicked and just threw the burning remnant to the floor where I stamped it out, which left a small black mark. I looked up and said, "The good news is we retired the debt. The bad news is we're starting a new campaign to replace the carpet." I like to think that most of the time the people I care for laugh with me, but I knew that morning they were definitely laughing at me. I was just grateful they were laughing.

Finally, the last aspect that's crucial to fully understanding a game is the payoff for each player. A payoff describes how much a player values a particular outcome.[8] Game theorists think of payoffs in two ways: ordinal and cardinal. Ordinal payoffs simply rank outcomes in terms of desirability. Cardinal payoffs allow game theorists to say more exactly how much each player values a particular outcome.[9] Normally, when looking at church conflict it's enough to use ordinal payoffs to figure out how players rank alternative options.

In my experience, church leaders are often uncomfortable talking about payoffs. At first blush discussing payoffs seems to imply a selfish, what's-in-it-for-me attitude. But this isn't the case. Payoffs describe preferences, and everyone has preferences. In thriving congregations, I suspect, players often prefer courses of action that serve the "least of these," for example. For such players decisions that benefit others offer a higher payoff than decisions that benefit them alone. So, just being aware of payoffs doesn't make players selfish.

8. Ibid., 19.
9. Ibid., 186.

Understanding payoffs is critical because they help leaders see what congregations actually care about rather than what we think they should care about. In other words, leaders fundamentally have to care enough about the people we lead to understand what is really important to them, especially when their values differ. Leaders don't have to like these values. We certainly don't have to agree with them. We can desire to change them over time. But before we can change anything, we must first have enough respect to understand it. My pastoral care professor in seminary, Bob Dykstra, taught me that we cannot change what we do not first love. Learning people well enough to understand their payoffs, what they really care about, isn't about calculation: it's an act of love.

Not taking the time to understand these payoffs can have terrible consequences. I once worked with a large established congregation with a history of conflict. In light of a string of pastoral exits, my hopes for their new head of staff were somewhat muted. Unfortunately, none of us knew how bad the situation would get. Concerns about the new head pastor emerged early, and I began working closely with the personnel chair and staff. In spite of numerous conversations between the pastor and the personnel chair, other leaders became increasingly convinced this new relationship wasn't working out. To their credit, the personnel team took an incredible amount of time and extended chance after chance, but ultimately they came to a unanimous decision that the match was a poor one.

All of this was lamentable but understandable. Sometimes the call process leads to a poor match. It happens. But the leaders on the personnel committee were so focused on the facts as they understood them that they forgot to take into account the payoffs of the pastor and the payoffs of the larger leadership body. The pastor acknowledged he had made mistakes but also believed God had called him to that church. If the personnel team had understood how much the pastor wanted to stay, they might have worked with him to offer a higher incentive to leave quietly. But it was the church governing board, the session, that actually had to vote to put into motion the process of terminating the pastor's call. Probably the worst mistake occurred when the personnel committee brought their recommendation to the session. The personnel team created an enormous report detailing the work they had done and the reasons for their recommendation to end the call. They called the meeting for the first week of Advent.

The timing could not have been worse. For one thing, churches tend to batten down the hatches during Advent, with all the extra work of the holiday season—not the best time to lose or anger a pastor from a purely practical standpoint. Second, many—especially church leaders—want to be generous and loving during the Christmas season. Rare is the Grinch who wants to vote to potentially fire someone right before baby Jesus' birthday. Payoffs are contextual. The preferences of a decision body in December can often be quite different than they might be in June. The personnel leaders were so focused on the data and the arguments supporting their conclusions that they never considered how the payoffs for the session might be affected by the holidays.

In what was a rancorous meeting, my sense was that many on the church board just weren't in a place to hear the report from personnel. They didn't want to be in an extra meeting during the holidays in the first place, and they certainly didn't want to be in a hostile meeting. When I called for the vote, the group was nearly split, with only a slim majority in favor of keeping the pastor. While hardly a mandate, he survived. And he would continue to survive for several more months until after Easter, when support for him collapsed. Was this shift due to leaders simply having more time to contemplate the situation? Did a greater awareness that problems existed allow them to see more evidence? I suppose both these questions factored into the change, but the largest reason was that payoffs for the session changed when the pressure of the high holy days ended. In ordinary time they could consider options that simply weren't on the table when they were in holiday mode.

Now that we know a little bit about what a game in game theory is, let's spend some time in the next two chapters learning about some specific games game theorists use in their experiments.

14

Playing Games and Telling Stories
Coordination Games

One of the intriguing connections between game theory and faithful leadership is the reliance upon story. Rich stories fill the Old Testament. Jesus taught using parables that teased the ears of hearers with tales of forgiving fathers, grateful (and grumbling) laborers, and wise and foolish girls. These stories delight and draw us into reimagining how the world could be. Something similar happens in game theory. Instead of sheep and goats, however, game theorists tell stories about hawks and doves, stag and rabbit hunters, and prisoners stuck in a dilemma.

Narrative permeates game theory because stories are an excellent medium for expressing that when it comes to conflict, little is new under the sun. Conflicts form patterns, and one of the ways we describe patterns is by telling stories about them. Over time the patterns of conflict in game theory became so easy to identify that iconic stories emerged as a kind of shorthand. It's similar to how people play roles in family systems theory. Many church leaders are already familiar with systems theory, which describes how individuals play predictable family roles such as the enabler, hero, or mascot. If you remove one person from a system without fundamentally changing the dynamics of the system, a new person can enter the system, but they will tend to take on the role of the person who left or also risk being removed from the system. The system is often more powerful than the personalities in the system.

In a similar way game theorists note that games are more important than personalities, and patterns of conflict in games tend to repeat. Think about the dollar auction described earlier: while the players may change, the game and its rules remain the same, so a game theorist can often predict the outcome. Just as we needed to limit our treatment of cognitive heuristics and biases in the first section, we will first discuss only the most important games here: the chicken game (also known as the hawk-dove game), the battle of the sexes, the stag hunt, the volunteer's dilemma, the prisoner's dilemma, the public goods game, and the ultimatum game. Then we will spend more in-depth time on the ultimatum game, the prisoner's dilemma, and the public goods game.

In *Rebel Without a Cause* James Dean's character, Jim, winds up in a chicken game with Corey Allen's character, Buzz. The standard chicken game features two cars racing toward a potential head-on collision, and in this scenario the chicken is the first car to swerve. But in this movie version both kids race their cars toward a high cliff overlooking the ocean. The first one to jump out is the chicken. The movie makes clear that chicken is not a game you want to be in. As Jim and Buzz race toward the cliff, Buzz catches his coat sleeve on the door handle, preventing him from escaping. Jim jumps out at the last minute and watches his car and Buzz's car hurtle over the edge, destroying both vehicles and killing Buzz. Chicken is a dangerous game: the potential for things to go wrong is always so much greater than the potential for anything to go right.

Game theorists use a game matrix to describe chicken. A game matrix elegantly describes all the possible strategies in a game. The simple games at which we will look have only four possible outcomes, but certainly it's possible to add much more complexity. The standard way of interpreting a game matrix is first to read the payoff of Player 1, the row player listed on the left side of the matrix, and then to look at Player 2, the column player listed above the matrix. In the standard game of chicken, if both players swerve, neither player gains nor loses. If one player keeps going while the other swerves, the one who keeps going gains a moderately positive payoff; the swerver receives a moderately negative payoff. But the big problem of this game occurs when both players refuse to swerve. In that case they share an enormously painful, possibly deadly, negative payoff—a classic lose-lose situation.

Chicken Game		Player 2	
		Swerve	Don't Swerve
Player 1	Swerve	0, 0	-2, 2
	Don't Swerve	2, -2	-10, -10

Unfortunately, chicken games happen all the time. It's easy to see these showdowns in the world around us. British philosopher Bertrand Russell compared the arms race in the Cold War to a game of chicken.[1] More recently the United States Congress has played chicken over the fiscal cliff and the debt ceiling. These games don't just happen on a global scale, either. Small groups and individuals can find themselves locked in a game of chicken, too. There is an especially high potential for confrontation when strong-minded people with deep commitments collide, which happens often in church environments.

Not long ago I welcomed a visitor who seemed absolutely delighted with our congregation. She loved the music and the warm welcome she received, and best of all, she loved the preaching. She was obviously a brilliant woman of refined taste. After about a month she asked if we could meet. Thinking we would be talking about how she might become more involved, I was surprised to find myself in a heated conversation about church politics. It turned out she was a refugee from another congregation where she had found herself at odds with their new pastor. After a bit of probing I began to sense, with some disappointment, that I probably held views more similar to that pastor than she realized. With even greater disappointment, I then listened to her tell me with great pride how she led a coup attempt against the new pastor. She organized all of her like-minded friends, and together they made a list of demands. At the end of this list they stated that if their demands weren't met, they would collectively take their membership and pledges elsewhere. She was hoping, of course, that the church would swerve. They didn't. Interestingly, her group did. Most of them backed down and, while they weren't thrilled with the direction their church was going, decided to stick it out. Just she and a couple of her friends decided to leave. Given her bullying, my-way-or-the-highway behavior, I breathed a sigh of relief when she figured out our congregation probably wasn't going to be a good fit either.

Surprisingly, the chicken game isn't always negative. Sometimes conflict can be a good thing. Take the biblical story of Solomon, who had to decide between the two women claiming to be the mother of one baby in 1

---

1. Russell, *Common Sense*, 30.

Kings 3:16–28. Solomon didn't have the benefit of genetic analysis to settle the conflict, so he created a game of chicken instead. Wielding a sword and dramatically threatening to split the child in two, Solomon set up a game in which he could swerve or cut the child in two, and both women could swerve or remain steadfast in their claim. One of the women flinched at the last moment. Solomon handed the baby to her, rightly concluding the true mother would prefer to see her child live with another woman than watch her child die.

What is fascinating about Solomon's move is that rather than shrinking from or de-escalating the conflict, he actually increased the level of tension. The default role that so many pastors play is to be the non-anxious presence attempting to calm every situation. While to be sure many situations do call for a calming presence, game theory pushes us to ask whether some situations might call for increasing tension rather than decreasing it. Game theory suggests that in some circumstances a wise leader will know her job is not to smooth every feather and please every constituent.

Fortunately, not every game is fraught with such drama. The battle of the sexes is another classic game, but unlike chicken the risk of destruction is far lower. In the story of the battle of the sexes we meet a happy couple with the unhappy problem of preferring different activities.[2] The couple is happy because they like each other and want to spend time together. Their unhappiness stems from the fact that they just can't seem to agree on what to do when they go out. In the hardest version of this game the couple are actually trying to show up at an event together but don't have the ability to communicate. This story was dreamed up before the ubiquity of cell phones. Today, you could just say they both forgot to charge their devices and had to guess. Let's say the couple agree they either want to go to a nice dinner at their favorite downtown restaurant or they want to go watch roller derby. The guy is something of a foodie and really prefers to go to dinner. He can't stand roller derby and only goes because of his undying love for his *undoubtedly* better half. The woman, on the other hand, loves roller derby. And she thinks their favorite restaurant is ridiculously overpriced and serves food she can't pronounce. She eats at this place only because she truly enjoys the company of her charming, if snobbish, beloved. What's our intrepid couple to do?

Here's how a game theorist would map the strategies of each player:

2. Dixit and Nalebuff, *Art of Strategy*, 116.

Battle of the Sexes		Player 2 (The Man)	
		Dinner	Roller Derby
Player 1 (The Woman)	Dinner	2, 3	0, 0
	Roller Derby	1, 1	3, 2

You can observe they are both the happiest, the payoff is the highest for each of them, when they are together no matter what they are doing. The woman would rather be with her husband even if she has to eat Portlandia chicken with a name and a story behind it. The man prefers to gaze at his lovely wife while tattooed women named Helen Killer and Genghis Mom tear into one another and zip around the track. Both of them are slightly happy if they wind up in the place they like the best even though they end up alone. The man is happy eating his gluten-free, locovore meal. The woman is happy watching the Girlzillas crush the Women of Mass Destruction. But neither is thrilled to show up to the place they don't enjoy by themselves.

The great challenge of such a coordination game, then, is how to find a meeting place. Finding common ground is a huge challenge facing many congregations, especially with regard to worship style. Although much is rightly made of the worship wars between traditional and contemporary music that continue to vex congregations, even congregations that successfully negotiate the music-style minefield can find themselves divided on other issues. Is it appropriate to clap? Is it right to display national flags? Is it OK to bring coffee into the sanctuary? No matter how healthy a congregation may be, it's just easier at times to focus on the things that divide us rather than all we have in common.

Political strategist and Nobel Prize laureate Thomas Schelling discovered that most communities navigate these coordination games by way of what are now known as Schelling points. When players have a stronger desire to coordinate than to opt for individual preferences, they find unspoken Schelling points to guide their behavior. An example of such a focal point is which direction to steer if you meet an oncoming car on a single lane. In the abstract it doesn't really matter whether you push to the left or pull to the right as long as the other driver moves in the opposite direction so you avoid a crash. In the particular, however, it matters greatly if you are driving in England or in most of the rest of the world. The Schelling point in England is to steer left; for most other places the convention is to turn to the right.

In a fascinating thought experiment Schelling asked a group of students to imagine they had to meet a stranger at some point tomorrow in

New York City without the ability to communicate. He asked them to write down a time and a place on a sheet of paper. For anyone who has been to New York City this task seems impossible. New York City is so vast, so filled with interesting places, how could anyone pull off such a stunt? And yet, over and over again, people playing this game do a pretty good job of coordinating. For the time, nearly everyone playing the game picks high noon. Not eleven o'clock. Not three thirty in the afternoon. High noon. Why? There is no logic to it. It just seems right to most people, which is what counts. And the place? There is more diversity regarding the place, but most people pick the information booth at Grand Central Station. Thomas Schelling would suggest that church leaders have to understand the deep focal points of their communities, the unspoken assumptions and gathering places, if they are to successfully navigate the normal tensions congregations experience when people have different preferences.

The easiest way to apply these Schelling points to the church world is to look at what leaders often derisively refer to as the congregation's sacred cows. Sometimes it's the case that congregations cling to sacred cows that might have served them in the past but have become golden calves that keep them from moving forward. But more often I think pastors, especially new pastors, roll their eyes too quickly at these sacred cows; they sometimes fail to look closely enough to understand the deep values that may be hiding underneath.

I'm only the second called pastor to serve Tualatin (pronounced Too-AH-luh-tin) Presbyterian Church. I followed a fantastic interim and a new church developer who successfully planted the congregation and then stayed for twenty-two years. Let's just say the founding pastor left a deep groove. In the deepest of these grooves lies what the congregation affectionately refers to as the birthday chicken—a wicker basket in the shape of a chicken. Every Sunday the pastor or liturgist invites all who have had a birthday in the prior week to come forward. Adults and children alike place coins in the basket to count their age; the money goes to mission support. Then the congregation sings a version of "Happy Birthday" in which God blesses them, and the celebrant finishes it all off with a prayer. How do I know this is a sacred cow?

The first time I led worship one of the members of my call committee approached me after service and said everything was great . . . except for the chicken. I did the chicken wrong. He assured me that I was the pastor now and could do whatever I wanted, but they were used to the chicken being done in a certain way. I told him I was more than glad to learn their ways. The full liturgy of the birthday chicken blessing involves saying the Aaronic benediction while touching the forehead of each person. The first time I neither touched foreheads nor prayed the Aaronic blessing. The second time

I got the blessing right but only touched them on the shoulder. Finally, on the third try, I got the right blessing and the right body part. They seemed baffled I didn't know about this tradition. Didn't everyone do the birthday chicken? As I told them more than once, as surprising as it seems, the birthday chicken liturgy isn't actually in our Book of Common Worship.

At first I resented the chicken. I resented the fact that my congregants seemed to care more about this chicken than what I was preaching. I didn't like how campy it was. Who sings "Happy Birthday" in church every Sunday? It was frustrating to me that I felt as if I could probably celebrate communion dressed like a clown and they wouldn't bat an eye, but when I prayed the "wrong" birthday prayer I was making a mistake. But in spite of my resentment I faithfully performed the rite of the chicken every Sunday. And I'm extremely glad I did.

After I had been there for a few years, I casually mentioned my dislike of the chicken to a leader I greatly respected. She looked at me and became quiet. Then she told me she could understand that, but the birthday chicken was extremely important for her. I asked her why. She said when she was a child she always had a birthday party; but when she became an adult, her family told her birthdays were just something for kids. She said now once a year she gets to stand in front of the congregation, celebrate her birth, and receive a blessing on her life. Moreover, she voiced that when I touched her and said the Aaronic benediction, she felt holy and loved. What seemed silly to me held profound meaning for her and many others. I have never since complained about the birthday chicken.

That moment is a gathering place for the congregation I serve. It was a touchstone from the very inception of the church. And I learned that day it isn't just a hokey ritual that outlived its purpose. It is a meeting place where adults feel touched, blessed, named, and claimed by God. Again, I'm not saying that every revered tradition a community holds dear is a good thing or worth keeping. I am saying that sometimes it takes a long time to understand the real meaning and value underlying some of these traditions. And leaders, particularly pastors in a hurry to be change agents, may not always take the necessary time to understand and protect these Schelling points. And protecting Schelling points, these gathering places, provides the way to weather disagreements over worship style and to modify what really does need to change. Our congregation struggles with music style from time to time. And don't get me started on whether it's OK to clap. But one of the reasons we endure through these challenges is we all agree that we prefer to be together than alone and have our own way. Practices such as the birthday chicken are tangible reminders of that togetherness.

Missing these Schelling points can be disastrous. United Methodist leadership expert Lovett Weems tells the story of a young United Methodist pastor just out of seminary who might have had the shortest pastorate in his conference. When he arrived at the church, he was dismayed to find a huge, ugly tree blocking one of the doors to the church. This tree was not only a safety hazard, in the pastor's opinion, but also such an eyesore that it probably kept new people from wanting to visit. So, he found a chainsaw and helpfully cut down this monstrosity, painted the door, and waited for people to come and thank him for his leadership. It turns out the tree had a name. It was called "the Wesley tree," because John Wesley himself had planted it when he visited long ago. This poor guy lasted a week before the district superintendent met with him and said maybe God wanted him to consider another opportunity.[3]

The last kind of coordination game is known as a stag hunt. Philosopher Jean-Jacques Rousseau came up with the stag hunt game as a way of describing how Western culture formed. The scenario he imagined was simple. Imagine there are a couple of hunters standing around. Both of them know that if they work together they can bring home a mighty stag, which represents the best bang for their (forgive me) buck. But working on their own, each of the hunters can easily come back home with a hare. Both of them are happy hunting hare on their own, but they are the happiest going after a buck together. The cooperative dilemma is this: what happens if one hunter goes after a stag and the other goes after a rabbit? The stag hunter will come back with nothing, but the rabbit hunter will be eating hasenpfeffer for dinner.[4]

Here's what a stag hunt looks like in a game matrix:

Stag Hunt		Player 2	
		Stag	Hare
Player 1	Stag	3, 3	0, 1
	Hare	1, 0	1, 1

The stag hunt is a cooperation game; the hunters are most happy when working together but are also happy when they are hunting separately. Stag hunts occur among people who want to work together but just aren't always sure what everyone else is doing. So, the main concern for leaders in a stag hunt is making sure people have the ability to communicate well.

3. Weems, *Church Leadership*, 83.
4. Skyrms, *Stag Hunt*, 1.

It's especially important for leaders in a stag hunt to assume the best intentions about all the parties involved, especially when mistakes occur. Staying positive and adopting a forgiving attitude creates the ability for players to repair any damage done when participants fail to cooperate. When failures happen, leaders at least need to ask whether the failure was intentional or simply due to lack of knowledge. It's easy to assume the worst, but my experience suggests that most people don't generally wake up in the morning trying to make life hard for others. Most people are fairly self-absorbed, busy, and make mistakes due to moving too quickly without enough information.

When I chaired our presbytery's Commission on Ministry, we experienced challenges with cooperation on a regular basis, and the pastoral search process was high on our list of headache-producers. Searching for a new pastor in our denomination is a complicated process involving a lot of people. Congregations would often act in ways that weren't in accordance with our polity. When I was new to the commission, my initial reaction was to assume these congregations were trying to get around the rules. Our rules are often cumbersome, and I just figured they didn't want to jump through all the hoops.

After spending time on the commission, however, I realized intentional disregard was rarely the case. Most of the time congregations, even pastors, simply weren't aware that many different people needed to be involved in these complicated decisions; they made mistakes through lack of knowledge. I myself didn't know there was such a thing as a Commission on Ministry manual until I began serving on the commission. Now, it's certainly true that sometimes congregations weren't interested in cooperating, and it's important to be realistic about that. Most of the time, however, they were willing—but the commission wasn't doing a very good job of making sure people had all the information they needed to make the best decisions. This awareness allowed me to enter into hard conversations with a conciliatory attitude rather than with guns blazing. In almost every instance, this softer approach was more productive.

Of course, not every challenge is related to coordination. Sometimes we find ourselves mired in more conflictual situations. In these more difficult situations we need to be, as Jesus put it, as wise as serpents even as we are trying our best to be gentle as doves. There is an entire category of these harder games in game theory known as social dilemma games. In the next chapter we'll turn our attention to them.

15

Playing Games and Telling Stories
Social Dilemma Games

In 1964 Kitty Genovese was brutally attacked and murdered in her home in Queens, New York. The story grabbed the world's attention because, although many of her neighbors reported hearing her screams for help, no one called the police or acted to intervene.[1] Psychologists use the phrase bystander effect to describe this counterintuitive and disturbing finding: the higher the number of people witnessing a crime, the lower the likelihood that anyone will act to intervene. Responsibility becomes diffused among a crowd in a way that doesn't happen when a smaller number of people witness a crime. Part of the problem is people assume someone else has probably already called for help. Another factor is that it takes time and effort to intervene, and it would be nice if someone else would step up and save you the trouble.

Social dilemmas such as the volunteer's dilemma happen all the time in the church. Congregations seem almost designed for social dilemmas. You have things that need to get done, and some person or small group of people has to step up and do what needs to be done. When the job is especially challenging, you sometimes feel the heavy sense of church members standing around just wishing someone will relent and volunteer. In the volunteer's dilemma game matrix, instead of two individuals and two

1. Fisher, *Rock, Paper, Scissors*, 78.

outcomes, the dilemma is between your action and the crowd's. Unlike other game tables a volunteer's dilemma only shows the payoffs from the perspective of the individual. You are happiest if someone from the crowd acts and you don't. You are fairly happy if you volunteer, and someone else steps forward. At least you have help. You are not very pleased if you step forward alone. But the worst case for everyone is if you all stand around doing nothing, and the community suffers from things left undone.

Volunteer's Dilemma		The Crowd	
		Someone acts	No one acts
You	You act	2	1
	You don't act	3	0

There is a word for what we feel when we are trapped in such a dilemma. The Yaghan people of Tierra del Fuego give us one of the most amazing words in the world: *mamihlapinatapai*. *The Guinness Book of Records 1994* claims *mamihlapinatapai* to be the most difficult word in the world to define succinctly. This beautiful term translates as "looking at each other hoping that either will offer to do something which both parties desire but are unwilling to do."[2]

The Scriptures portray the period chronicled in the book of Judges as an ongoing volunteer's dilemma. The twelve tribes of Israel act with great independence from one another in a constant cycle between observance and doing what was evil in the sight of the Lord. When their behavior became very bad or when the threat against the people from without was great, God would raise up a judge from among the people. This charismatic leader would temporarily organize the Israelites until the threat was eliminated. Ultimately, this cycle was destructive, and the people finally clamored for a king to permanently unify the nation. Although Samuel warned the people that kings come with their own set of problems, the people clamored all the more for someone to unite them, so Samuel figured he'd better call Saul.

The church I serve is currently dealing with a volunteer's dilemma. The larger governing body that organizes the churches in our district is known as a presbytery. Our presbytery, the Presbytery of the Cascades, extends all the way from Vancouver, Washington, to Tulelake, California. Like most presbyteries ours experienced its heyday in the late fifties and early sixties. Flush with support from growing churches, the Presbytery of the Cascades

2. Matthews and McWhirter, *Guinness Book of Records*, 392.

became a programmatic institution, organizing mission and ministries that brought together multiple congregations. With declining church membership and tanking revenues, our presbytery, like so many other denominational bodies, has fallen on hard times. Barely able to afford staff, we now talk openly about the inability of our presbytery to continue its programmatic role.

One of those presbytery programs is something called family camp. Every year people from various churches descend on Honeyman State Park, a few miles south of Florence on the Oregon coast, for a week of fellowship, worship, and education in one of the most beautiful areas of the world. Florence is blessed with the most unusual mix of giant sand dunes, towering Pacific Northwest conifers, and the Pacific Ocean. But recently, presbytery officials have told the folks who organize family camp that they need to find another entity to provide them with a bank account and insurance. Leaders from family camp contacted the church I serve. Would our congregation be willing to volunteer our tax identification number, allow family camp to run upwards of twelve thousand dollars through our accounting system, and cover them with our insurance? You can imagine the immediate response from our session: Uh . . . why should we do what presbytery is no longer willing to do? And isn't there some other church, a larger church perhaps, that would be a better choice? It's a classic volunteer's dilemma. And I don't think I've ever seen so many faces with that *mamihlapinatapai* look in their eyes. I suspect we'll find a solution to continue this shared family camp ministry; but if we don't, we'll all be the poorer for it.

Along with the chicken game, the prisoner's dilemma is probably the most recognized game in game theory. The prisoner's dilemma pits individual benefits against the collective good. Melvin Dresher and Merrill Flood, mathematicians working at RAND Corporation, conceived of the prisoner's dilemma game during the dark days of the Cold War era.[3] Princeton mathematician Albert Tucker gave the prisoner's dilemma its name and parabolic story.

Tucker's story starts with two prisoners being held separately in a police station. Although the police have enough evidence to convict both prisoners on a small charge, without further cooperation and testimony from at least one of the men the police will not be able to convict either on the most serious charge. So, the police offer each prisoner the same deal: testify against your partner and go free. Three possibilities arise from this situation: the prisoners cooperate with one another and say nothing to the police, resulting in both being convicted on the lightest charge; the prisoners both give evidence (known as "defecting"), causing each to be convicted

3. Poundstone, *Prisoner's Dilemma*, 117.

on the serious charge; or, diabolically, one of the prisoners maintains silence while the other defects, which results in the loyal partner being convicted on the most serious charge while the betrayer goes free.[4]

Prisoner's Dilemma		Player 2	
		Cooperate	Defect
Player 1	Cooperate	3, 3	0, 5
	Defect	5, 0	1, 1

On the surface, a prisoner's dilemma game has the feel of a stag hunt. Both games have two players who have to make a simultaneous decision, and in both games it would be better for each player if they agreed to cooperate. The terrible difference between the prisoner's dilemma and the stag hunt, however, is what is called the sucker's payoff—one player gains by defecting, the other (the "sucker") loses. Why cooperate when you can do even better by defecting? In the stag hunt there is no motivation to defect because both players are happy hunting together or alone.

Sometimes the prisoner's dilemma is criticized for being too contrived. This is a fair criticism. It's hard to imagine a real-life scenario playing out exactly like the prisoner's dilemma where two people have to make a simultaneous decision with similar cooperation and defection incentives. But it's a mistake to write the prisoner's dilemma off because it seems artificial. What's incredibly important about the prisoner's dilemma is it reminds leaders that the people we lead are not always interested in cooperation. If the stag hunt reminds us to assume the best of intentions, the prisoner's dilemma teaches us to sleep with one eye open. The unfortunate truth every pastor knows is that sheep bite, and what many church leaders have experienced is that too many pastors behave like hired hands or even wolves rather than good shepherds. The prisoner's dilemma stands as a reminder that some people will always be wondering how to get others to work hard while they reap the benefits—what economists refer to as a free rider.

OK, I love the prisoner's dilemma. It's been studied so often that there is an enormous amount we know about this dynamic of pure conflict. When I first met with Dan Ariely to talk about conducting an experiment for my graduate research, I suggested observing prisoner's dilemma games with pastors and church leaders. But Dan quickly steered me in another direction—to a multiplayer version of the prisoner's dilemma called a public goods game. Frustrated at first with Dan directing me away from the

4. Ibid., 118.

prisoner's dilemma, I can now see he was totally right. If the weakness of the prisoner's dilemma is the unreal nature of the thought experiment, the best thing about the public goods game is it takes the abstract dynamic of the prisoner's dilemma and makes it real.

In "The Tragedy of the Commons" ecologist Garrett Hardin offers the classic version of a public goods game.[5] Hardin describes how in England farmers were allowed to graze their cattle on land known as the commons. The commons were land held for use by all. There were rules about how many cattle an individual farmer could graze on the commons, but there was little oversight. If every farmer cooperated and grazed the number of cows they were allowed, the land would sustain such use on an ongoing basis. However, each individual farmer stood to personally benefit by over-grazing. Given lax oversight, the farmers were unafraid of being punished. It is not difficult to imagine what happened. All the farmers decided if others would overgraze and benefit personally, they would be foolish not to do so as well. Most of the farmers overgrazed the commons, and within a short period of time the fields became a trampled wasteland of no use to anyone. As in a prisoner's dilemma, this public goods game pits the individual good of one farmer against the common good of all. The farmers as a collective would have benefited most by cooperating and working together; however, the farmers as individuals benefited more in the short term by defecting.

Have you ever been to a church potluck? Have you ever led a steward-ship campaign? Church potlucks and stewardship campaigns are both congregational examples of public goods games. It's best for the whole gathering if everyone brings food and helps clean up afterwards. But there's a temptation at every church potluck to show up even if you've forgotten to bring a dish, then enjoy the food and quietly slip out, leaving others to clean up after you. Or what about stewardship? Most churches jealously guard the privacy of how much individuals contribute. Many pastors I know choose not to know individual giving amounts, arguing they don't want to be swayed by how much a member does or does not contribute. This anonymity turns church giving into a public goods game. Of course, it would be best for the whole group if everyone gave generously, but there's always the temptation, especially when it's reasonable to believe few will know, to enjoy the benefits of a church family without helping support it.

Fortunately, the good news is that people are far more willing to coop-erate and play nicely when actually playing these games than game theorists say we should be. Next we'll move on to John Nash and learn why I say he has a beautiful, but wrong, mind.

5. Hardin, "Tragedy of the Commons," 1243–47.

16

John Nash's Beautiful (but Wrong) Mind

Some may be wondering at this point what all of this game theory stuff has to do with the predictable irrationality stuff from the first section. It's a fair question. To answer it, let's start with a simple game known as the ultimatum game.

To play the ultimatum game all you need is two players and a pile of twenty one-dollar bills. We will call one player the divider and the other player the decider. The job of the divider is to divide up the money however she likes. She can divide it up equally, so that she would get ten dollars and her partner would receive the other ten. Or, she could be more selfish and divide it up with nineteen dollars for herself and one dollar for the other player. Or, she could be generous and give the other player more. The decider, on the other hand, gets to decide whether the duo walks away with the money or whether no one gets the money. So, how should the divider play?

I say *should*, because classical game theory is normative, meaning classical game theorists say there is a correct, rational way to play this game. Since rational players will always maximize their self-interest, there is a correct way to play. The divider should give herself nineteen dollars and give the other player one dollar. And the decider should accept this lopsided deal. Why? Because one dollar is better than nothing, which is what the decider would get if he rejects the deal.

But is this correct, rational way really how you would play? If you are a living, breathing human being, then hopefully you said no. No, of course you wouldn't play this way. Not only would you not be such a jerk as to give yourself nineteen out of twenty dollars if you were the divider, but if you were the decider, you would probably prefer to get nothing than to see the divider get away with such unfairness. Is this irrational behavior? Sure it is. Is it what makes us human and care about fairness and justice? Absolutely.

After the success of his first book, *Predictably Irrational*, Dan Ariely followed up with *The Upside of Irrationality*. Relying on studies of games such as the ultimatum game, he writes,

> In most cases, the word "irrationality" has a negative connotation, implying anything from mistakenness to madness. If we were in charge of designing human beings, we would probably work as hard as we could to leave irrationality out of the formula; in *Predictably Irrational*, I explored the downside of our human biases. But there is a flip side to irrationality, one that is actually quite positive. Sometimes we are fortunate in our irrational abilities because, among other things, they allow us to adapt to new environments, trust other people, enjoy expending effort, and love our kids. These kinds of forces are part and parcel of our wonderful, surprising, innate—albeit irrational—human nature (indeed, people who lack the ability to adapt, trust, or enjoy their work can be very unhappy). These irrational forces help us achieve great things and live well in a social structure.[1]

This distinction between how rational players should play these games and how real people actually play these games is crucial for understanding the rest of this section. To really understand it means getting to know John Nash, one of the giants of game theory. Like John von Neumann, John Nash was affiliated with Princeton; in fact, his doctoral adviser was Princeton's Albert Tucker, who named the prisoner's dilemma game. My interest in game theory probably stems from the fact that I attended Princeton Theological Seminary from 1998 to 2001 and regularly walked past the filming of John Nash's life story, *A Beautiful Mind*, on the Princeton campus in 2001. I felt a personal connection with the movie that led me to be more interested in Nash's work.

John Nash was born in Bluefield, West Virginia, in 1928. Nash escaped the coalfields to attend Carnegie Institute of Technology, now Carnegie Mellon University, in Pittsburgh, where he graduated with two degrees in math. His recommendation letter to graduate school simply stated, "He is

---

1. Ariely, *Upside of Irrationality*, Kindle location 194.

a mathematical genius."[2] Nash received a full-ride scholarship to Princeton, where he wrote his dissertation on what would come to be known as the Nash equilibrium, for which he was awarded the Nobel Prize in 1994. Nash is probably most famous for his struggle with depression and paranoid schizophrenia, as depicted in the movie version of Sylvia Nasar's biography *A Beautiful Mind*. In Nash you see the full drama of the heights and depths of genius and madness. What is so remarkable is that in spite of his inner turmoil, no one can study game theory without at least a passing knowledge of his justly famous equilibrium theory.

A Nash equilibrium exists whenever one player is unable to improve their situation by unilaterally switching their strategy.[3] In other words, a Nash equilibrium exists whenever each player is making the most rational, self-interested choice they can make in light of the other player's rational, self-interested strategic possibilities. The Nash equilibrium for the ultimatum game, for example, exists when the divider allocates the most they possibly can to themselves and the least to the other player. The Nash equilibrium in a prisoner's dilemma exists when both players defect. Even though both players would benefit more if they cooperate, the specter of the sucker's payoff is so costly that according to Nash's theory the rational, self-interested individual has to adopt a defensive, uncooperative position.

It makes sense when you think it through. If you cooperate and the other player cooperates, that is fantastic. According to the prisoner's dilemma game matrix you both wind up with an outcome of three. But if you cooperate and the other player defects, that is a disaster. You wind up with nothing, and the other player winds up with five. In that case it would be a smarter play for you to defect because if you defect, you protect yourself from the sucker's payoff and still get at least a payoff of one. For rational players, one is always better than nothing.

To complicate things slightly, in coordination games such as the battle of the sexes and the stag hunt, there are two Nash equilibria. For example, in the battle of the sexes the players are equally happy between their alternatives as long as they wind up at the same place at the same time. In a stag hunt both players are equally happy hunting a stag together or hunting rabbits alone. Thus, for these coordination games it's crucial to discover the unspoken Schelling points because it is these intuitive meeting places that help you arrive at the same decision as the other player.

But as important as it is to understand Nash's equilibrium, it's even more important to ask whether it matters when it comes to actually playing

2. Duffin, recommendation for John Nash, doc. 22, para. 2.
3. Nasar, *Beautiful Mind*, 95.

these games with real people. Nash says people should be perfectly selfish in the ultimatum game—but studies have shown that to be a phenomenally bad way to play the game. In experimental trials with real people most dividers split the amount fifty-fifty, and most deciders are quite happy to accept that deal. When dividers give themselves a little bit more than the deciders, most deciders are OK with slightly less. If the split becomes too uneven, however, most deciders would rather get nothing than feel as if they're being taken. And, much to the frustration of game theorists and champions of rationality everywhere, even when people understand the *right* way to play, there is always a stubborn minority who actually give the other player more than they give themselves.[4] The generous nerve of them! A rationalist will argue that such players derive some kind of benefit from playing generously—that it's really just self-interest in disguise—but this explanation seems hopelessly cold and out of touch with real people. Dan Ariely is right: we're a little irrational, and it isn't always a bad thing.

In his intriguingly titled book *Economic Fables*, game theorist Ariel Rubinstein argues game theory is important, but only when taken with a grain of salt. Game theory models can help us understand the conflicts we're experiencing, but they can also give us the false impression of thinking we understand too much. In addition, the formal language of game theory has its disadvantages. It creates the illusion of being scientific. Rubinstein suggests that those unfamiliar with formal models tend to regard them as representing absolute truth, though they are nothing more than tales.[5] With this assertion, Rubinstein isn't denigrating narrative but lifting up the importance of human intuition in figuring out which story we're inhabiting.

Rubinstein's perspective is that game theoretic models are tools primarily useful for stimulating our imagining and thinking. In other words, we should use game theory to help understand and describe our world. But when we begin to predict and even dictate how people ought to behave, these rationalistic models leave us hopelessly out of touch with basic human behavior. Part of his heterodoxy stems from actually meeting John Nash on several occasions. In every instance Rubinstein perceived Nash as awkward (in spite of his beautiful mathematical mind), with the flat affect and lack of social intelligence often seen in people suffering from schizophrenia. Nash knew numbers like few ever will. But knowing numbers and understanding people are two entirely different things.

Unfortunately, this overly rational approach has made classical game theory a poor subject for church leadership or biblical interpretation. As

4. Rubinstein, *Economic Fables*, Kindle locations 1333–34.
5. Ibid., Kindle locations 243–44.

far as I'm aware only one book has been published that attempts to pair classical, rationalist game theory with biblical interpretation: Steven Brams' unusual *Biblical Games: Game Theory and the Hebrew Bible*. Brams, a game theorist, analyzes stories such as Adam and Eve's early adoption of the whole foods movement and Abraham's questionable parenting moment with Isaac, among a host of others. While Brams shines as a game theorist, his theological conclusions suffer from treating God as merely a rational player in conflicts that can be mapped out and understood.[6] In comparison with the depth of Kierkegaard's existentialist reading of Abraham's sacrifice, Brams' insistence that this story can be figured out with payoffs and matrices seems hopelessly simplistic. This kind of game theory doesn't engage our imagination and lead us into mystery—it attempts to know too much.

But the problem of classical game theory is the promise of behavioral game theory. The problem of classical game theory is the desire to make normative predictions of future events based on how rational people should behave. As we've seen over and over again, people aren't terribly rational and are highly unpredictable. So, when people try to use game theory as a practical solution to decision-making, they are often disappointed. But when game theory is used descriptively to help us discern in what story we are living and how we might work to change that story, it is immeasurably helpful. And when game theory is used experimentally, as a means of exploring human behavior, it is powerful indeed.

One major theologian knows the power of experimental game theory firsthand. Sarah Coakley, who writes and lectures at Cambridge University, previously teamed up with game theorist Martin Nowak at Harvard; together they made an incredible, if unlikely, pair exploring for the first time the connections between game theory and theology. Their collaboration led to Coakley's 2012 Gifford Lectures entitled "Sacrifice Regained: Evolution, Co-operation, and God";[7] the second lecture in the series explored game theory, altruism, and evolution. Coakley and Nowak also released a groundbreaking book together: *Evolution, Games, and God*. Coakley was heading toward her current research focus, forging a kind of chastened natural theology that creates space for religion and evolutionary biology to mutually inform one another, but along the way she participated in the first-ever collaboration between a behavioral game theorist and a theologian. Coakley joined forces with Nowak and others to observe two groups of participants play a

6. Brams, *Biblical Games*, 174.

7. Available on the Gifford Lectures website; see: http://www.giffordlectures.org/lectures/sacrifice-regained-evolution-cooperation-and-god.

prisoner's dilemma game to test for cooperation when presented with different religious texts.[8]

Here's what they did. The first study actually took place in a congregational setting. Those attending a service of worship at Parish of the Good Shepherd in Waban, Massachusetts, were presented with an unusual opportunity at the conclusion of worship. As they remained seated in the sanctuary, some of the congregants were given a passage from First Corinthians to read; the rest were given a passage from Matthew. Both passages emphasized the importance of giving. Then, the participants ranked how much they resonated with the reading. Finally, they played a prisoner's dilemma game with a fellow participant for a small amount of money. The study results would have been a source of chagrin for John Nash because about 70 percent of the players chose to cooperate rather than pursue the rational strategy of defection. The researchers were pleased to find a significant relationship between how much a player identified with the text they read and their willingness to cooperate. The hope is, pastors, that what you do every Sunday really does matter. Preaching and teaching the word can help worshippers form connections between the Scriptures and everyday actions. These connections significantly affect how people behave in real life.

But maybe all of these people were predisposed to cooperation in the first place because they were churchgoers in a sanctuary. So the researchers ran a second, online version of the study; they split 547 participants into groups identifying as Christian, Hindu, and Atheist. Coakley and Nowak designed the study so that participants played a prisoner's dilemma game with strangers under neutral conditions with no reading, a secular reading encouraging giving, a Christian reading, and a Hindu reading. The Christian group was significantly more likely to cooperate after reading a Christian passage encouraging giving but not after reading similar passages from other traditions. Neither the Hindu group nor the Atheist group seemed influenced by any of the readings; however, the researchers pointed out those groups were smaller than the Christian group, which could potentially negate the statistical significance.

The conclusion of the team is that formation of connections between words and actions is important. The more closely a person identified with a passage encouraging cooperation, the more likely a person was to cooperate. For our purposes, though, it's important to notice how Coakley and Nowak are using the prisoner's dilemma. Unlike Nash, they aren't using it to analyze a situation and then tell others how the game should be played.

---

8. Rand et al., "Religious Motivations for Cooperation," 31–48.

They're using it as a way of testing how cooperative people are in different situations. Like Ariely, these researchers know people are predictably irrational. What they're interested in is how different conditions will encourage positive irrational behavior such as cooperation and what conditions discourage it.

This interest in the conditions that encourage cooperation is precisely what the next chapter regarding the iterated, or repeated, prisoner's dilemma is all about. And that discussion leads directly to seeing the Apostle Paul for the irrational leader he was.

17

The Surprise of Tit for Tat

We've looked at several different games, from the chicken game to the stag hunt to the volunteer's dilemma, as a way of understanding a variety of conflictual relationships. From this point on, however, two games—the prisoner's dilemma and the multiplayer version of the prisoner's dilemma, the public goods game—will take center stage. There are two really good reasons for concentrating on this pair of games. First, these games get straight to the heart of a challenge nearly every church experiences: how do you get busy people with many, sometimes conflicting interests to cooperate and pull in one direction? Second, these games have been studied exhaustively, giving us an enormous amount of information about how cooperation emerges, or doesn't, under different conditions.

University of Michigan political science and public policy professor Robert Axelrod pioneered our understanding of how the conditions for cooperation can emerge even in the midst of conflict. Since cooperation among relatively self-driven individuals without a strong central authority is exactly the climate in mainline denominations these days, I was immediately interested. To test what influences cooperation, Axelrod has devoted much of his professional life to the study of iterated, or repeated, prisoner's dilemmas. Wanting to model human behavior in the most realistic way, Axelrod decided to study open-ended, iterated prisoner's dilemmas pitting two players against each other for a repeated game of unknown length. In order to model a world of egoists, nothing demonstrates humanity at its most venial like the prisoner's dilemma.

Axelrod wanted as much data as possible, so rather than studying human subjects, he held a tournament inviting specialists from such diverse fields as political science, mathematics, and biology to enter a strategy encoded into a computer program that would compete against other programs. Some programmed strategies were incredibly complicated, taking into account nuances in the opponent's patterns of behavior; other programmed strategies were simple, composed of just a few lines of code. Some were aggressive, seeking to defect as much as possible, while others were conciliatory, showing a willingness to cooperate. Axelrod compiled all of these programmed strategies, carefully played them against one another, and detailed his findings. The surprising results led to his groundbreaking work *The Evolution of Cooperation.*

Axelrod and his research team assumed that the most successful program would be the most cutthroat, the one most willing to use subterfuge, and the one most willing to defect.[1] In others words, Axelrod and his research team hypothesized the program most resembling a stereotypically Machiavellian personality would dominate in this competitive game of total conflict. In a twist no one expected, the dominant program, coming from University of Toronto mathematician and peace advocate Anatol Rappaport, was not only the most simple, but it was among the most cooperative strategies as well. Rappaport's program, entitled Tit for Tat, is as simple as it is powerful. Tit for Tat always begins the game by cooperating. It retaliates exactly one time in the event the other program defects and then returns to cooperation. Tit for Tat never deviates from this pattern. Axelrod was so surprised that Tit for Tat won the first tournament he suspected it might have been a mistake. To test for a possible mistake and to see how Tit for Tat fared against competition that had a chance to prepare, Axelrod published the surprising results and welcomed more than twice as many competitors to a second tournament. Even when the competition had a chance to prepare, Tit for Tat cleaned up again. Sometimes nice guys really do finish first.

This pattern is considered nice because Tit for Tat begins by cooperating and continues cooperating as long as the other player doesn't defect. Far from an anomaly, this willingness to cooperate was the norm for successful strategies: "Each of the eight top-ranking entries (or rules) is nice. None of the other entries is. . . . The nice entries received tournament averages between 472 and 504, while the best of the entries that were not nice received

1. Axelrod, *Evolution of Cooperation*, 33.

only 401 points."[2] Tit for Tat is no doormat, however. When another program attempts to take advantage of Tit for Tat's willingness to cooperate by
defecting, Tit for Tat immediately retaliates by defecting as well. However,
and this is key, while Tit for Tat is willing to retaliate, the strategy it employs
is what the researchers termed a forgiving strategy; immediately after defecting in retaliation, Tit for Tat returns to cooperation. Axelrod highlighted
the significance of forgiveness, pointing out that of all the nice rules the one
that was the least competitive was the rule that was the least forgiving. Axelrod noted that "even expert strategists do not give sufficient weight to the
importance of forgiveness."[3] Finally, the last virtue of Tit for Tat is clarity: the
simple clarity of Tit for Tat allows other strategies to understand it, predict
its behavior, and therefore make a free, independent decision whether or
not to cooperate. Today, talk about transparency is commonplace. Axelrod
knew about transparency before transparency became trendy.

Scholars in political science, evolutionary biology, and history have
utilized Axelrod's work to recommend strategies to world leaders, explain
why some species dominate biomes and others die out, and elucidate how
cooperative behavior can emerge without centralized control in the unlikeliest of circumstances. Indeed, Axelrod included a brief study of the known
truces that occurred spontaneously during World War I. Axelrod showed
how the unique nature of trench warfare created an iterated prisoner's dilemma. In opposition to the high command on both sides, the English and
German soldiers at the front created the live-and-let-live system by being
willing to cooperate, retaliate, and forgive when mistakes occurred. In one
instance a visiting English officer described a German officer rushing forward when German artillery mistakenly fired on the English: "All at once
a brave German got on to his parapet and shouted out 'We are very sorry
about that; we hope no one was hurt. It is not our fault, it is that damned
Prussian artillery.'"[4] Unfortunately, as powerful and useful as Axelrod's
work has been in other fields, it has been all but completely ignored in biblical and theological studies.

I became fascinated with this behavioral form of game theory for
three reasons. First, as I mentioned, the situation Axelrod addresses, where
individuals try to cooperate in the absence of a strong central authority, describes most congregations and denominations today. It's true that in small
congregations pastors may have the bandwidth to weigh in on every conflict
and act as a centralized authority, but most church leaders don't have the

2. Ibid., 33.

3. Ibid., 39.

4. Ibid., 85.

time or energy to do so. They lead congregations in which individuals and teams have to work together without a lot of direct guidance. Most pastors have to think more about creating the conditions in which cooperation can emerge than solving every little challenge that arises.

Second, Tit for Tat appealed to me as a surprisingly biblical pattern of behavior. What characterized Tit for Tat is a balance of care for others with maintenance of a healthy boundary. Jesus said whoever would lead must become the servant of all. Tit for Tat sought cooperation as often as possible, a vital part of any community-building effort. Even when Tit for Tat played patterns that were so naively nice they exposed themselves to exploitation, Tit for Tat never took advantage. In this sense Tit for Tat manifested a servant heart. Further, the fact that the pattern was forgiving is obviously extremely evocative from a Christian point of view. But as nice and forgiving as the pattern was, I also loved that Tit for Tat had boundaries, which is especially important in pastoral ministry. When other patterns defected, Tit for Tat didn't just roll over—it pushed back. This pushback pattern made me think about Jesus turning over tables in the temple or calling the religious authorities "whitewashed tombs." It made me think of the Apostle Paul defending his ministry in Corinth against the incursion from those he sarcastically referred to as the super-apostles.

Third, I recognized this Tit for Tat behavior pattern not only in the Scriptures but also in good pastoral leaders. In the next chapter I'll focus particularly on the Apostle Paul and see how this pattern marks his ministry. But first, I want to highlight how I see this pattern of cooperation and selective defection operating in concrete ways in the church. When you play a repeated prisoner's dilemma, cooperating and defecting are clear choices you make. You either click a box to cooperate or defect in a computer scenario, or you use your thumb to signal thumbs up for cooperate and thumbs down for defect in a real-life game with another person. But checkboxes and thumbs are an abstraction for the purposes of a game. What does it look like for leaders to cooperate or defect in real life?

In a great episode of *This American Life*, Ira Glass interviews a flight attendant about the challenges of living with other coworkers in close quarters.[5] These flight attendants flew international flights for hours on end and had to maintain a professional demeanor in front of the passengers at all times. But any time you have people living in close proximity, tempers will flare. In their case, however, they flared in subtle ways. One flight attendant, Jill, grew to despise one of her coworkers for talking incessantly when they were on break. Jill acknowledged that her own silence probably got on her

---

5. *This American Life*, "Same Bed, Different Dreams," prologue.

colleague's nerves, too. Anyway, it became apparent to both of them that they really couldn't stand one another. But they couldn't express their dislike on the flight in a direct way. So, they would make these moves that were absolutely clear to them but not understood by the passengers. When they were in the aisle with the drink cart, for instance, and her nemesis would ask her for cokes, Jill would sometimes look at her and say, "Oh, we're out of cokes." Jill said she knew they weren't out of cokes, and her coworker knew they weren't out of cokes. But the other flight attendant was stuck behind the beverage cart and powerless. To the passengers nothing sounded out of the ordinary, but without anyone else knowing about it those two flight attendants were silently conducting war.

This pattern describes so many interactions you experience in congregational leadership. In the church people don't openly conduct war because they, too, want to maintain a professional demeanor. They avoid open war because they've been taught they have to behave nicely in church situations; and because they have to live with these other leaders, it's just easier to try to get along. But conflicts abound all the time, and leaders have opportunities in every interaction and every meeting to cooperate with another leader or instead choose to not cooperate and defect. And generally we do this in the subtlest of ways.

Let's look at some of the most common ways leaders cooperate with one another. If a leader does not entirely agree with another's idea, he may concede the point just to create a more positive attitude. When leaders express agreement with one another in public meetings, it's an even stronger form of cooperation. Cooperative leaders also often thank people by using written notes, by praising them in worship, and by giving gifts. Leaders pull together by returning emails and phone calls quickly; and in ways that can be incredibly subtle and vary by generation and context, correspondents indicate cooperation by writing in kind tones and using polite formalities or positive emoticons and emojis. Other ways of showing positive cooperation include the gift of your presence—just showing up to a meeting or offering to take someone out to lunch. And this is just the tip of the iceberg. Eye contact, body posture, and tone all convey whether leaders are pulling together in a spirit of cooperation or whether they are pulling away.

But like flight attendants, we church leaders don't always cooperate with one another. And just as there are limitless ways leaders cooperate, there is an infinite number of ways leaders defect. I have seen leaders defect by simply "forgetting" to return a call or an email. Or, in written communication, by choosing inflammatory or challenging language to not so subtly convey their frustration. And let's not forget the ever popular choice leaders make of voting with their feet. You set up a meeting or simply have a regular, stated meeting, and a leader in defect mode always finds an excuse not to be there. Of course, what's challenging is sometimes leaders legitimately can't make a meeting so you must always exercise judgment and discretion when figuring out whether these nonverbal actions constitute defection or not. Savvy leaders always contemplate the possibility that someone may be defecting when they stop showing up.

The main idea in corporate virtue advisor Dov Seidman's *How* is that how we behave impacts our relationships more than what we do and produce. It used to be the case that people became successful by focusing on making things, or focusing on what Seidman calls the "what." Due to the flattening effects of information technology, however, the "what" matters less today. Advances in manufacturing and communication have enabled people to replicate things more easily than ever before. Therefore, the key to success today, Seidman argues, isn't what we do but how we do it. The more emotionally intelligent, relational, and service-oriented we are the more likely it is we will thrive, which means paying attention to all the little things that improve or impair our relationships.

Seidman doesn't use the language of cooperate and defect, but when he speaks of microinequities—small lapses—he might as well be speaking of defection:

> Bad body language in a meeting, a question asked in a mocking tone, an off-color joke told at an inopportune moment—all lapses in how you fill the spaces between you and those with whom you work—can subtly leech productivity from any organization. Checking your messages while speaking with colleagues devalues their time and thus them. Glancing at your watch while someone makes a presentation dismisses his or her effort. . . . In the past week or two, how many times have you opened an email and had one of the following reactions: This is not what we agreed to. This pisses me off. Why did you cc: my boss? Are you trying to make me look bad? I'm offended. I don't find this all that funny. Why are you filling my in-box with this stuff?[6]

With all the myriad ways people can choose to cooperate or defect when living in community, leaders have to figure out in real time how to foster the conditions under which the community will seek cooperation rather than unravel in defection. Given that individuals and communities are constantly in flux, encouraging cooperation is incredibly difficult work. My sense is that great leaders do it intuitively. But knowing patterns like Tit for

6. Seidman, *How*, 111.

Tat can give all leaders a powerful framework when they find themselves in the midst of challenging personalities. Tit for Tat reminds us to always seek cooperation. But good leaders recognize that it's not only appropriate but also effective to push back against a defection with a measured retaliation before returning in forgiveness to cooperation once again. Congregational bullies won't appreciate such reasonable, tough-love behavior, but everyone else will notice and appreciate it. With this Tit for Tat pattern of behavior in mind, we'll see how cooperation and defection show up in the ministry of the Apostle Paul in the next chapter.

18

The Irrational Paul

Even though the most rational way (from the perspective of the standard economic model) to behave in a conflictual, prisoner's dilemma type of relationship is to always defect, Robert Axelrod's work suggests that the way to create a lasting, cooperative relationship in a noncoercive environment with weak central authority is for one party to behave in a consistent pattern of cooperation, retaliation, and forgiveness. Thus, Axelrod's work demonstrates that irrational behavior is not only nice but also effective. New Testament scholar Bengt Holmberg paints a picture of Paul doing ministry in a complicated environment with low central authority that fits Axelrod's imagined conditions like a glove.[1] While Paul's ministry can't be reduced to a Tit for Tat pattern, enough of this structure emerges in Paul's letters to think of him as an irrational leader. And given the continued fracturing of mainline denominations, this context of diffuse authority that existed in Paul's world increasingly characterizes the context in which contemporary ministry exists as well—making the irrational Paul all the more relevant today.

While Axelrod's team first assumed the most successful programs would be the most cutthroat, they were surprised to find that the most successful, most robust programs were what they came to term "nice." Nice in Axelrod's terminology doesn't indicate politeness but denotes a willingness to cooperate. Paul epitomizes "niceness" in this sense. In every community

1. Holmberg, *Paul and Power*, 70.

Paul met resistance and could easily have heeded, had he known about it, Jesus' advice to shake the dust from his feet. And yet Paul is the quintessential community builder, enduring challenge after challenge to start churches all over the Mediterranean.

Where the issue of niceness plays a significant role in the Corinthian correspondence is within the Corinthian community itself. To complicate the picture here, a prisoner's dilemma exists not only between Paul and the Corinthian community but also between factions within the community itself. As New Testament scholar Gerd Theissen has argued, one of the most important divisions fracturing the church in Corinth involved socioeconomic class.[2] While the Roman Corinthian culture was highly stratified according to a patron and client system, the Corinthian church seems to have manifested an incredible, if uneasy, socioeconomic diversity.[3] The wealthier members of the community felt a constant temptation to defect from their poorer brothers and sisters and from Paul's teachings, wanting to be members of Christ's body and members of Corinth's civic elite at the same time.[4]

The prime example of socioeconomic defection occurs in the controversy over the Lord's Supper. Paul admonishes the church in Corinth, "For all who eat and drink without discerning the body, eat and drink judgment against themselves" (1 Cor 11:29). Traditionally, the church in America has interpreted this text to indicate the importance of individual moral rectitude. More recent scholars view Paul's injunction to the Corinthians differently in light of better understanding of the ancient socioeconomic reality. Duke Divinity School professor Richard Hays and others shed light on what was most likely going on to cause the abuses. Unlike the symbolic meal shared by most mainline Christians today, the Lord's Supper in the Corinthian community was an actual common meal. The meal would be hosted in a home large enough to accommodate such a gathering, meaning in the home of one of the wealthier members of the community. It is also likely the wealthier members would dine in the triclinium, or formal dining room, while the poorer members would be relegated to an outside room. Finally, it seems that the wealthiest members not only divided the body by dining privilege but, even worse, ate and drank all the provisions before the poorer members even had a chance at the scraps.[5]

2. Theissen, *Social Setting of Pauline Christianity*, 96.

3. Johnson, *Writings of the New Testament*, 273.

4. Ibid.

5. Hays, *First Corinthians*, 196.

From a game theoretic perspective what is taking place is that the divided Corinthians face a prisoner's dilemma. All factions desire the integrity of the community. However, the wealthier Corinthians are tempted to defect from the poorer faction and eat and drink more than their fair share. To defect in this way, to use the language of Robert Axelrod, is to violate the first rule of community behavior: to play "nice." Violating niceness provokes a sharp response from Paul.

A similar example of defection in the Corinthian community surrounds the dilemma about whether or not to eat food sacrificed to idols. Wealthier members of the community would be highly tempted to continue to partake of this food due to their familiarity with it and the civic connections such meals offered, whereas the less well-connected, poorer members of the community viewed this meat and those who consumed it with great suspicion. As in the situation with the Lord's Supper abuses, a dilemma exists for the wealthier Corinthian Christians. On the one hand, these members would like to maintain the integrity of the community, which in this case would require abstention from this food. On the other hand, they prize the civic relationships that idol-sacrifice meals confer and are tempted to defect, once again, from their brothers and sisters.

Paul threads the needle more carefully in the case of the food sacrificed to idols than the abuses at the Lord's Supper. But the way in which he acts out his provocation confirms the issue underneath is primarily the integrity of the community more than it is a theological issue. Paul offers an extended conversation regarding eating food sacrificed to idols that begins in 1 Corinthians 8 and then is picked up again explicitly in chapter 10:14–22. However, what is most significant isn't the obvious content in chapters 8 and 10 but the bridging material in chapter 9. In chapter 9 Paul's topic concerns his rights as an apostle. Paul speaks about his right to stop working for a living, but emphasizes that he has refrained from demanding that right: "Nevertheless, we have not made use of this right, but we endure anything rather than put an obstacle in the way of the gospel of Christ" (9:12). And the reason Paul eschews his right is for the good of the community: "For though I am free with respect to all, I have made myself a slave to all, so that I might win more of them" (9:19). Put simply, Paul's underlying point about food sacrificed to idols is this: just because you *can* do something doesn't necessarily mean you *should*. Community only exists when members tempted to defect choose to play nice, that is, they voluntarily choose to cooperate.

When this niceness breaks down, the second step in Axelrod's pattern is provocability. Provocability is just what it sounds like: it is the willingness to retaliate against another player when they defect from the relationship. The key to provocability in Axelrod's findings is that the retaliation is commensurate. With Tit for Tat, for instance, the program retaliates only once for a single defection. Programs that modeled more harsh behavior were unsuccessful at creating the conditions for community to emerge. But patterns that failed to retaliate at all weren't competitive either. The willingness to be provocable and defect commensurately is absolutely vital for the establishment of conditions for cooperation, and the Apostle Paul shows a great willingness to retaliate.

Sometimes Paul retaliates by what he doesn't say rather than what he does say. In the letter to the Galatians, for example, Paul omits the thanksgiving section. More often, though, it is by what he does write that Paul sends his harder messages. In the first letter to the Corinthians Paul claims he is not writing to shame the Corinthians but to admonish them as a loving father (4:14). And does he admonish! Paul offers sharp rebukes to the community several times throughout the correspondence, proving himself provocable, indeed.

We've already noted Paul's willingness to criticize the Corinthians over the abuses at the Lord's Supper, stating to them in no uncertain terms that if they continue in their behavior, they eat and drink to their own destruction. And he offers correction regarding eating food sacrificed to idols, allowing for the possibility of eating meat purchased in the marketplace but under no circumstances eating it in the temple or eating such meat in the presence of church members who would be offended by this practice. But Paul reserves his strongest language for the brother who is sleeping with his father's wife, an action that truly seems to shock Paul. He orders the community to exclude this man from their fellowship as well as "anyone who bears the name brother or sister who is sexually immoral or greedy, or is an idolater, reviler, drunkard, or robber. Do not even eat with such a one" (1 Cor 5:11). While this behavior may seem harsh to contemporary ears, from the perspective of game theory Paul simply proposes retaliation in response to the defections of those unwilling to abide by the standards of the community.

In a similar way Paul offers harsh words against the practice of taking church members to court (1 Cor 6:5) and against those practicing glossolalia for self-aggrandizement rather than the building up of the entire community (1 Cor 14:19). Again, the pattern is clear: Paul is not criticizing to be cruel; Paul is offering a commensurate, retaliatory correction to members who have already defected against the body.

Another great example of Paul's provocability rears its head in his second letter to the Corinthians. Scholars widely agree that Second Corinthians is a composite letter, perhaps comprising at least six individual letters.[6]

---

6. Barrett, *Second Epistle to Corinthians*, 13.

The main problem in the second epistle stems from leaders infiltrating from without rather than factions within the body. Yet these outsiders, these super-apostles, and the response of the Corinthians to them constitute an existential threat to which Paul responds sharply.

In what some suggest is the first letter (2 Cor 2:14—7:4), Paul offers a warning against other leaders and defends his own apostleship. Then, Paul visits the community and, not liking what he discovers after his visit, writes his "furious letter," also known as his "letter of tears" (2 Cor 10-13). Not only does Paul defend himself in this furious letter, but he further attacks the credibility of the super-apostles and offers the Corinthians a stern warning indeed: "I warned those who sinned previously and all the others, and I warn them now while absent, as I did when present on my second visit, that if I come again, I will not be lenient" (13:2). And while in that verse Paul makes it sound as if he is only thinking about returning, he makes it clear that the Corinthians should expect him: "So I write these things while I am away from you, so that when I come, I may not have to be severe in using the authority that the Lord has given me for building up and not for tearing down" (13:10).

In confirmation of Axelrod's pattern, Paul's furious letter—his retaliation against the community for their defection—seems to pay off. The third letter Paul writes, his conciliatory letter (2 Cor 1:1—2:13 and 7:5-16), demonstrates not only Paul's pastoral heart but also the fact that the community responds positively to his retaliation. Rather than escalating the situation, the Corinthians respond by choosing community again, which is exactly what should occur, according to the pattern of Tit for Tat.

The importance of commensurate retaliation may be the single most significant element of Axelrod's theory that the mainline church needs to hear and consider today. In response to decades of decline the mainline church has often lowered standards, opting for a lukewarm message void of judgment. As Niebuhr wrote prophetically about the mainline church in 1937, we preach that "a God without wrath brought men without sin into a Kingdom without judgment through the ministrations of a Christ without a Cross."[7] And while sociologists such as Mark Chaves point out that the story of mainline decline is largely demographic in nature,[8] Axelrod's findings would also predict decline due to the church's unwillingness to be provocable and maintain community standards—an unwillingness on the part of clergy and members to faithfully challenge one another in love.

7. Niebuhr, *Kingdom of God*, 137.
8. Chaves, *American Religion*, 91.

The third part of the Tit for Tat pattern is what Axelrod terms the willingness to show forgiveness. As important as it is for Tit for Tat to be tough and provocable, to create the conditions necessary for cooperation to emerge it is equally important to be forgiving. What this means technically is that as soon as Tit for Tat retaliates against a defecting program, Tit for Tat immediately moves back to a conciliatory posture and chooses to cooperate. Tit for Tat therefore signals to the other player that there is nothing to be gained by defecting and everything to be gained by cooperating. As with niceness and provocability, Paul also demonstrates this willingness to forgive, wanting only for the community to live as a cooperative reflection of Christ's body.

The prime example of Paul's demonstration of forgiveness occurs in Second Corinthians regarding a brother who caused pain to Paul and the body (2:5–11). The actual offense of this brother is unknown. What is clear is that Paul first urged the community to discipline a brother who caused harm to the body, and now Paul acknowledges that the punishment is sufficient: "This punishment by the majority is enough for such a person; so now instead you should forgive and console him, so that he may not be overwhelmed by excessive sorrow. So I urge you to reaffirm your love for him" (2:6–8).

For me this moment encapsulates what makes Paul such a compelling figure. He manifests niceness by planting the church and nurturing it in the first place. However, Paul is no doormat. When a brother causes him pain, Paul acknowledges that this person causes pain to the whole body. While Paul may be willing to suffer a private attack upon his person, he is absolutely unwilling to roll over when an attack is leveled at the community. Paul then marshals every resource to discipline this brother. Paul, in other words, is as provocable as they come. But what makes both Tit for Tat and Paul compelling is that neither is content to remain in a retaliatory stance; both push forward to the ultimate goal: the restoration of the community. Paul shows incredible compassion for this brother who caused harm, and as forcefully as Paul demanded that he be punished when he defected, he urges with equal strength that the community surround this brother and restore him when he shows willingness to return to cooperating with the community. Paul is a kind of Dutch uncle to the Corinthians: he's the first to lash out at them when they defect, and he's the first to put his arm around their shoulder when they're willing to return to the fold. We can say, then, that Paul's ministry mirrors the highly successful—and irrational—Tit for Tat strategy of cooperating, defecting, and forgiving.

19

SuperCooperators and Reciprocity Styles

We've seen how Robert Axelrod recommends being a combination of nice and tough and how Paul certainly seems to embody such tough love. To me as a fairly progressive mainline Protestant, tough love intuitively seems right. Often it feels as if at least some of our denominational decline stems from wanting to be so nice we offer up cheap grace in place of appropriate confrontation. But there are others researching the prisoner's dilemma who question whether this Tit for Tat strategy is always helpful. Is the answer to our woes really just to grow a spine and push back harder and more often than we normally do? Remember Harvard's Martin Nowak, who worked with Sarah Coakley to test whether priming study participants with religious texts encouraged cooperation? Nowak isn't so sure pushing back harder is the answer.

By employing sophisticated models with computational power Robert Axelrod couldn't have dreamed of in the seventies, Nowak built upon Axelrod's work and took it to the next level. Nowak directs most of his attention to evolutionary biology, using game theory to model how species and culture evolve. For Sarah Coakley, the primary motivation for collaborating with Nowak was his successful challenge to the "selfish gene" theory of evolutionary biologist Sir Richard Dawkins. Nowak defends altruism: he acknowledges that selfish, punishing behavior can be an effective strategy in the short term; however, his research suggests that individuals and groups

that practice loving-kindness flourish in the long run. Nowak is so committed to this view that he has coined the phrase "punish and perish."[1]

It's not that Nowak is naive and unaware of how effective punishing
behavior can be in establishing cooperation among groups. Everyone knows
the power of the stick. Every time I see a police officer on the highway, I
instinctively slow down even if I'm going the speed limit. Two of Nowak's
most interesting conversation partners, Austrian economists Ernst Fehr and
Simon Gächter, argue that punishment is a vital aspect of creating the conditions for cooperation. Fehr and Gächter believe you can't have cooperation
without some form of societal punishment. Without it you'd have *Lord of
the Flies* or what happens in just about every third children's sermon I offer.

Being game theorists, these folks don't just assert things. They observe
people playing games and hope to find confirming evidence. Fehr and
Gächter watched people play four different versions of a repeated public
goods game.[2] In two of the versions they watched friends and strangers
play a basic public goods game. Friends played with friends and strangers
played with strangers. In the other two versions they observed the same
conditions, only this time people could spend some of their own money,
and they were using real money, to punish other players. In both versions of
the game without punishment, cooperation deteriorated as it does in most
public goods games. In both versions with punishment, friends and strangers employed punishment and created environments where teams continued to cooperate. What was particularly interesting to Fehr and Gächter is
that strangers were willing to spend their own money to punish strangers.
They termed this "altruistic punishment" since a person who spent their
own money to punish strangers showed a willingness to sacrifice themselves
on behalf of the group.[3]

Now, again, it's not that Nowak and his colleagues dispute that punishment can effectively make people more willing to pony up in a group
situation. But he noticed that while Fehr and Gächter allowed for players
to punish one another, they didn't allow for players to reward one another.
He wondered what would happen if you gave players both options. The title
of one of Nowak's books is *SuperCooperators*, and this title, in part, comes
from this study. Nowak and his team found that when people played games
without the ability to punish or reward, cooperation plummeted predictably until individuals were hardly contributing anything. This tragedy of
the commons almost always occurs when people play a public goods game.

1. Nowak and Highfield, *SuperCooperators*, 221.

2. Fehr and Gächter, "Cooperation and Punishment," 981.

3. Fehr and Gächter, "Altruistic Punishment," 137.

When people were allowed to punish only, groups that punished did better than groups that didn't. When people were allowed to reward only, groups that rewarded excelled over groups that didn't. But, importantly, when groups were given the option to both reward and punish fellow players, groups that tended to reward one another crushed those that relied more on punishment.[4]

So, it's not that Nowak doesn't know Axelrod's work. He's an expert in it. And it's not that he's a Pollyanna who only wants people to be nice. He knows Fehr and Gächter's results. He knows punishment can work to keep people in line. But what he also shows is that communities that can figure out how to create cooperation without punishing avoid wasting valuable resources in negative ways and flourish in comparison with communities committed to the stick.

My own doctoral research built on this conversation. Over the course of a year I studied ninety-eight Presbyterian elders in eleven congregations scattered from Oregon to North Carolina. I observed them playing two versions of a public goods game. The second version of the game included the ability for elders to anonymously punish or reward one another. In larger membership congregations I saw a statistically significant correlation between membership growth and cooperative, rewarding behavior.[5] This small study suggests in church leadership there really is something to Nowak's "punish and perish" maxim, and leaders should think twice about being punitive in their responses to negative behavior.

But wait a minute. Robert Axelrod says leaders need to be nice but tough. Leaders need to be willing to push back against negative, defecting behavior with temporary, equivalent defective behavior. But Martin Nowak's research suggests organizations that rely on punitive behavior will lose out to institutions that use positive, rewarding practices to support cooperation. Who is right? What's a leader supposed to do? Are we supposed to be tough or forgiving? Are we supposed to be like Jesus when he thrashes the money-lenders or like Jesus when he tells us to forgive again and again?

Well . . . yes.

This seeming contradiction puzzled me for a long time. Ultimately, business professor Adam Grant comes to the rescue with his understanding of different reciprocity styles. In his book *Give and Take* Grant shares his counterintuitive research: after identifying leaders who exhibited different reciprocity styles, Grant asked their peers to rank them on a success scale. Grant studied professions as diverse as medicine, law, and marketing and

4. Nowak and Highfield, *SuperCooperators*, 231.
5. Evers-Hood, "Playing Church," 160–91.

asked participants to rank their colleagues in terms of their influence; his team had already assessed the participants as givers, takers, or matchers.

Givers are people who prefer that others get more from interactions than they get themselves. Givers are happiest when the people around them are thriving. Takers are the exact opposite. We've all known takers. Takers will do anything to get to the top; takers will beg, borrow, and steal as long as in the end they climb the ladder of success. Matchers prefer a balance. They don't want to take advantage of others, but neither do they want to be used. Matchers prefer fairness in their relationships: they are willing to help others as long as they receive help, too.

First, the bad news: Grant divided the data into three success categories—the laggards at the bottom, those doing moderately well in the middle, and the high-flyers at the top. Unfortunately, the givers wind up comprising most of the bottom third. In this case, according to Grant's study, the truism that nice guys finish last has some truth to it. Less surprisingly, takers and matchers mostly fill the middle third. The great surprise in Grant's work is who comprises the top third. When I ask groups to guess, while a few optimists guess the matchers, most people assume the takers are the most successful. This assumption certainly fits with common perceptions about the Wall Street wolves who were responsible for the financial collapse and still ended up with huge bailouts. Indeed, psychologists recently made a splash arguing psychopaths and sociopaths are overrepresented in top echelons of leadership.[6]

Now for the good news: our instincts about takers and power don't hold. Most of the people rated at the top of the heap? Givers. While it's true that some givers wind up on the bottom, givers also largely make up the top.[7] What accounts for this dichotomy? Grant argues the difference between the givers on the bottom and the givers on the top is the givers on the top learn how to change their reciprocity styles depending on the kind of people they are around.

The challenge is people don't run around with labels on their foreheads telegraphing their preferred reciprocity style. It's not obvious who the givers and takers are. Worse, because we tend to associate givers and takers with certain traits, it's easy to make the wrong assumptions about people. Grant notes that we tend to think of the world in terms of affable givers and mean takers. If someone appears to be nice and kind, we tend to unreflectively assume they have a generous nature.[8] If someone is pushy and gruff, we

6. Steinberger, "Psychopathic C.E.O.'s," para. 1.

7. Grant, *Give and Take*, 7.

8. Ibid., 192.

often think the worst. If you remember back from the first section, this is a classic representativeness heuristic error. Because some givers are obviously nice and some takers appear to be selfish, our inner Esaus see all givers and takers similarly. Unfortunately, this affect mismatch allows kindly takers to exploit us and permits gruff givers to remain undetected. Anecdotally, I suspect the church is full of both kindly takers and gruff givers.

The late Ken Lay, former CEO of Enron, represents a kindly taker as well as anyone. Lay's smooth-talking, Bible-carrying persona with the reputation of being able to create compromise contrasted greatly with Jeffrey Skilling's know-it-all arrogance. But after the dust settled, it was clear that Skilling didn't dupe the kindly Lay, nor was he more corrupt; Skilling was simply easier to spot as a taker. Because they fit our profile of a taker, the Jeffrey Skillings of the world aren't as dangerous as Ken Lay, who quoted Scripture after being found guilty but never once publicly admitted his crimes.[9] Wise givers have to learn how to identify the kind-seeming Ken Lay types.

On a more hopeful note, not every person who seems unfriendly is a selfish taker. Some of the most important gifts come to us from disagreeable givers, people who appear hard and gruff on the surface but are full of love. The first time I learned Greek I enrolled in what became one of the hardest challenges of my life. In one summer at the University of Texas at Austin I took a class that crammed two full years of Greek into one summer. The class started at 8:00 a.m. and didn't let out until 5:00 p.m., and we had homework every night.

The man behind this incredible experience, Professor Gareth Morgan, was a formidable presence. One of our tests fell on the Fourth of July. I asked him if I could take the test on another day as I was planning to be out with family that day. "Why?" he demanded in his Welsh accent. "Well," I stammered, "it's the Fourth of July?" "What's that?" he thundered. "It's a holiday?" I said meekly. "A holiday?" he roared. "Yeah, it's Independence Day." "Mutiny day, you mean!" he shouted, an impish smile on his face.

I wound up taking the test early instead of later. He argued giving me more time to prepare wouldn't be fair to the other students. Gareth Morgan was one of the toughest professors I ever knew. But he was also one of the best. He was willing to meet early and stay late. He would meet over lunch. At one point he invited everyone to his home for a staged reading of Aristophanes' play *The Birds*. He was crusty and tough, but Professor Morgan was no taker. He might have been a somewhat disagreeable giver, but he was most definitely a giver.

9. McLean and Elkind, *Smartest Guys in the Room*, Kindle locations 9906–7.

Because it's difficult to distinguish between affable givers and affable takers and between disagreeable takers and disagreeable givers, Grant writes that successful givers use rules to help them identify givers, matchers, and takers. One person Grant profiles, Jason Geller, practices a kind of screening process to help him discover givers among the new hires at Deloitte. While Geller doesn't have to do this, he offers to meet with all the new hires. He tells them if they find the meeting helpful, he would be willing to meet with them again on a monthly basis. He notes that because the value of his offer is not immediate, takers tend to meet only once or twice. Over time he's able to discover the givers among the rest of the group. He notes that once he suspects someone of taking behavior, he doesn't immediately cut them off; however, he is more cautious in terms of how much time he devotes to them.[10]

Such screening processes are as old and biblical as the book of Judges. During the dark days when judges led Israel, one of the judges, Jephthah, went to war successfully against the Ammonites. Jephthah asked the people of Ephraim to help, but they refused. Later, the people of Ephraim rose up against Jephthah, who roused the tribe of Gilead against them. Gilead routed the Ephraimites. Some of the defeated men of Ephraim tried to defect and join the ranks of the Gileadites to cross back into their own land. The men from Gilead, though, knew there was a way to tell the difference between the two tribes. The word *shibboleth* in Hebrew literally means the part of a plant containing grain. The importance of the word for the Gileadites lay in its pronunciation rather than its definition, however. In Gilead people pronounced *shibboleth* with an "sh" sound, as you and I would. In Ephraim, however, people pronounced the word with an "s" sound as in "sibboleth." In order to screen unknown people to determine whether they were true Gileadites or Ephramite refugees, Gileadite sentries forced unknown men to pronounce the word.

I have found that talk of screening often brings objections from church leaders. Who are we to judge? Indeed, screening involves actively choosing to help some people and not others. Screening raises complicated issues, not least of which is the thorny issue of power. Church leaders are a diverse group, but I have observed that the plain exercise of power poses an emotional challenge for many of us. Many in the church carry Lord Acton's dim view of power deep in our hearts: power tends to corrupt, and absolute power corrupts absolutely.

Andy Crouch's masterful *Playing God: Redeeming the Gift of Power* should be required reading when it comes to exercising power in the church.

---

10. Grant, *Give and Take*, 200.

Crouch sees this negative view of power throughout the church. In interviews with church leaders, he encounters many who see power as a sad reality that can at best be controlled to limit the damage it may cause.[11] Perhaps this aversion to power is part of what's behind the general desire for at least the appearance of niceness in the church, which can make leadership so difficult. Crouch bravely and deftly poses another possibility: perhaps power is a gift from God to be used in the support of flourishing communities.

Crouch points out that God exercises power when it comes to the creation of the world, separating dark from light and water from dry land. The prophets exercise power in speaking truth to both leaders and people when their actions are in opposition to the flourishing of communities. Indeed, Jesus himself exercises power in restoring bodies, in teaching minds, and most visibly in the resurrection from the dead. Crouch sums up his positive view of power as a fundamental drive: "All true being strives to create room for more being and to expend its power in the creation of flourishing environments for variety and life, and to thrust back the chaos that limits true being. In doing so it creates other bodies and invites them into mutual creation and tending of the world, building relationships where there had been none: thus they then cooperate together in creating more power for more creation."[12]

Crouch systematically analyzes the exercise of power, summing power up into violence, domination, force, and coercion. In the destruction of others we see violence, the total distortion of power, in Crouch's view. Domination expresses itself in the few living above the many—and again, in Crouch's view domination and domination systems represent a terrible distortion of power. But in force and coercion (the threat of force), however, Crouch sees the potential for good. It was by force that God established the boundaries of creation and Jesus cast out demons. Force resulting in flourishing is power rightly used. And coercion, the threat of force, can sometimes be used in healing ways. Crouch lifts up the painful example of ethicist John Howard Yoder, an advocate for peace who abused his position by sexually violating students in his care. Without coercion, the threat of sanction, Yoder would not have entered into the restorative processes by which victims were given voice and he was rightly removed from his position.

It is in this sense—using power for the purpose of nurturing flourishing communities—that I argue it is vital for leaders to practice screening in their communities. When we lavish time and energy on givers, this energy will be multiplied and returned to the community. When we give

11. Crouch, introduction to *Playing God.*
12. Ibid., 51.

our attention to matchers, at the very least our energy will be returned. But when we cast our pearls before swine, as it were, and invest in takers, we squander the gifts entrusted to our care. To be sure, leaders have to be open to the possibility that people could change their reciprocity styles, but leaders also have to be aware of the necessity of being good stewards of our very limited time and energy.

However, I've learned an important distinction has to be made when it comes to the screening processes we use to identify takers. When I was talking this idea over with a friend and colleague, the Reverend Aric Clark, he immediately expressed discomfort with the idea of some kind of foolproof screening test to identify takers. Aric pointed out that people view men and women experiencing homelessness, people struggling with addiction, and others in need of help as takers. The screening process I was advocating sounded to him like an attempt to justify avoiding Christ's challenge to feed, clothe, and care for him by feeding, clothing, and caring for the least of these.

Aric's point is well taken. It's important to remember that Adam Grant, a professor at the Wharton School of Business at the University of Pennsylvania, is writing from a place of privilege. The men and women comprising his study were all employed. Even the givers at the bottom of the scale most likely had undergraduate or graduate education and enjoyed health care benefits and salaries, which afforded them access to safe housing and at least a couple of weeks of vacation. The takers in Grant's study and imagination are powerful people. These are men and women who are climbing the ladders of success and are still hungry for more. When Grant recommends careful behavior by givers to screen out takers, he is absolutely not speaking to the question of caring for the least of these.

Responsibly caring for people in need in a way that is truly helpful and sustainable requires more time than I have to devote to it in this book. Aric Clark and two seminary friends, known as Two Friars and a Fool, have written a book, *Never Pray Again*, that offers a good start.[13] What is clear for our purposes here is that screening for takers implies deciding how much to give to someone who already has a great deal of agency and power and who may be trying to take advantage of kindness out of their own greed. Screening for takers says nothing at all about giving to people in challenging circumstances.

To sum up, rewards work the best to foster cooperation, givers must keep an eye out for takers, and power used to create flourishing communities is a good thing. At this point, we're going to shift gears from game theory to

13. See Clark, Hagler, and Larson, *Never Pray Again*.

alternate reality games and gameful thinking. I will introduce you to game designer Jane McGonigal and her world of empowerment and hope.

20

Putting the Fun Back into Game Theory

One summer I led a retreat for a Portland area church. We gathered on the Oregon coast, and the energy in the group the first night was palpable. When we were planning the retreat, the church's leaders talked with me about starting with something fun, and that first night folks were ready for fun. Since my presentation topic was behavioral theology and game theory, I thought we'd start with an iterated prisoner's dilemma. I believed the game would be pretty simple to explain—after all, it only requires people to use their thumbs to indicate whether they are cooperating or defecting. After going over the rules of the game, I held up three Starbucks gift cards worth twenty dollars each. The highest-scoring team and individual would walk away with the cards. How do you think it went?

Well, let's just say my idea that this game was easy to explain was more than optimistic. And, as we have already learned, the prisoner's dilemma introduces a dark, competitive element. While groups that cooperate do outscore groups that compete with one another, the fact that I included a gift card for the highest-scoring individual ensured that at least some in the group defected any time they thought they could get away with it. So, what was supposed to be a fun game to introduce our topic for the weekend turned into a chaotic mess leaving most people with confused looks on their faces. The rest of the weekend ended up going fine, but this "game" definitely did not get us started on the right foot. One person approached me after the game was over and said, "When I heard we were doing game theory I was excited. I normally like games. But that wasn't really all that fun. Do people usually have more fun playing that game?"

This person is not alone in noting game theory's ironic lack of fun. Even game theorists have noticed a certain tedium associated with these games. Israeli economist Ariel Rubinstein writes, "Whoever came up with the name 'game theory' was a genius not only in mathematics but also in public relations. Imagine if it had been called the 'Theory of Rationality and Decision Making in Interactive Economic Situations.' Would this book and the theory as a whole have enjoyed the same degree of popularity? The word 'game' has a young and familiar sound. All of us play games—board games, computer games, political games. But game theory is not a box of magic tricks that can help us play games more successfully. . . . These games are only used in game theory as convenient illustrations."[1] You know you have a "fun problem" when your own thought leaders call you out.

Fortunately, today we live in a golden era of gaming and of what people who study games refer to as gameful thinking. Sometimes this gameful thinking is incredibly simple. When it comes to our health, should we take the stairs instead of riding an escalator? Of course we should. Yet the creators of The Fun Theory—part advertising campaign, part initiative to change human behavior—videotaped people negotiating public stairs in a subway station and found that nearly everyone chose the escalator over the stairs. I suppose we could post signs telling people about the importance of exercise. We could appeal to their reflective inner Jacobs and hope to persuade them. But my guess is the inner Esaus in us wouldn't even notice such a sign when we're thinking about other things. So the creators of The Fun Theory tried a different idea. They transformed the stairs into a giant piano. They turned the steps into working black and white keys; each step sounded a different note. As people ascended the stairs the notes became higher in pitch, and as they descended they got lower.

The difference was astounding. When the stairs were normal steps, people picked the escalator nearly every time. When the stairs were fun piano keys, people flocked to them. The video footage showed people going up and down the stairs in different patterns to make songs. People were laughing. Children jumped on the stairs with two feet. Suddenly, something that seemed like a chore became a game. And when the stairs were "gamified"— a neologism for using games to motivate real-world behavior—people chose the stairs over the escalator 66 percent more often.

1. Rubinstein, afterword to *Theory of Games*, 633–34.

In the first section of the book we learned that behavioralists describe how people actually behave in contrast to how rationalists say they should. Game designers simply put into practice what behavioralists call the Mary Poppins principle.[2] When Jane and Michael didn't want to take their medicine, Mary Poppins could have sternly ordered the children to swallow it. She could have threatened them with sanctions if they refused. But Mary Poppins found a far more effective way: she sang a catchy tune ("Just a spoonful of sugar makes the medicine go down"). By adding sugar to medicine, by turning the chore of cleaning their room into a game, Mary Poppins found a perfectly fun way to take care of business. Of course, if we were perfectly rational people, our intellect and our actions would match and we would easily do such things as take medicine, clean our rooms, eat in moderation, and exercise regularly. But we already know enough about our predictable irrationality to know we need the kind of motivational help games provide.

And games are far from being mere entertainment. Game designers are using games of all kinds now to tackle some of the world's most serious problems. Jane McGonigal is a leading designer of alternate reality games, or ARGs. An ARG aims to immerse players in an imaginary situation with real-life consequences. One of the best examples is *World Without Oil*, created in 2007 by Ken Eklund and Jane McGonigal, among others. Over the course of thirty-two days, more than sixty thousand people from all over the world signed up to participate. Each player received daily updates from the game's designers regarding the price of oil and imaginary real-world consequences. The players then made different decisions in their actual lives based on these updates. Players created more than fifteen hundred blogs, videos, and other reports about the actions they were taking to cope with the oil shortage.

The catchphrase for games such as *World Without Oil* is "play it before you live it." And the idea is to get a glimpse of how real people would respond during a peak-oil crisis. While the designers could have predicted some of the behaviors players exhibited, no one could have imagined all the creative ideas and solutions that emerged from actually playing the game.[3] Most importantly the benefits didn't end when the game ended. Months after, the game players reported maintaining many of the good habits they developed while they were playing the game.

Furthermore, even though the narrative of the game became increasingly dire and bleak as the world collapsed, the players reported incredibly

2. Williams, "Mary Poppins Principle," para. 5.

3. McGonigal, *Reality Is Broken*, Kindle location 5022.

high levels of optimism. McGonigal tells us one of the most powerful gifts games give us is a sense of empowerment and hope. McGonigal believes the control that players feel over their own choices in games endows them with a powerful mindset they bring to all the challenges they face—they become "super-empowered hopeful individuals," a term she borrowed from futurist Jamais Cascio.[4]

Jane has created games that address institutional decline. Church leaders often bemoan the shrinking number of people interested in participating in our congregations, but we aren't alone in this. The New York Public Library contacted Jane to use her gaming superpowers to increase the number of youth using the library. Knowing McGonigal is a gamer and believing young people would be attracted by video games, library staff proposed filling the main room with Xboxes on a Friday night and using what game designers call PBLs (points, badges, and leaderboards) to keep the kids interested. Jane thought game night at the library was a terrible idea. A simple game night had no connection with the fundamental mission of the library, and she seriously doubted whether young people really were just dying to play *Halo* in a library. And even if they were, what would playing video games in a library do to increase the desire on the part of the kids to actually use the library?

Rather than guess at what young people were interested in, McGonigal asked them. She created a short poll for the targeted kids and discovered that one of the things these kids were most interested in was writing a book. They agreed that one of their top goals in life was to become an author. Armed with this knowledge, Jane examined a multilevel map of the New York Library and recognized that the floor plan resembled a mash-up of *Donkey Kong* and *Assassin's Creed*. Jane then designed a game called *Find the Future*. More than five hundred young people descended on the New York Public Library. Their mission, Jane told them, was to spend all night in the library, completing various quests in order to write and publish their very own book. The young people worked together all night long, compiling their work using medieval bookbinding techniques.

At the end of the night, the leaders of the library declared their work such a success the book was placed in the permanent collection between copies of the Declaration of Independence signed by Thomas Jefferson and the Gutenberg Bible. Every young person who was a part of the project is allowed to enter that room with a guest whenever they please. I don't know what the ultimate, long-term results of this game will be, but every person who participated walked away with an incredibly different relationship

---

4. Ibid., Kindle location 5155.

with the library. Churches, too, need to foster new relationships with young people—and if they took a page from McGonigal's book, using creative games to engage curious minds, it's possible they would no longer wring their hands, wondering where all the young people have gone.

The ARG for which Jane is probably best known, *SuperBetter*, also has incredible relevance for the church. *SuperBetter* isn't just another game for McGonigal. McGonigal created *SuperBetter* when she failed to recover from a concussion. She realized, during some of the darkest days of her life, that she needed to rely on everything she had learned from her gaming career to survive her injury. *SuperBetter* draws upon the best current science from medicine and positive psychology on increasing physical, mental, and emotional well-being. Using deeply biblical words such as "spirit" and "gratitude," *SuperBetter* creates an online environment marking individual progress through badges and leveling up. Community plays a central role in *SuperBetter* as well. The game recommends that players find allies in their lives to play support roles and enables them to send formal ally requests via email.

Church leaders should care about *SuperBetter* because this community seeks to meet many of the same needs church communities do. Both aim to support people in growth and positive behavior, connect us to a community beyond ourselves, serve others in need, and foster a sense of hope. Church communities could use *SuperBetter* as is or create more theologically framed alternatives to leverage their own caring ministries.

Games and gameful thinking aren't just tools to motivate us. Theologically, games help us tap into our most creative and playful selves—the selves most clearly made in the image of God. Mystic Meister Eckhart writes, "Do you want to know what goes on in the heart of the Trinity? I will tell you. In the heart of the Trinity the Father laughs and gives birth to the Son. The Son laughs back at the Father and gives birth to the Spirit. The whole Trinity laughs and gives birth to us."[5] In his book *The Third Peacock: The Goodness of God and the Badness of the World*, the late American Episcopal priest Robert Farrar Capon chimes in, "The Trinitarian bash doesn't really come *before* creation; what actually happens is that all of creation, from start to finish, occurs within the bash—that the raucousness of the divine party is simultaneous with the being of everything that ever was or will be. . . . The world is not God's surplus inventory of artifacts; it is a whole barrelful of the apples of his eye, constantly juggled, relished and exchanged by the persons of the Trinity. No wonder we love circuses, games and magic. They prove we

---

5. Quoted in Ward and Wild, *Resources for Preaching*, 158.

are in the image of God."[6] One of my professors in seminary, Dan Migliore, writes about God's act of creation as the play of God: "It may be more helpful, therefore, to think of the creation of the world as the 'play' of God, as a kind of free artistic expression whose origin must be sought ultimately in God's good pleasure."[7]

A full history and theology of play in light of today's emphasis on gameful thinking still needs to be written. But theologians such as Hugo Rahner, Harvey Cox, and Jürgen Moltmann have given us a good start. Moltmann actually anticipates the alternate reality games in his *Theology of Play* when he sees in games the space to creatively dream up a different world that may result in real-world changes: "The significance of games is identical with that of the arts, namely to construct 'anti-environments' and 'counter-environments' to ordinary and everyday human environments and through the conscious confrontation of these to open up creative freedom and future alternatives. We are then no longer playing merely with the past in order to escape it for a while, but we are increasingly playing with the future in order to get to know it."[8]

My own call to ministry was deeply influenced by theologians of play. Theologian and monk H. A. Williams builds on Harvey Cox's image of Christ as a harlequin, jester, and clown to tie both death and resurrection together, making one of the most memorable connections to Jesus' life as a divine comedy. Williams casts the Pharisees as the serious people of business and Jesus as an annoying jester: "No wonder the Pharisees, who seem to have been always wholly serious, had to have Jesus put down. He couldn't be allowed to go on indefinitely standing everything on its head and making their piety look ridiculous. Why, in the end, they might even laugh themselves, and that would be the ultimate catastrophe. . . . So the Jester had to be crucified."[9] Williams goes so far as to cast Jesus' resurrection as one enormous, wonderful, cosmic joke: "But behind their backs, . . . the fool has popped up again like a Jack-in-the-box and is dancing about even more vigorously than before and even more compellingly. . . . If that isn't funny, nothing is. It is the supreme, the final, the ultimate joke—that than which nothing could be funnier. And since laughter, although not irresistible, is none the less highly contagious, perhaps the brass hats themselves will in

6. Capon, *Third Peacock*, 13–14.

7. Migliore, *Faith Seeking Understanding*, 93.

8. Moltmann, *Theology of Play*, 12–13.

9. Williams, *Tensions*, 117–18.

time catch the disease, turn round, see the joke, and laugh with the rest of creation because the kingdom of God has drawn near."[10]

When I was contemplating entering into ordained ministry, I encountered Williams through Reuben Job's classic devotional *A Guide to Prayer for Ministers and Other Servants*.[11] I fell in love with this playful sense of Jesus turning everything upside down. I included Williams' image of Jesus as a jack-in-the-box in the first draft of the long information form I would send to the Committee on Preparation for Ministry—the people who would ultimately determine whether they shared my inward sense of call. My pastor at the time wisely suggested that maybe that wasn't the best image to use for my first impression. I agreed and removed it. Somehow, though, I managed to send the original version. When I came before the committee, one of the first questions they asked was about this jack-in-the-box image. I tried to explain that I had taken that out in the second draft, which didn't exactly help my case. Fortunately, even Texas Presbyterians have a sense of humor, and my playful theology, while suspect, passed muster that day.

The most compelling theologian of play, believe it or not, is the Apostle Paul. Paul provides the strongest connection to the importance of games, particularly games as sport. In 1 Corinthians 9:24–27, Paul employs the metaphor of the Isthmian Games, held in Corinth every two years, to describe his apostleship and encourage excellence in the community. Just as the athletes practice discipline and run to win, so too should disciples of Christ practice the way they intend to follow.

And this analogy to the Isthmian Games is not unique. In Galatians 2:2, Paul describes meeting with the other apostles to ensure that he is not running his race in vain. In Philippians 3:13–14, Paul frames living into his call as a goal and a prize. The Pauline community continued using this gaming metaphor even after Paul's death. Second Timothy 2:5 compares faithful teachers to athletes who play by the rules. Paul and the Pauline community are not only unafraid to draw from the world of games; they lift up games as a way to understand discipleship in the real world.

And it's no wonder Paul's language is so steeped in the language of games and gaming: in his day job Paul was a tentmaker. I've always heard the term "tentmaker" used in the context of modern pastors who work outside the church in order to support their ministry. I never really thought about why Paul was making tents. After all, the first-century Greeks knew how to build *oikoi*—sophisticated, two-level home structures. And the Roman settlers of Corinth knew all about the *domus*, the open-roofed staple of

10. Ibid., 118–19.

11. Williams, "Tensions," in Job and Shawchuck, *Guide to Prayer*, 240–42.

Roman domestic architecture. The ancients created architectural techniques we are still using today. They didn't live in tents. REI wasn't around just yet, so why did Paul have so much work? Scholar Ben Witherington and others tell us Paul made tents for spectators as well as athletes at the periodic gaming events not only in Corinth but in Thessalonica, too.[12] In a very real way Paul lived and breathed games and gaming. His ministry was supported by the gaming industry of the day. He most likely came into contact with game lovers and game participants on a regular basis. It's no wonder this close contact and love for the games became woven into Paul's language and metaphors for discipleship.

This kind of respect for and love of gaming keeps us from the deadly kind of seriousness that led me to botch the opening night of that church retreat. In the fall of 2014 I met Jane McGonigal at what may be the very first formal interaction between the game design community and the church: a symposium hosted by San Francisco Theological Seminary to launch its brand-new Center for Innovation in Ministry. Here's how Jane opened the night. She asked us if we wanted to play a game in which we would experience ten positive emotions. Well, of course we did. The game is called massive multiplayer thumb-wrestling, and it was created by the art-technology-philosophy group monochrom.

You probably already know how to play the simple, two-person version of thumb war. You lock opposing hands with another player, move your thumbs back and forth while saying, "One, two, three, four, I declare a thumb war," and then try to pin the other person's thumb down. No problem. Ever considered adding other hands to the mix? In massive multiplayer thumb-wrestling, players connect to other players with both hands or link two or three hands together to create a node of several players. In a node of more than two hands, whichever thumb pins another thumb first is considered the winner. What's even more fun is you can keep adding other hands.

First, Jane demonstrated the game with a few volunteers and then invited the entire audience to participate until the whole room, maybe one hundred people, was connected. Then, we wrestled. Every time people play this game you see smiles, hear laughter, and feel the energy level in the room go through the roof. The congregation I serve, Tualatin Presbyterian Church, actually played massive multiplayer thumb-wrestling on World Communion Sunday in 2014 to demonstrate the connected nature of the body of Christ. I do believe it may be the first time this game has ever been played in a worship setting.[13]

12. Witherington, *Paul Quest*, 128.

13. Evers-Hood, "Never Just a Game," 02:27/25:35.

The ten emotions? People feel *curiosity* when they hear about the game. It takes creativity to connect all those hands. Players experience *joy*. There is *surprise* and *excitement* in the room. People feel *relief* at standing up and not sitting and listening to someone talk, especially if they've been listening to speakers all day. There is *contentment*: no one checks their iPhones when playing this game. And we can't forget Jane's favorite emotion: *love*. She points out that one of the best ways to produce oxytocin, the hormone associated with love, is to hold hands with another person for at least six seconds. Most people hold hands for far longer than six seconds when they play this game. *Pride* results when people win: some people win one thumb to make it to the grandmaster level; some even win two and can style themselves as legendary grandmasters. Most importantly for the church, people feel *awe* and *wonder*. It's an incredible experience when an entire group of people physically connect. In Christ, we say, we are connected to each other. In this game we actually see and feel the connection.

Now that's the kind of game you can use to open a retreat.

21

Les Jongleurs de Dieu

The humility and kindness of Saint Francis continues to inspire us today. Even the current pope, Jorge Bergoglio, himself a Jesuit, adopted the name of Francis to indicate the service-oriented direction in which he is leading the church. We honor Saint Francis for many things. We honor his care for the least of these, remembering how he kissed the hand of a leper. We honor his preaching to the birds and continue the tradition of blessing animals in his name. We honor him for starting both the Franciscan order and the Order of the Poor Clare Sisters. We honor him for organizing the first crèche, and we carry on that tradition today, making images of the Holy Family out of everything from Israeli olive wood to (Saint Francis forgive us!) characters from *The Simpsons*. Few today, though, honor Saint Francis for the title given to him and shared by his followers: *le jongleur de Dieu*, "the jester of God."

G. K. Chesterton writes that Francis and his followers were known as holy jesters for their joyful abandon and for the freedom afforded by their poverty.[1] Like troubadours they wandered wherever they felt the Holy Spirit blowing them. Like tumblers they stood the typical order of the world on its head. And like jesters they took a position on the edge of culture and criticized power in oblique rather than direct ways. Toward the end of his life, as Francis was passing through a certain town, people came to tell him of a notorious priest living in a scandalous relationship with a woman. When

1. Chesterton, *St. Francis of Assisi*, 73.

151

they hauled the priest before the famous friar, everyone expected Francis to punish the man or at least speak harshly to him. On the contrary, Saint Francis fell to his knees, held the priest's hands, and said he held the hands of Jesus. Surprised and overwhelmed by this unexpected compassion, the priest was converted and changed his ways.

As the church in North America and Europe continues to encounter massive disestablishment, we need to recover our identities as *les jongleurs de Dieu*, as holy jesters. In *Feast of Fools*, Harvey Cox emphasizes the importance of recovering the church's biblical and historic connection with playfulness and festivity, lost as a direct result of its becoming an institution: "A church that actually holds power and reigns has little capacity for self-caricature or irony. . . . Only now, in our secularized, post-Christian era, is it able to emerge again. A weak, even ridiculous church, somehow peculiarly at odds with the ruling assumptions of its day, can once again appreciate the harlequinesque Christ. His pathos, his weakness, his irony—all begin to make a strange kind of sense again."[2] Cox is right that a weak church at odds with the culture can again provide a helpful voice of critique and hope, but only if church leaders embrace our identities as holy jesters rather than forever trying to find a way back to an imagined golden day when the pews were full and the institution respected.

Accepting the new circumstances of the church is challenging for us. Church leaders still want to learn techniques to grow their membership, and institutional leaders even now pine for the past. Recently I spoke with a committee seeking to hire a seminary president, and one of the primary concerns of the committee was whether this candidate had the gifts and skills needed to help restore the status of clergy so that we would once again be seen as the equals of doctors and lawyers. Not only is no seminary president anywhere capable of such a feat, but what an opportunity we would miss to learn the deep, Franciscan, playful power of giving up on being powerful. I still don't know what candidate the seminary is going to choose, but my guess is this leader will probably not be the person who will lead the conversation about becoming fools for Christ. Sometimes we won't embrace a new direction until circumstances force us to do so.

Fortunately, there are *les jongleurs de Dieu* leading in the church today. There are holy jesters embracing play and tapping into the power of games. At one end of the spectrum there are individuals and movements that simply embrace playfulness without engaging game theory, game design theory, or gaming culture specifically. Like The Fun Theory and Mary Poppins, these voices link the element of fun to the accomplishment of a

---

2. Cox, *Feast of Fools*, 170.

task. Retired Presbyterian minister J. Barrie Shepherd would restore Augustine's wisdom by suggesting that good preaching should teach, exhort, but also delight.[3] Preacher and stand-up comedian Susan Sparks, who is the very embodiment of a holy jester, writes, "If you can laugh at yourself, you can forgive yourself. And if you can forgive yourself, you can forgive others. Laughter heals. It grounds us in a place of hope."[4] Influential movements such as the Episcopal Godly Play Foundation merge the best scientific research on cognitive development and biblical teaching to shape curricula that engage children in a way their particular brains can comprehend and taps into their natural gift of learning through play. There are also Christian clowning ministries and Christian magicians, both of which are numerous enough to support formal associations with local chapters.

Other voices have said it is time to connect with gamers and their culture. As with so many technological innovations, this connection emerged as youth leaders responded to changes happening among the kids they served. Youth leaders saw gamers move from a fringe movement to the mainstream. On the least intensive end, youth leaders simply utilize games as a way of gathering youth together. Game nights that used to center around board games now feature an Xbox or PlayStation. Game Church, however, represents a more intensive connection with gaming. If you attend a Comic Con or game conference, chances are you will encounter a booth with a picture of Jesus playing a video game. You can pick up a free copy of *Jesus for the Win*, a short book mainly articulating the Gospel using gaming language, and meet some interesting people. Without knowing it you have walked into Game Church. Mikee Bridges started Game Church almost by accident, simply by doing ministry with kids entirely uninterested in Jesus.[5] His was a relational ministry; Bridges just spent time with kids, playing games and telling them Jesus loved them without any judgment. Today Game Church continues this very basic ministry, avoiding hot-button social topics in order to simply convey the love of Christ to an intensely unwelcoming culture.

But movements such as Game Church, while engaging heavily with gamer culture, still represent fairly traditional efforts to translate a core message into another language. There is little theological engagement regarding how game theory and game design could help us recover or critique elements of our tradition and offer us ways to refocus our practice. This evaluation isn't a negative criticism of a Game Church type of engagement;

3. Shepherd, *Whatever Happened to Delight?*, 4.

4. Sparks, *Laugh Your Way to Grace*, Kindle locations 391–92.

5. Dixon, "Videogames, Bibles, and Beer," paras. 3–5.

it simply acknowledges that some leaders are beginning to test more sub-stantive approaches. Of course, game design is incredibly difficult. A good game is as much an art as a science, and some of the church's early attempts to delve into gameful thinking are more fruitful than others.

One of the most well-known and controversial efforts at gameful thinking in the church wasn't a conscious attempt at play but accountability. As a bishop of the United Methodist Church serving in the North Alabama Conference, William Willimon used a staple of game design, the leader-board, as an innovative tool to drive ecclesial excellence. The leaderboard simply posted attendance and giving records for all the churches in the con-ference. While the numbers aren't specifically tied to things such as clergy promotion, they certainly were taken into consideration. Some heralded the attempt as nothing less than taking the church as seriously as John Wesley did, while others questioned what seemed to be the quantifying of ministry "like so many hamburgers sold."[6] On the one hand, as a member of an-other mainline denomination facing decline, I can't fault Bishop Willimon for trying something, anything, to create change. But on the other hand, using game design elements without serious reflection on game design is potentially disastrous.

Game designer Margaret Robertson criticizes the practice of using game design elements to change behavior without consciously and actively considering what game is really being created, derisively referring to this as "pointsification":

> Gamification isn't gamification at all. What we're currently terming gamification is in fact the process of taking *the thing that is least essential to games* and representing it as the core of the experience. Points and badges have no closer a relationship to games than they do to websites and fitness apps and loyalty cards. They're great tools for communicating progress and ac-knowledging effort, but neither points nor badges in any way constitute a game. . . . They are the least important bit of a game, the bit that has the least to do with all of the rich cognitive, emotional and social drivers which gamifiers are intending to connect with.[7]

Agreeing with Robertson, game designer Ian Bogost blasts institutions that use game design to manipulate behavior: "More specifically, gamifica-tion is marketing bullshit, invented by consultants as a means to capture the wild, coveted beast that is videogames and to domesticate it for use in

6. Byassee, "Bishop's Dashboard," para. 7.

7. Robertson, "Can't Play, Won't Play," para. 4.

the grey, hopeless wasteland of big business, where bullshit already reigns anyway."[8]

Even proponents of gamification agree that leaderboards represent one of the more divisive and problematic game design elements. In their fantastic book *For the Win*, Wharton professors Kevin Werbach and Dan Hunter cite studies showing gamification can sometimes backfire and create problems that didn't exist in the first place. This is particularly true of leaderboards: "Game mechanics such as leaderboards can actually demotivate workers when the mechanic is entangled with traditional rewards such as salary and bonuses. When they see how low on the totem pole they are, many workers will give up. The climb up the ladder is too daunting. Others will internalize that the work is less important than the game and treat the work less seriously."[9]

Fortunately, better examples exist of church leaders using gameful thinking. The Reverend Mike Mather pastors Broadway United Methodist Church in Indianapolis, Indiana, and reads the Bible in one hand and Jane McGonigal's *Reality Is Broken* in the other. In the chapter on evidence-based ministry, we'll see that Mike is a game-changing pastor in the most profound sense of the term. In this chapter I just want to highlight Mike's creative use of a leaderboard in a way that helps rather than hurts. In order to playfully encourage community involvement, Mike and his ministry team agreed on several practices they thought were important. They came up with twelve great ideas, including visiting people in their homes to lay hands on them and bless them, praying with people wherever they found them, sharing meals to remind people of Christ's presence at the table, and throwing parties to celebrate the power of God's love.

Each player gets one point for every action (except pulling together a party, which is worth five points). What makes Mather's game effective are the dozen creative ways his church is trying to engage people in their community. And what makes it fun is that at the end of each month, the "winner" gets to buy all the other players a round of cupcakes. Because the winner really turns out to be a servant and because everyone likes cupcakes, Mike's leaderboard avoids creating an anxious, overly competitive environment. Jesus' saying "whoever wishes to be great among you must be your servant" (Matt 20:26) is especially true when dessert is involved.

Now, Mike simply uses the office wall as a leaderboard. It was just an idea he had, and he doesn't take it too seriously. But Dutch gamification expert Johan ter Beek created an incredibly sophisticated online game

8. Bogost, "Gamification Is Bullshit," para. 5.

9. Werbach and Hunter, *For the Win*, Kindle locations 608–11.

called *YourStory* connecting people with churches, schools, governments, and businesses to gamify personal, spiritual, and community development. *YourStory* works much like *The Extraordinaries*, a volunteer matching game Jane McGonigal chronicles in *Reality Is Broken*.[10] *The Extraordinaries* is a web- and mobile-based app that presents volunteers with small, doable, actual projects such as translating a document, locating and mapping defibrillators within a given building, or adding photos and tags for a museum. *YourStory* uses a web platform to present players with different volunteer missions. As missions are completed, a visual dashboard shows badges, levels, and an avatar that improves with growth. Missions can be assignments such as helping seniors, improving school playgrounds, and spending time in prayer.

This connection between the church and gamification is so cutting-edge that projects are still in the development stage. Professor Mary Hess at Luther Seminary, Executive Presbyter the Reverend Sarah Moore-Nokes, Professor Heidi Campbell, Dr. Sybrina Atwaters, and I are currently working on *Remnants*, an alternate reality game similar to *World Without Oil*. As churches in North America continue to decline in membership, this group wonders about a future in which remnants of the Christian tradition remain but the institutional church is but a memory. The question is, with only fragments of the Christian tradition remaining, how will people celebrate a marriage or grieve a death? How will they honor major life passages? Leaders could sit around and dream up responses on their own, but as *World Without Oil* reveals, a small group can't imagine the myriad solutions a larger collaboration can. The Center for Innovation at San Francisco Theological Seminary supported an incubator at which an early version of a possible game was beta tested. This effort is in its infancy, but it represents one attempt of church leaders to engage in gameful thinking. My guess is it's only the beginning.

10. McGonigal, *Reality Is Broken*, Kindle locations 4065–66.

22

Let's Get Real (Again)

At the end of the first section we looked at the case study of young pastor Alex and used the language of predictable irrationality to think about the forces shaping his relationship with a declining congregation. This time we're going to look at an actual gaming experiment carried out in the fall of 2014 at a district meeting of Presbyterians.

If you had been attending the fall meeting of the Presbytery of the Cascades, you would have seen two pastors, yours truly and my good friend the Reverend Paul Belz-Templeman, running around Westminster Presbyterian Church. We would have been the two carrying a wooden board with a line marked down the center and a seemingly bottomless bag full of stacks of ten one-dollar bills. If we approached, you would have seen the wild gleam in my eyes as I invited you to play an ultimatum game. Remember the ultimatum game?

In case you don't, here is a refresher. The rules, Paul explained to our willing victims, are quite simple. One person plays the role of the divider; the other plays the role of the decider. The divider splits the ten dollars into two portions: some to keep for themselves and some to give away to the other player. The decider then chooses whether to accept this division. If the decider accepts the deal, both players walk away with the money; if the decider rejects the deal, the money stays on the table and the game is over. As you can imagine, people wanted to know if they really got to keep the money. Yep, we told them. Some wanted to know the origin of the money.

We told them it was self-funded, and we were hopeful we'd be able to make up the money by publishing an article. (My wife, Melissa, was thrilled about that part.) Some wanted to know why we were conducting this experiment. What were we hoping to learn? Was there a trick? When we finally answered all the questions, we made it to the game.

You might remember that standard game theorists say the most rational way to play the game is for the divider to give themselves nine dollars and offer the decider one dollar. The decider should accept this division, because one dollar is still better than none. But as behavioral game theorists have learned, something different happens when living, breathing human beings play the game. Even when players understand the rational strategy, the average splits are closer to six for the divider and four for the decider.

For our study we observed fifteen pairs of pastors, known as teaching elders, and fifteen pairs of ruling elders for a combined total of sixty participants. When I tested a version of the game with small groups of pastors, I noticed some unusual behavior. Pastors tended to play in a strangely generous way. Pastors offered splits of nine dollars for the other person and one dollar for themselves. Sometimes they offered the whole amount to the other player. To me this behavior felt inauthentic and overly generous. I suspected that pastors who led churches with such an overly generous attitude would subject themselves to abuse from those who would take advantage of their generosity. And other church leaders might not appreciate what they perceived as pastors giving away the farm to free riders.

In contrast to the pastors, we hypothesized that the ruling elders, many of whom were business professionals, would play more like participants in other studies: slightly self-interested. Because of my preliminary tests, we postulated that pastors would play more generously: as dividers they would offer the deciders more than they gave themselves. I was hoping to write about reciprocity styles and show that pastors tend to behave more like givers and other congregational leaders act more like matchers. I would argue that pastors should be thoughtful about how such generous behavior in meetings might be perceived by the teams with whom they serve. While other givers often see such behavior as generous and positive, those with matcher styles might view them as foolish. It was going to be a great article.

To some the game was a welcome distraction from the serious business facing the presbytery that meeting. Our national body, known as the General Assembly, already allowed for openly gay and lesbian pastors and ruling elders, but in the summer of 2014 just before this meeting, the national body voted to approve the blessing of same-sex marriages. Because of these changes, many more socially conservative Presbyterian churches were seeking to leave the denomination, which is complicated because we have a trust clause in our *Book of Order* that states that church property is held by the presbytery. Presbyteries play a vital role in starting most congregations and invest heavily in the beginning. While congregations ultimately shoulder the greater part of the financial burden, no church can claim they made it to where they are without help. So, when a church desires to leave, a negotiation takes place between the leaders of that congregation and leaders from the presbytery to determine a fair arrangement. On the one hand, the presbytery wants to avoid the expense of a lawsuit and desires to be generous, but on the other hand, no one likes to be a sucker. After already dealing with many churches leaving, one of the first items of business at this meeting was coping with yet another congregation desiring to go their own way.

So, what do you think happened? Did the pastors play more generously than the ruling elders? Did we get to write that article on pastors and reciprocity styles? In a word . . . we were wrong. One of the most powerful aspects of behavioral game theory is the experimental nature of it. As soon as you start playing a game, anything can happen. And the data will lead you where it will, regardless of your hypothesis.

Both groups played more generously than studies would predict. In the pastors' group, the dividers gave themselves an average of $4.14 and offered the deciders an average of $5.86. Ruling elders were even more generous on average, with the dividers giving themselves a mere $3.93 and giving away $6.07. But unlike the pastors, who walked away with the money 80 percent of the time, the ruling elders left a lot on the table, accepting the deals only 60 percent of the time.

Why were the ruling elders seemingly more generous yet also so unsuccessful at taking the money? No doubt many reasons might account for the generous behavior of the ruling elders. Perhaps the amount of money was too paltry to entice them. Or they might not have believed they would really receive the money. To Paul and me, one reason stands out. We believe the religious nature of the meeting and the sacred space greatly affected the ruling elders. The games took place in and around a sanctuary. Many have demonstrated the impact religious space and imagery can have. We saw earlier in Sarah Coakley and Martin Nowak's research that religious priming—reading a religious text about generosity before playing a game—can increase giving behavior. These ruling elders weren't just playing a game; they were playing a game in a church. We think the setting helps make sense of why the ruling elders were more generous than the pastors. For the ruling elders the day was a visit to an unfamiliar sanctuary and charged with meaning. It wasn't an ordinary business meeting either; it was business interspersed with worship. The pastors, however, given the amount of time they spend around religious spaces, were less likely to be influenced by these sacred spaces. For pastors it was another day at the office, for many of them on their day off.

But why did the ruling elders experience such a challenge in receiving the money? We believe the story here lies in the distribution of offers. The most common offer for both groups was absolute fairness: $5 for the divider and $5 for the decider. The ruling elders offered more lopsided deals than the pastors. Twice ruling elder dividers gave away the entire $10, once the split was $1 and $9, and once the division was $3 and $7. But in all but one of these extreme cases the ruling elder deciders rejected the offer. The ruling elders were uncomfortable with unequal deals even when they would benefit from them personally. The ruling elders preferred fairness.

This penchant for fairness is important because while we were playing these small games, the presbytery itself was playing a similar game—only one with far higher stakes. As I said in the introduction to this example, Cascades Presbytery, like all presbyteries, continues to experience churches that want to leave the denomination over polity changes. The process usually begins with presbytery leaders striking a deal with the departing congregation; then this arrangement is put before the whole presbytery body to either accept or reject. Does the process of working out a tough deal in a small group only to present it cold to a larger body for a vote sound familiar?

Conversations about money are never easy. But because of the importance of these agreements and the likelihood presbyteries will continue to face the "ultimatum" of congregations wanting to leave, Paul and I believe we can improve how we handle these situations. First, we recommend that presbytery leaders strive to craft financial arrangements that are not only gracious but also fair. The good news from our ultimatum game findings is that both pastors and ruling elders seem to prefer fair to slightly generous offers, giving presbytery leadership a lot of room to negotiate. The harder news is that presbyters have to be mindful of the possible cost of not reaching a deal with a local congregation. Even though our presbytery won a legal case against a departing congregation, the legal bills from this win were significant. Indeed, that was a game in which a player could win and still very much lose. The cost of potential legal action must be factored into the arrangements and explained plainly.

Second, because of the strong priming effects of sanctuaries where most presbytery meetings are held, we recommend that presbytery leaders send the relevant financial details of proposed settlements with departing congregations in advance and ask the ruling elders to read these reports in their places of business or home offices. Further, because of the difficulty people have carrying over thoughts and feelings from one affective state to another, we recommend that these leaders write down a brief reflection on any offer as soon as they read it. After analyzing the terms in the cool light of day in their office or home, would this be a deal they would accept personally if it were their money?

Finally, we recommend that the presbytery leadership exercise transparency and present comprehensive financial information for these offers, including the value of the assets and the amount to be paid by the departing church. We believe it would be helpful to make a strong case for how the agreement is based on facts as well as feelings. Currently, in our presbytery we emphasize the amount of prayer that occurs during the meetings and how cordial both parties are as they work through these painful conversations. These are outstanding practices, and we commend our leaders for their time and care. But we believe it would ease these difficult moments in our presbytery slightly if our leadership would appeal to heads as well as to hearts—to the riders as well as the elephants, to the Jacobs as well as the Esaus.

We will always have difficult decisions to make. If it isn't around congregations leaving with property, it will be something else. Our great hope isn't that we might someday avoid difficult decisions but that we will learn how to better discern together as both church people *and* businesspeople at the same time. Presbyterians are proud we don't ask people to check their brains at the door when it comes to theological questions. We should carry on this proud tradition of valuing the intellect when it comes to financial questions as well.

"I can't decide to play as a businessperson or a church person," said one woman playing the ultimatum game we conducted. We suspect this ruling elder was wondering whether she should play generously or more fairly. Given these results we'd like to answer her question by saying, "Yes!"

23

Ten Game Ideas and Concepts to Remember

1. **Strategy**: A strategy in game theory means drawing out all the possible outcomes given different decisions. This matrix encourages leaders to think through all the possibilities and not just focus on the few outcomes they desire.

2. **Payoff**: A payoff in game theory represents the value players assign to different outcomes. What's important about payoffs is thinking empathetically and honestly. We have to step into the shoes of the people around us and honestly think about what they might prefer, not just what we wish they would prefer.

3. **Chicken Game**: Chicken is a common, dangerous game in which two or more players compete in such a way that winning represents a small gain and losing constitutes a catastrophic loss. While chicken games can be designed to create anxiety for good ends, generally these are destructive games that should be changed or avoided.

4. **Schelling Point**: Schelling points are unspoken agreements around which communities coalesce. Thomas Schelling's original research concerned strangers meeting up in New York City without the ability to communicate; most people guessed noon at Grand Central Station. In church situations Schelling points include important practices and rituals revered by the community. Because of the often unconscious

and sensitive nature of these points, it's important for new leaders to learn them as quickly as possible.

5. **Prisoner's Dilemma Game** and **Public Goods Game**: Prisoner's dilemma games and public goods games represent games in which individuals are better off cooperating but are sorely tempted to defect and go their own way. These games help model trust in challenging environments.

6. **Ultimatum Game**: In the ultimatum game two players square off over a pot of money. One player, the divider, gets to divide the money up; the other player, the decider, chooses whether to accept or reject the division. If the decider accepts the decision, both players walk away with their share. If the decider rejects the division, both get nothing and the money stays on the table. While rationally the divider should be selfish and the decider should accept any offer but zero, real human beings don't behave this way. Games such as the ultimatum game model fairness and justice in communities.

7. **Alternate Reality Games**: In alternate reality games (ARGs) people play games with real-life social value. *World Without Oil* represents one of the most significant ARGs—more than sixty thousand players responded to prompts to make changes in their own lives based on an imaginary oil shortage. Games such as these help us imagine and change the future.

8. *Les jongleurs de Dieu*: Saint Francis and his followers were known as *les jongleurs de Dieu*, or "jesters of God." The name arose from their joyful acceptance of poverty and their way of turning the conventional idea of power on its head. They remind us of a theology of play that has always existed at the margins of the church. I am calling for leaders to become *les jongleurs de Dieu* once more.

9. **Gamification**: Gamification is a controversial tool describing the use of games for real-world purposes. Game designers employ gamification in creative and fun attempts to improve behaviors such as physical exercise, but they also warn of potential dangers such as manipulation and the creation of bad games that are neither fun nor helpful.

10. **Points, Badges, and Leaderboards**: Points, badges, and leaderboards (PBLs) are some of the most common tools game designers use to give players feedback. Games award points for various actions, assigning more points to more important actions. Games award badges, or visual icons, for various achievements. Leaderboards show how players are progressing in comparison to one another. The most significant

thing to remember about PBLs is that as important as they are in game design, PBLs are not games. Simply using points or leaderboards without thinking more deeply about a game can be counterproductive.

Interlude

ISAIAH, COMMUNITY, AND THE PRISONER'S DILEMMA

Sermon given at Tualatin Presbyterian Church, February 6, 2011

Isaiah 58:9b–12: If you remove the yoke from among you, the pointing of the finger, the speaking of evil, if you offer your food to the hungry and satisfy the needs of the afflicted, then your light shall rise in the darkness and your gloom be like the noon-day. The LORD will guide you continually, and satisfy your needs in parched places, and make your bones strong; and you shall be like a watered garden, like a spring of water, whose waters never fail. Your ancient ruins shall be rebuilt; you shall raise up the foundations of many generations; you shall be called the repairer of the breach, the restorer of streets to live in.

When Melissa and I lived in Princeton, I remember one day I was walking around the university campus when I saw an unusual sight. There were a whole bunch of large trucks scattered around, workers carrying long metal poles with various attachments, and a fair number of people dressed in suits and hats who looked as if they had stepped out of a time machine from the 1940s.

I asked somebody what the heck was going on, and they told me it was a film crew shooting what would become the 2002 Academy Award winner for Best Picture: *A Beautiful Mind*. If you saw the movie or read the book by Sylvia Nasar, you know it tells the story of John Nash, one of the most brilliant mathematicians of the twentieth century. When Nash applied to graduate school, his adviser from Carnegie Tech wrote his recommendation in one sentence: "He is a mathematical genius." What makes Nash's story so much more compelling, though, is that for nearly all of his adult life he also suffered from paranoid schizophrenia, which almost ended his career time and time again.

But Nash hung in there in spite of his disease, and he eventually won the world's most prestigious recognition for intellectual work: the Nobel Prize. Nash won the Nobel Prize in economics for his work in what is known as game theory. Game theory is a branch of practical mathematics that attempts to describe any kind of group behavior where an individual's success is related to the choices others make. Another way of saying that: Nash studied what was likely to happen anytime two or more people tried to figure out how to live together.

One of the most famous types of scenarios Nash described is called the prisoner's dilemma. Here is the dilemma: imagine that two prisoners conspired to commit a crime. Now they are caught and being held in separate jail cells, unable to communicate. The police don't have enough evidence to convict and offer them both the same deal. Here's the deal:

A. If both of them are loyal to one another and stay silent, they will each serve a short sentence on a minor charge.

B. If both of them rat on one another—or "defect," as Nash calls it—then they will each serve a full term. Not good.

C. But—and here's the wrinkle—if one of them defects and rats the other out, but the other one stays silent and loyal, then the defector goes scot-free while the other serves the full sentence.

So, again, if both prisoners are loyal and cooperate, they will each pay a small price. If you think of them as partners or a community, cooperation is the best option. Each suffers a little but not too much. And, of course, if they both betray one another, they both wind up serving the full sentence, which is lousy. But at least they're in it together. Let's put it in personal terms: the most interesting possibility, what really makes this game fascinating, is that you could be loyal, and that rat fink could betray you. Then you would serve the whole sentence, while that turncoat would go absolutely free and pay nothing at all. And then, there's always the possibility in the back of your mind that if he stayed silent, you could defect and walk—and really, if you're honest with yourself, you never liked him all that much in the first place. You don't like to think of yourself as a traitor, but hey, you've got to be practical, right?

Now, here's the thing: even though the best decision for both would be to clam up and have one another's back, Nash would tell you loyalty is not the best decision. The best decision, the most logical decision, is to defect. Check it out. Because if you choose to trust, you know you will serve a little time; but you might get betrayed and get stuck with the whole sentence alone. If you defect, sure you might serve the sentence, but the other guy will, too, which feels fair. And you might even go totally free. So, for Nash it's a no-brainer—you and I shouldn't trust and cooperate with one another in most cases. It's just too risky. We should look after our own interests. No one else will.

And experimentally, is double defection what happens when psychologists study people who actually play this game? In one experiment where strangers come in and play the game, people do defect. The very possibility that the other person might betray you and send you down the river while they could get away scot-free is enough for most people to forgo the win-win choice.

And we see this in the real world, too. Globally, the prisoner's dilemma was used to understand the arms race between America and the Soviet Union after World War II. It wasn't in the best interest of either of us to spend so much money on weapons that we could destroy the planet one hundred times over. But neither side trusted the other. I mean, anyone who has ever seen *Rocky IV* knows you can't trust Russia! And so both sides kept making more and more weapons just in case and taught a whole generation of schoolkids how to duck and cover. (How crawling under your desk was ever supposed to help you in a nuclear blast, I have no idea.)

And this dilemma is equally true on the personal level. Any relationship you enter requires some amount of personal sacrifice on your part: you are always having to give this or that up to keep the peace and make the relationship work. But if one of the partners starts to feel as if they are doing all the giving and adjusting, it doesn't take long before they get tired and think about defecting, too. When the other person seems to always think of themselves first, you start to feel foolish and taken advantage of when you keep trying to sacrifice for the team. I think it's safe to say that in nearly every relationship that falls apart, it's rarely one giant breach that does it. No, it's the thousand tiny little moments where one partner had the opportunity to deepen the trust or repair damage done, and they just didn't do it. Until over time the love just gets choked out.

Well, this way of thinking, this prisoner's dilemma, this is what was going on with the people of God to whom Isaiah is writing in the text for this morning. The part of Isaiah we're reading from is what scholars call Second Isaiah—and it comes from the restoration period in the fifth and early fourth centuries before the time of Jesus, after the exiles returned home. So, you know the backstory: Babylon came in and destroyed the temple and in two waves carried almost all the Israelites into exile. In the first wave the

Babylonians carried off the leaders, and in the second wave they carried off the regular folks. But sometimes we forget that they didn't actually exile the entire population to Babylon. They left a group of people behind to tend the fields and shepherd the flocks, a people who came to be known as the 'am ha'aretz, the people of the land. These people were the poorest and the least educated, but for seventy years they were the only Israelites living in the land.

So, what happens next? When Cyrus of Persia rises up and smacks down the Babylonians and sends the Jews back home, the story isn't quite as simple as sometimes it's told. It's not as if all of Israel comes marching back to a completely empty land. The exiles come back and discover a Jewish community that has been doing all the cooking and cleaning while everyone else has been living it up in the hanging gardens of Babylon.

Now the exiles could sit down with the 'am ha'aretz, the people of the land—they could sit down and decide to work together. They could decide to trust and to cooperate. But they don't. The exiles march back in, and they don't thank the 'am ha'aretz for running the place. They say, "What do you think you're doing trying to lead? Go back to the fields; go back to the sheep. We'll let you know when we want to hear from you. But don't hold your breath." You hear this hinted at in Isaiah's text—about the yoke, the finger-pointing, the speaking of evil, and the hungry and afflicted. The exiles could have cooperated, but they chose to defect.

But don't think that the 'am ha'aretz are somehow innocent. The books of Ezra and Nehemiah record the history of this period. And Nehemiah records a letter that the 'am ha'aretz write railing against the exiles—telling the Persians that the exiles are really up to no good, and the Persians better come in and intervene against the exiles and knock heads. The people of the land would rather have the Persians come in and leave all the Jews with nothing than watch the returning exiles lord it over them again.

So both sides are locked in this prisoner's dilemma, and they are behaving exactly like Nash tells us is logical. They aren't trusting one another; they are not cooperating. They are not choosing relationship; they are circling the wagons and choosing defensive self-protection.

And after awhile, after reading this text again and again, and thinking about it all week, I have to admit I was left wondering at times if there's any hope for community, for relationship. Nash is a genius. I'm not. I can't deny his analysis. I can't deny that it's probably more rational not to trust each other. I can't deny the experience of the exiles and the 'am ha'aretz. I spent a lot of time this week wondering if relationship, community, is even possible, or if we just fool ourselves and make do with pretend communities as long as they are convenient.

But then I did the only thing I know to do—I kept reading. And thank God for the rest of Isaiah. Isaiah, who is as realistic as you can get, who has seen the absolute worst in terms of what we humans are capable of—Isaiah absolutely sings to the exiles. And his message is to try, to trust. His message is to reach across the lines—not because of what you might get out of it, not because of your dreams for yourself, but because of God's dream of a more beautiful community, a kind of community the people can't even imagine yet.

Listen again to Isaiah 58:9b–12: "If you remove the yoke from among you, the pointing of the finger, the speaking of evil, if you offer your food to the hungry and satisfy the needs of the afflicted, then your light shall rise in the darkness and your gloom be like the noonday. The LORD will guide you continually, and satisfy your needs in parched places, and make your bones strong; and you shall be like a watered garden, like a spring of water, whose waters never fail. Your ancient ruins shall be rebuilt; you shall raise up the foundations of many generations; you shall be called the repairer of the breach, the restorer of streets to live in."

Isaiah says there is something better than just clinging to our interest groups and only hanging out with the people who already agree with us on pretty much everything. Reach out, he says. Reach across. Take the risk of trusting the Other. Could you get hurt? Absolutely. But if they reach back, together, and with the Spirit of God, you will be capable of a kind of healing that can change the world—you might someday be known as repairers of the breach, restorers of the streets.

And do you know what? As smart as Nash was . . . as smart as he was—it turns out even he didn't fully understand the prisoner's dilemma. It is true that when psychologists observed strangers coming in and playing a prisoner's dilemma game, they would defect and betray one another. That's true. BUT. What Nash didn't foresee was a slightly different experiment by a guy named Robert Axelrod called the iterated prisoner's dilemma. *Iterate* just means to repeat. And in the iterated version players come together and agree to play not just a few times—but hundreds of times. In other words, they decide to form a kind of community with one another. And when people form community, something fascinating happens. What happens is that, more often than not, people take the risk of trusting the other player—knowing full well they could get hurt. But they take the risk of trusting knowing that if they cooperate—if, over the long haul, they work together—both will be better off than if they defect.

And so, relationship and trust: it's true, it's hard. It's rare. And maybe it isn't even natural or logical. But by some beautiful miracle of God—it is possible. We are capable of it. We just have to decide whether we want to point the finger and speak evil or whether we would rather be known as a repairer of the breach, a restorer of streets.

The most beautiful thing I have heard in a long time came from Nicholas Kristof in his *New York Times* column this week (February 3, 2011). Kristof has taken his own life in his hands to travel into Egypt when everyone else is trying to get out. And he's not just reporting from a distance; he and a cameraman have walked right into the heart of Freedom Square.

The protest started out peacefully, but this week pro-government forces, largely made up of ex-cons who came armed with weapons, have been wreaking havoc. And for a protester, it's a classic prisoner's dilemma. If you're an individual protesting—if you decide to stay loyal to the group— the best that can happen is you add your voice; but the worst that can happen is you might be killed, which is an all too real possibility. If you leave, there's always another day. The logical choice based on rational self-interest for an individual is to back away. To defect.

But here's what Kristof saw this week:

> Inside Tahrir Square on Thursday, I met a carpenter named Mahmood whose left arm was in a sling, whose leg was in a cast and whose head was being bandaged in a small field hospital set up by the democracy movement. This was the seventh time in 24 hours that he had needed medical treatment for injuries suffered at the hands of government-backed mobs. But as soon as Mahmood was bandaged, he tottered off once again to the front lines. . . . I was awestruck. That seemed to be an example of determination that could never be surpassed, but as I snapped Mahmood's picture I backed into Amr's wheelchair. It turned out that Amr had lost his legs many years ago in a train accident, but he rolled his wheelchair into Tahrir Square to show support for democracy. . . . Amr was being treated for a wound from a flying rock. I asked him as politely as I could what a double-amputee in a wheelchair was doing in a pitched battle involving Molotov cocktails, clubs, machetes, bricks and straight razors. "I still have my hands," he said firmly. "God willing, I will keep fighting."[1]

This month is Mission Month here. We're going to be hearing about different possibilities, different opportunities. But fundamentally mission means making the choice not just to keep to yourself—but to reach out,

---

1. Kristof, "We Are All Egyptian," paras. 1–4.

to risk. It means not hoarding our time, and talent, and treasure for our-selves—but offering it up, on the hope that God really is doing new things in our midst every single day.

And the question for each one of us is this: do we want to be disciples of John Nash? Do we want to be known as reasonable, rational, and risk-averse people who piled up as much stuff up as we could? Or do we want to listen to Isaiah and that other Middle Eastern carpenter, the one who laid down his life for others? Can we step into an uncertain future together, trusting that in God's hands we may someday be known as repairers of the breach and restorers of the streets? Who do you want to be? Amen.

The Irrational Leader

24

Decisions, Decisions, Decisions!

Pastors and other church leaders wear a lot of hats. As resident theologians of their communities, they study the Scriptures, church history, and theological tradition. They practice spiritual disciplines, praying for the institutions and people they serve. They listen, offering their ears to those carrying heavy burdens. They advocate for justice, organizing efforts to care for the least, the last, and the lost. They preach, teach, and lead worship. One of the most important roles pastors and other church leaders play, a role that provides the foundation for all others, is that of decision-maker. Leaders themselves make decisions, and they help the bodies they serve make decisions. This role is so crucial I would venture to say that it is in decision-making that we find the very essence of leadership. In decision-making we see the insights of behavioral economics and game theory meet. This meeting point is the place where everything we've been learning about in section 1 and section 2 comes together.

Over and over the Scriptures lift up the importance of decision-making. Proverbs repeatedly urges people of faith to "not let these escape from your sight: keep sound wisdom and prudence, and they will be life for your soul" (3:21–22). This theme of judgment and discretion connected to life and death marks the entire Deuteronomistic history all the way from Deuteronomy through Second Kings. Before his death, Moses explains to the people that the choice they have to follow in the ways he has led them is nothing less than a choice between the ways of life and the ways of death.

Joshua repeats this scene at the end of his life; he tells the people that while his family has chosen to serve the Lord, they must all make their own decision. In the Scriptures everything hangs on good decision-making.

The very relationship between God and God's people, as set down in the Scriptures, is fundamentally a record of the decisions both God and the people make along the way. Throughout the Scriptures, leaders continually make tough decisions that take them into unknown territory. Abram and Sarai make the decision to trust in God's promise and leave everything they know to find a new land. Shiphrah and Puah first take their lives in their hands by defying Pharaoh's orders to kill the Hebrew male children and then compound their defiance by lying to him when questioned. Moses decides to turn aside to marvel at the burning bush and then return to Egypt even after killing that Egyptian overseer. Nearly every prophet, when approached by God, responds with the same decision as Isaiah: "Here am I; send me!" (Isa 6:8). The men and women who follow after the way of Jesus leave their previous lives to walk with him even into Jerusalem. Jesus himself, facing certain death, asks for the cup to be taken from him yet decides to submit.

Certainly, decision-making is difficult. It's easy to make poor choices. Some children of the eighties will remember the *Saturday Night Live* (*SNL*) parody of a commercial for Bad Idea Jeans. A bunch of guys are getting ready to play a pickup game of basketball when one admits to spending money on renovating an apartment he's renting; another says, "Now that I've got kids, I feel a lot better having a gun in the house." Being *SNL*, the bad ideas go downhill from there, but the scope of those bad ideas barely touches the spectrum of poor decision-making in the Scriptures.

While the tradition unfairly assigns more blame to Eve than Adam, both decide to take a bite out of that apple. In Numbers, Moses strikes the rock twice to bring water from it even though God ordered Moses to speak to it. Many interpretations exist for why God punishes Moses so harshly for this one contrary act, but underneath all of them is the fact that Moses makes a poor decision. King Saul offers sacrifices that were not his to make, makes a collective vow of hunger that his son breaks, and refuses to wholly destroy the Amalekites and all their belongings so that he can keep some of the spoils for himself. These decisions cause Samuel to anoint David even while Saul remains on the throne.

David himself, of course, was certainly no stranger to poor decision-making. While his choice to murder Uriah to cover up his adultery with Bathsheba captures our lurid imagination, it is David's earlier decision to remain at the palace in the springtime—the time when kings normally go to war—that places him in a context where he is less likely to be the king he wants to be. Later kings make decisions that lead to the destruction of the northern and southern kingdoms and ultimately to the Babylonian exile. In the New Testament Judas betrays Jesus with a kiss. Peter denies knowing Jesus not once but three times. If you could ask Paul, I suspect he might tell you the leaders of the Corinthian community couldn't make a good decision if their lives depended on it.

Given the fundamental importance decision-making holds for church leaders and how replete the Scriptures are with critical decisions, it's surprising how little guidance most leaders receive regarding the art of decision-making. Think about it for a moment. Of all the classes you have ever taken, have you ever enrolled in an entire course devoted to decision-making? Have you even had one class or a week of education devoted to the question of what constitutes a good decision? Most church leaders I know receive a great deal of training in various disciplines important to their work, but precious few receive any training in how to translate this expertise into wise decision-making. Our church culture operates with the assumption that everyone just knows how to make a decision; thus, the important thing is to make sure we train people to think theologically and biblically. Since we think everyone just kind of naturally knows how to make decisions, then what's important is to make sure people are making decisions on a solid foundation of ecclesial knowledge. While I understand this perspective, I hope that having read the first two sections about behavioral economics and game theory, you might now question how natural wise decision-making really is given all the ways our perception and thinking are shaped by our bodies and the contexts, or games, in which we find ourselves.

Currently, Stanford University in Palo Alto, California, supports one of the most robust programs in decision-making. Throughout his long career at Stanford, Professor Ron Howard met a lot of brilliant, powerful leaders, and he discovered that being a great engineer, software developer, or financial analyst does not make one an intuitively, naturally good decision-maker. I would posit that this absence of intuitive decision-making ability is equally evident in the ecclesial world. Being a gifted theologian, preacher, or pastoral caregiver does not necessarily mean a leader will naturally make wise decisions. Stanford's Strategic Decision and Risk Management (SDRM) program incorporates the cognitive heuristic and bias awareness from behavioral economics, the strategic thinking of game theory, and adds a level of analytical sophistication with the goal of improving decision quality in organizations. Up to this point, I can find no one in church leadership who has taken the insights of SDRM and paired them with the challenges facing church leaders. Given the significance of decision-making and the powerful insights the Stanford model offers, it's about time we started.

25

Discernment vs. Decision-Making

In the church we run into two main problems when it comes to decision-making before we even get to the decisions themselves: we confuse discernment with decision-making at the beginning of the process, and we conflate the outcome of the decision with the quality of the decision itself. Because of the long and rich history of discernment in the church, we'll tackle the question of discernment and decisions in this chapter. Then, in the next chapter, we'll explore the problems that arise when we fail to distinguish between the outcome of a decision and our evaluation of the decision itself.

Some readers may have found themselves pushing back against my claim in the previous chapter that church leaders receive little training in decision-making. These leaders would rightly point out that they were taught discernment practices such as the clearness committee that not only have a rich theological heritage and strong traditional place in the history of the church but also provide incredible guidance for decision-making. I myself was taught to practice a version of the Quaker clearness committee and agree this is an important tool for leaders.

While we don't have time here to provide an exhaustive list of other spiritual discernment practices, I commend books such as Elizabeth Liebert's *The Way of Discernment*. Liebert envisions discernment as a rich, multifaceted process of silencing oneself until one is able to sense God's Holy Spirit and listen for God's still, small voice. Liebert recommends steeping oneself in prayer and Scripture; she also advocates following practices such as the Jesuit examen, the Quaker clearness committee, and embodied prayer in a series of steps as one works through a question. Each practice reveals a different layer of the question until, after a time, a decision just begins to emerge. The weight of the decision drives the time of the process: a more simple decision may take a few days, while a decision with greater impact may take months or years.[1] Unlike others who focus exclusively on spiritual approaches, Liebert does allow for the role of reason; however, she uses the example of the traditional pros and cons list, which is a method of decision-making particularly vulnerable to confirmation bias.

The main disagreement I have with Liebert's approach stems from how she defines discernment and decision-making. Liebert views discernment as the process whereby we carefully separate out what we believe God wants us to choose from what we as humans desire. She writes, "Discernment, then, is the process of intentionally becoming aware of how God is present, active, and calling us as individuals and communities so that we can respond with increasingly greater faithfulness."[2] She relegates decision-making, however, to a merely human-centered process of choosing what we want. Discernment is about God; decision-making is about us.

This distinction is an unfortunate one. In one fell swoop Liebert and others in the discernment tradition assert a theological contrast between discernment and decision-making: God is present in the religious practice of discernment, whereas we encounter only human will and desire in the baser realm of decision-making. This kind of thinking severs us from the deep wisdom of nonreligious traditions and exalts the church in a way that is self-aggrandizing. It also confines God to religious spheres when, if God is God, the Holy One of Israel can and will speak through Barthian dead dogs and even (gasp!) some of the best practices in the business world.

The real difference between discernment and decision-making is not theological but practical. Liebert rightly reminds us that the Latin root of the word *discern* is *discernere*, which means "to distinguish and separate apart." Liebert narrows this definition to mean that in discernment we are sifting out human will from the divine. Discernment can also mean to simply separate apart the various layers that complicate the challenges we face. When we discern, in other words, we sit, we listen, and we carefully separate and pull apart the tangle of feelings and voices around something important in our lives. Yes, God's voice is a part of these steps, but so are many other

---

1. Liebert, *Way of Discernment*, 145.
2. Ibid., 8.

factors. What's important is that the act of discernment is a process of separation and untangling.

In decision-making, however, we cannot be content to merely untangle the difficulties facing us. In decision-making we have to make a choice. The roots of the word *decide* are *de-* and *caedere*, meaning "to cut off." When we make decisions, we are making what the founder of decision analysis, Ron Howard, calls "a choice between two or more alternatives that involves an irrevocable allocation of resources."[3] By describing this choice as an "irrevocable allocation," Howard acknowledges that with a decision something really is at stake in the action of deciding. When we choose one path, in other words, we are not choosing others. Abram and Sarai could ignore God and stay in Haran; they could pay lip service to God, go on vacation and later return; or they could follow God's promise and leave their home. They could not do all of these things at the same time.

Discernment and decision-making, in this sense, are mutually dependent. Good decision-making requires that leaders spend as much time as the situation allows in prayer, in studying the Scriptures, and in separating out their thoughts, feelings, and sense of where God's Holy Spirit is nudging them. They also, at some point, preferably as late as they possibly can without losing the opportunity, have to make a call. They have to make a decision. Just as Faulkner is commonly given credit for saying that great writers have to learn to kill their darlings, great leaders have to learn to eventually kill off options initially open to them in order to commit to the path on which they believe God is leading them. And God is not, then, in just the discernment mode or just the decision-making mode. God was, is, and ever shall be inextricably intertwined in the whole process.

When I have presented this material to Christian leaders and people of faith, I find people consistently prefer the term *discernment* to *decision-making*. The easy distinction spiritualists assert between faithful discernment and businesslike decision-making carries a strong appeal. I suspect some of this appeal comes from the suspicion the church harbors toward the business world. Church leaders often perceive the business world as driven by greed, and the church sees itself as led by truth.

One respected leader who has shown this kind of antipathy toward the business world is the pastor and author Eugene Peterson. In his memoir he writes,

> I was watching both the church and my vocation as a pastor in it
> being relentlessly diminished and corrupted by being redefined
> in terms of running an ecclesiastical business. The ink on my

3. Howard and Abbas, *Foundations of Decision Analysis*, 8.

ordination papers wasn't even dry before I was being told by experts, so-called, in the field of church that my main task was to run a church after the manner of my brother and sister Christians who run service stations, grocery stores, corporations, banks, hospitals, and financial services. . . . This is the Americanization of congregation. It means turning each congregation into a market for religious consumers, an ecclesiastical business run along the lines of advertising techniques, organizational flow charts, and energized by impressive motivational rhetoric. But this was worse. This pragmatic vocational embrace of American technology and consumerism that promised to rescue congregations from ineffective obscurity violated everything—scriptural, theological, experiential—that had formed my identity as a follower of Jesus and as a pastor.[4]

To be sure, Peterson makes a valid point when he warns us to keep a watchful eye on the unreflective and idolatrous assumption of techniques from the business world that would usurp God's fundamental and primary role in leading the church through Jesus Christ in the person of the Holy Spirit. But Peterson's scorching rhetoric—he later refers to the application of business practices to the church as "blasphemous desecration" and "a vocational abomination of desolation"—overdoes it.[5]

So, then, what has Palo Alto to do with Jerusalem? When church leaders put the clear thinking of Stanford decision-quality leaders into the service of Christian practice, Palo Alto can indeed have quite a lot to do with Jerusalem.

4. Peterson, *Pastor*, Kindle locations 1839–48.
5. Ibid., Kindle locations 1849–50.

26

Decision Outcome vs. Decision Quality

In the middle of the wilderness God made a decision, and it didn't go well at first. God made the call to summon Moses up to the top of Mount Sinai and give him the law inscribed on two stone tablets. In Moses' absence the people grew anxious and demanded immediate gods. To mollify them, Aaron took their jewelry and fashioned two golden calves. Ready to celebrate, the people ate, drank, and were very merry indeed. God, angered by this betrayal, determined to destroy the people, but Moses talked God down off the ledge. Yet when Moses descended and saw for himself what was going on, he threw the tablets down and destroyed them.

There's no other way to say it: the first attempt to give Israel the law was an epic failure. But was it a bad decision? Was the decision to give Israel the law in the first place a poor one?

Failure is a hot topic in church leadership today, and for good reasons. For one thing, as Duke Divinity's C. Kavin Rowe provocatively puts it, "Failure is at the heart of what Christian leaders have to offer the world."[1] Here is what Rowe means: the leaders Jesus trained abandoned him in his hour of need; Jesus himself died a tragic death; and when he rose again, he didn't stick around but left a struggling organization. The Christian story is not a string of successes going from (as business guru Jim Collins titles his book)

1. Rowe, "Failure as Christ-Shaped Leadership," para. 3.

good to great.[2] So, theologically we have incredible resources to draw upon when thinking about failure.

Also, we know that permission to fail is vital for faithful innovation. Great ideas rarely arrive fully baked. Faithful institutions support experimental cultures that allow leaders to fail until they get it right. In their *Faith and Leadership* article "Failure to Learn," L. Gregory Jones and Kelly Gilmer write, "We have problems to fix in and across our institutions, and fixing them will require us to dream big and to create cultures of experimentation, innovation and learning. Addressing our key challenges might involve some spectacular failures, but those failures will teach us what we need to learn and do for a more sustainable future."[3]

Today, church leaders are taking this call to experiment to heart. In the fall of 2014 San Francisco Theological Seminary's Center for Innovation in Ministry featured a training led by Smallify, which bills itself as an innovation capacity-building firm. Smallify works with organizations to introduce a process for fostering institutional creativity. One of the firm's key ideas is the small bet, a modest risk that encourages institutions to take chances and learn from failure. The following year, NEXT Church demonstrated a similar willingness to experiment when, at its national gathering, it connected church leaders with FAILURE:LAB, a counterintuitive approach that features personal stories of failure to reduce the fear of failure that so often cripples us and keeps us from testing new ideas.

With all of this talk, however, we're still missing one crucial element in our conversations around failure: we don't know how to assess the quality of our decisions. We rightly talk about the importance of creating cultures of trust and experimentation. We point out the importance of differentiating between good experimental failures and catastrophes resulting from leaders' bad ethical behavior. But even more fundamental is assessing the decisions themselves. How do we distinguish between good decisions that happen to turn out poorly versus bad decisions that also result in failure? Or how do we tell the difference between a bad decision that just happens to turn out well versus a good decision that goes according to plan? How do we assess the quality of our decision without resorting to merely judging it by its outcome?

Distinguishing decision quality from decision outcome is one of those things that is easy to say and nearly impossible to do. Our default is to assume that good decisions result in good outcomes; bad decisions result in

---

2. See Collins, *Good to Great: Why Some Companies Make the Leap—and Others Don't.*

3. Jones and Gilmer, "Failing to Learn," para. 29.

bad outcomes. If something goes well, it must have been a good decision. If something fails, there must have been a mistake. But it doesn't always work so simply. Leaders at SDRM remind us we can make terrible decisions that still result in good outcomes, and we can make great decisions that, unfortunately, head south on us.[4] If we fail to see this subtle distinction, we will continue practices we shouldn't and pull the plug on projects that merit more patience.

Let's say my high schooler attends a wild party, drinks, and then makes the epically bad decision to drive home. This is a terrible decision. If he makes it home without incident, the outcome is good—but we would never say his safe arrival home means he should repeat the initial decision to drink and drive. No. He was lucky. He made a bad decision and experienced a good outcome. On the flip side, if my kid drinks at this party but calls me to come pick him up, we would commend him for at least having the sense to call for help. If, on the way home, a cat darts out in the middle of the street and causes me to swerve and run our car into a tree, then this trip ended with a terrible outcome. But this bad outcome doesn't mean the decision to call me for help was wrong. It was a good decision that just happened to lead to a bad outcome. These things happen.

Church leaders rarely make this distinction, and it's a problem. I started out in ministry leading a new church development. I had no idea what I was doing, which is probably the only reason I agreed to try. You learn to fail in new church development. A lot. Planters learn very quickly to separate their sense of self from whether they succeed or fail, or they won't be planters for very long. Unfortunately, few on the outside understand this concept. We know that vastly more new church developments fail than succeed. But we have less understanding of why some fail while others thrive. Every startup group believes they have a chance, or they wouldn't invest the time, energy, and resources. Yet, every time a new plant fails, people come out of the woodwork to say it was a mistake all along. If the outcome is bad, it must have been the wrong decision in the first place. We have to stop this flawed reasoning. Good decisions can and will sometimes lead to bad outcomes.

Instead of reasoning from the outcome, we have to spend more time thinking about the quality of the decisions we make. What goes into making a decision that's high-quality? How can you tell when the board on which you are serving is making a low-quality decision? These are questions we will address in the next chapter. Currently, church leaders aren't talking about decision quality versus outcome at all. If we don't start this

4. Howard and Abbas, *Foundations of Decision Analysis*, 18.

conversation, we will continue to face an uphill battle in creating cultures that nurture experimentation and tolerate good failures. When we don't make this distinction, we almost can't help punishing good leaders who fail well and need to keep trying.

Remember how God's first attempt to give the people the law constituted an unmitigated disaster? I asked whether it was a bad decision. What do you think? I say the answer is absolutely not. While the first outcome of golden calves and smashed tablets was terrible, it was still a good decision for God to give the law. When leaders face good decisions that result in poor outcomes, they have to persevere and try again, which is exactly what God and Moses do. Just two chapters after Moses destroys the first tablets, God tells Moses to cut two more tablets. God again inscribes the tablets with the law. God doesn't modify the plan. God doesn't say they made mistakes earlier. The first decision really was a good one. It just had a bad outcome. And so God and Moses try the same idea again, and happily, the second attempt results in the same Ten Commandments that continue to guide us today.

27

Decision Quality and the Decision Quality Chain

With the benefit of hindsight it's obvious God's decision to bestow the law was a good decision. Rare is the decision that endures for thousands of years. But leaders don't have the benefit of hindsight. How can leaders discern whether a decision is a high-quality one regardless of the outcome without the long view? Let's remember that lofty advice in Proverbs 3 that we read in the first chapter of this section—for people of faith to hold fast to "wisdom and prudence"—judgment and discretion—and see what Stanford's decision-making program suggests for actually doing it.

SDRM offers an invaluable guide for leadership bodies making decisions together. Leaders at SDRM call this guide the decision quality chain. The chain as they teach it contains six elements: appropriate frame; creative, doable alternatives; good information; values; sound reasoning; and commitment to action. These facets of decision quality aren't ordered, although it does make sense to evaluate the frame as early as possible. Depending on the situation, however, a group may spend more time thinking through alternatives than they do seeking good information, or vice versa. But at whatever point a group enters the chain, it is important to remember that the overall quality of the decision depends, like the strength of a chain, on the weakest link. A group can spend adequate time on five of the six elements of the chain, but one weak link can doom the quality of the decision. For instance, if a team worked incredibly hard on all the facets except

186

whether the larger organization was committed to action, the team is potentially spending a lot of time on a decision that will never come to pass.

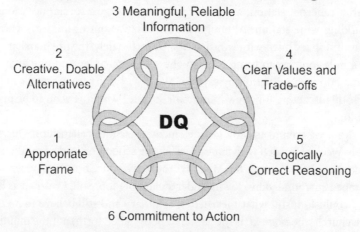

Elements of Decision Quality

3 Meaningful, Reliable Information

2 Creative, Doable Alternatives

4 Clear Values and Trade-offs

DQ

1 Appropriate Frame

5 Logically Correct Reasoning

6 Commitment to Action

It's worth spending more time to understand each of these links in the chain. When looking at the element of appropriate framing, leaders consider whether they are solving the right problem. The right solution to the wrong problem will only lead to frustration, and it happens all the time. I realize now that one of the reasons I concluded it was time for me to leave my first call, a new church development outside of Austin, Texas, was a framing issue.

If there is a good way to start a new church, this wasn't it. The leader, a pastor of a theologically moderate congregation who dreamed up the idea in the first place, left her church before the plant started. After her departure two theologically conservative congregations agreed to partner with the original congregation, which added the burden of social-issue conflict on top of the challenge of just starting a new community. While the leadership was in flux, district denominational leaders ran an ad on the local cable access station basically inviting anyone from the community interested in starting this church to show up. The marketing campaign didn't target people with the gifts and temperament for starting a new congregation; it simply brought in the curious. We wound up with the gamut: from people who wanted praise songs and hands in the air to one musician who considered Mozart contemporary and only Bach legitimate. And then there was me, a wet-behind-the-ears seminary graduate who knew absolutely nothing about leading a congregation, much less starting one. What could possibly go wrong?

Perhaps the greatest challenge for this new church development was worship space. We were elated to start off our venture in a winery located on Lake Travis—humorously imagining serving communion by intinction with a cabernet station, a pinot noir station, and, on special occasions, a sparkling wine station. Although the winery was out of the way, it was a beautiful space lined with wine barrels. Unfortunately, the fire marshal gave us a mile-long list to bring it up to church-space code. And one architect summed up the situation by saying, "Well . . . I don't feel unsafe standing near this structure for a few minutes or so, but I wouldn't want to be inside for long."

So, we wound up at a local elementary school cafetorium. Our first Holy Week coincided with circus week at the school. Instead of candles and a contemplative setting for Maundy Thursday and Good Friday, we worshipped surrounded by clowns under a giant big top. Still, I worked as hard as I could to instill what I learned in seminary and still believe to be true: the church, the *ekklesia*, is the gathered body called forth, not the building.

It turned out that the good people I was leading gave me the very best start in ministry. We prayed together, laughed together, and stumbled together. Author Neil Gaiman advises, "Make new mistakes. Make glorious, amazing mistakes. Make mistakes nobody's ever made before."[1] We followed his advice to the letter. But I would learn over time that no matter how often I preached and taught that we already were the church, this idea many of them had in their heads and hearts—the idea of building a nice little building on a beautiful piece of Texas hill country—would never go away. One day, about three years after we had started on our adventure together, I was talking with one of the members I considered particularly wise. He told me offhand that he was looking forward to the day when he would be able to invite more of his friends. I asked him why he wasn't inviting them now. He immediately replied, "Oh, when we have a church. I'll invite them when we have a church. That's all."

And just like that I realized in my heart, if not in my head just yet, that we had a framing problem. I had accepted the fact that we weren't going to find the millions of dollars it was going to take to buy land and build a building, and I was working my tail off to solve the problem of becoming a church without a building. Indeed, I had even been to conferences where they handed out books such as *When Not to Build*,[2] the answer to which in

---

1. Gaiman, "My New Year Wish," para. 9.

2. See Bowman and Hall, *When Not to Build: An Architect's Unconventional Wisdom for Growing the Church*.

almost every case is not to build. Few people in new church development were interested in the old model of land and building. So, I was working hard to help the people I was serving live into this brave new world. That was the problem I was solving. But that was not the challenge that interested my members. They were land-and-building people. They always had been. They knew it wouldn't be easy, but they were signed on to meet an entirely different challenge: how to build the church of their dreams.

I didn't survive this framing challenge. I left not long after that conversation. I felt like a failure, although together we had accomplished some pretty amazing things. Just in terms of numbers: we started out with sixteen people and grew to around ninety. I honestly believed the problem they were trying to solve was an impossible one; and when I left, I felt as if I were killing whatever small chance they had. But God is God, and I, most certainly, am not.

Part of the reason the language of biases and heuristics makes so much sense to me, I think, is that I've experienced being wrong so many times. Not only did they survive, but they have thrived. And that pastor who had the original idea for starting the new church but left for another call? She actually returned with her husband to lead the congregation, and one of her great gifts is fundraising. *Serious* fundraising. She was able to see opportunities where all I saw was barrenness. In 2013 Presbyterian Church of Lake Travis celebrated worship in a beautiful limestone sanctuary on their own little corner of Texas hill country that, for me, will ever stand as a reminder to never say impossible when it comes to the mischievous and persistent Holy Spirit.

In the second component of the decision quality chain, SDRM pushes leaders to articulate creative and doable alternatives. Especially when we feel convinced we're on the right path, it's easy to avoid thinking through alternatives. That is a mistake. Without several creative, doable alternatives, including not doing anything at all, we should question the quality of our decision. The emphasis here is on creative and doable. Ever been in that meeting where people throw out absurd alternatives like selling the church property and going to Bermuda? Though it can take incredible patience and a strong will to keep pushing ourselves to seek and find other faithful pathways, we must do it if we wish to arrive at a sound decision.

Developing alternatives is hard in part because the intelligence it requires is different than what is required for addressing frame and information. Framing is all about concentrating our focus until the group can agree on the one problem that's really in front of us. Getting good information requires analytic work comparing different approaches in a way that hopefully limits the field. These kinds of activities are convergent: they work at isolating the one right path from a host of alternatives. But dreaming up creative alternatives requires divergent intelligence, the capacity to entertain opposing ideas, or what strategy consultant and business professor Roger Martin calls "integrative thinking."[3] Divergent intelligence refers to the ability to think expansively. The classic test for divergent intelligence involves a brick: how many ways can you think of to use a brick?

The Scriptures offer a deep way to strengthen our divergent capacities. Here I don't mean examples of people thinking creatively within the Scriptures, although Ezekiel's visions do spring to mind. What I am referring to are classical ways people have approached interpreting the Scriptures. Although today many have the perception that a literal interpretation of the Scriptures is traditional and therefore fundamental to the faith, narrow literalism is actually a very recent phenomenon. While the Reformers such as Calvin certainly placed more value on plain sense literalism than on allegorical readings, none of the Reformers held the naively simplistic literalist hermeneutic expressed in the bumper-sticker mantra "The Bible says it. I believe it. That settles it." Early and medieval traditions were even more open with their fourfold sense of Scripture.

The fourfold sense of Scripture refers to the four layers of meaning words and images possess in the Scriptures. The literal sense refers to the plain sense meaning, which is the most basic and simple of the four meanings, but it is emphatically not more important than the others. The second sense, the allegorical sense, refers to deeper meanings possibly hidden in the Scriptures where some figures stand for or represent others. The tropological or moral sense points to the instructive value the Scriptures can hold for an individual. When a word from Scripture seems to be speaking just to you and offering you a lesson, you are experiencing the tropological sense of the Scriptures. Finally, the anagogical sense refers to the future-oriented sense of how the Scriptures lead us up into contemplating the kingdom in the fullness of time.

The Christian monk and theologian John Cassian first formally proposed this fourfold sense of Scripture. What I think is most intriguing about it is that readers aren't forced into picking just one level of meaning for each word or verse. Words and verses may contain what philosopher Paul Ricoeur calls a "surplus of meaning." Take Jerusalem, for example. Cassian writes that Jerusalem can be understood in a fourfold manner. The literal meaning of Jerusalem refers to the city in Israel. The allegorical meaning for him points to the church. In the tropological sense Jerusalem represents

---

3. Martin, *Opposable Mind*, 6.

the human soul. And in the anagogical sense Jerusalem symbolizes the very kingdom of heaven.[4]

What's significant about this approach isn't simply the complexity and multiplicity of meaning in the Scriptures but the expansive habits of the mind that deep reading of the text can cultivate. This exegetical habit, this deep way of searching for multiple ways of reading one word or verse, is a transferable skill. When we learn how to search for a plurality of meanings in the Scriptures, we can apply this habit of heart and mind to the challenges that face us in the church. Gracious, if the Scriptures can contain at least four meanings, shouldn't we assume God might offer at least that many pathways through the challenges we face in community?

The third part of the decision chain is assessing the value of our information: is our information based on the intuition of the loudest person in the room, or is it rooted in something more solid? Evidence-based management proponent Jeffrey Pfeffer, about whom we'll learn more later, argues that basing decisions on good information is a comparatively recent development in medicine and barely in its infancy in the business world. Rather than basing decisions on good information, most leaders look to previous experience.[5] Regardless of whether the conditions today are similar to the past, most of us believe that if something worked once, it will probably work again. In churches we experience a similar phenomenon: the we've-always-done-it-that-way principle. To me it's heartening to discover that church leaders aren't the only ones who suffer this aversion to facts.

Pfeffer also observes leaders eschew facts in favor of what he calls "casual benchmarking."[6] By this term he means leaders who look to other successful institutions and copy what they are doing whether those contexts have much in common with theirs or not. In the church I might call this the Willowback problem because so many leaders look to large congregations like Willow Creek and Saddleback and think if they just copy their practices, they can reproduce the results. In her sermon "Preaching during a Recession: Rick Warren, Charlamagne, Survivor-Man, and You," Anna Carter Florence notes that Rick Warren, the pastor of Saddleback, even publishes what he describes as "sermons that work," a resource for preachers everywhere—as if preaching could be context-neutral.

Finally, Pfeffer suggests that most leaders make decisions without evidence by simply adhering to untested, anecdotal beliefs.[7] This kind of rea-

4. Cassian, *Conferences of John Cassian*, Kindle location 7279.

5. Pfeffer and Sutton, *Hard Facts*, 5.

6. Ibid., 6.

7. Ibid., 10.

soning pervades congregational decision-making. Most volunteer leaders and even many pastors have limited experience with the vast breadth and depth of congregations in North America, let alone the world. And yet how often have leaders said, "In all my experience I've never heard of a church doing something like this." The reality is the actual breadth of their experience normally boils down to deep, personal experience with only a small number of churches, rarely a representative sample size for drawing much of a conclusion. This discussion is so important I've reserved another chapter for more about evidence-based ministry later in this section.

The fourth link in the chain focuses on core values. Are the proposed solution and creative, doable alternatives to the challenge we face grounded in the core values of the body we serve? The principle of traditioned innovation holds that new ideas must be rooted in who God has always called us to be and not just the latest and greatest trend or desperate Hail Mary pass. When bodies are anxious, it's tempting to embrace new ideas from consultants exuding confidence, but leaders have to ensure the next big idea is consistent with values one would expect from people of God. Former senior strategist for leadership education at Duke Divinity School L. Gregory Jones often says that if an idea is entirely new, then it really isn't Christian. What he means by this claim is that traditioned innovation connects new ideas to forgotten or neglected ideas in our past and repurposes them for a new day.[8]

There are times when leadership bodies make decisions rooted in their core values that won't always make sense to those on the outside. One of my favorite examples of the people of God making a decision rooted in their core values happened when the exiles returned to Palestine from Babylon. In this period known as the Restoration the biblical books of Ezra and Nehemiah follow the story of the exiles returning home. Much like the homecoming of Odysseus, the return of the exiles was far from easy. For one thing, the Babylonians hadn't taken everyone from Israel. A group known as the "people of the land" had remained behind to work the fields. They weren't exactly thrilled when the exiles came back acting as if they owned the place. For another thing, the other nations surrounding Israel wanted the land for themselves and rightly saw those returning as a major threat.

The very first thing an ancient people did when trying to establish a new camp or city was build a wall. Before anything else—before building shelter or establishing water and food supplies—an ancient people erected walls around their location. Walls make perfect practical sense. There's little point in trying to sleep or eat in an undefended location. If a people didn't build walls, they probably wouldn't be there long enough to build much else.

---

8. Jones, "Traditioned Innovation," paras. 7–13.

The normal priority of erecting walls makes the building decisions of the returning exiles all the more stunning. According to Ezra, the very first thing the returning exiles do is make sacrifices on the place the first temple stood and resume regular worship. Worship is the very first thing the people of God do. What's even more remarkable is in the very next chapter the returning exiles decide to start rebuilding the temple, which would take years and massive resources. And all the while the walls of the city lie in ruins. It isn't until we get to Nehemiah, the second book narrating the Restoration, that the Jews turn to the labor of rebuilding the walls.

The books of Ezra and Nehemiah don't make a big deal out of their building priorities, so it's easy to miss, but to most observers Ezra and Nehemiah would have seemed like irrational leaders, indeed. Everyone knew you had to take care of the basics, such as defense, before you attended to "luxuries" such as worship. Except Ezra and Nehemiah knew they had it right. For them and for God's people worship wasn't a secondary luxury, something they did when they had the time to get around to it. Worship was primary, more fundamental even than defense itself. Had Jesus been around at the time he would have approved—and confronted any doubters with the question, "What's the point of gaining the whole world if you lose your soul?" This question is a good one to keep in mind when we're asking whether the decisions we are making are grounded in our core values.

The fifth component of the decision quality chain is sound reasoning. When SDRM refers to sound reasoning, they are asking leaders to apply their knowledge about cognitive heuristics and biases, which we explored in the first section, to the decision at hand. Are we being led astray by loss aversion, confirmation bias, or any of the many ways we think we see clearly when we really don't? There are at least two major camps in decision-making: the rationalist, normative camp emphasizes how people *should* make decisions; the behavioralist, descriptive group lifts up how people *actually* make decisions.[9] Most of the leaders of SDRM hail from the rationalist, normative camp, and it shows in this step. While they acknowledge the importance of understanding bias, they treat bias as relevant to only one link in the chain. Limiting the discussion of bias to the sound-reasoning element gives the impression that bias can be dealt with as a single step in the process rather than as something that pervades every aspect of decision-making. As with evidence-based ministry, the pervasiveness of bias is such an important point that I'm devoting the next chapter to a modified decision chain that pairs each link with a significant bias to underscore how thoroughly cognitive bias influences us.

9. Peterson, *Introduction to Decision Theory*, 3.

Finally, the last element of the decision quality chain is commitment to action. If we make this decision, is there commitment to action? This last question brilliantly pushes leaders to think through all the parties who will ultimately need to embrace the changes ahead. If there isn't commitment to action, even the best decisions will be dead on arrival. Remember the story I told at the beginning of this book? I spent all that time with my leadership body discussing LGBT inclusion and then, without much warning, sprang it on the congregation as if I were giving them this awesome gift. Yeah, I was so focused on leading the people right in front of me through the decision-making process that I forgot there were others who would need as much time, or longer, to embrace the decision. I didn't know about the decision quality chain back then; but if I had, I might have given more thought to all the people it would take to ultimately ensure there was commitment to action.

28

The Modified Behavioral Chain

While deeply grateful for the efforts of SDRM, my work in behavioral theology led me to develop and use a modified decision quality chain. As mentioned in the previous chapter, when it comes to rationality, the leaders of SDRM invest greater confidence in our ability to identify and overcome cognitive heuristics and biases than behavioralists such as Dan Kahneman and Dan Ariely believe is possible.[1] The traditional decision quality chain only includes a single step inviting leaders to consider what biases may be influencing our thinking. This single-step consideration implies that heuristics and biases can be dealt with by simply being aware of them. Yet over and over behavioralists have shown cognitive bias is far more deeply rooted, coloring every perception and thought. To honor the humility of this approach I pair a particular bias with each step of the decision-making process, which reminds leaders that we need to be attentive to bias from start to finish.

I credit Chip and Dan Heath for this idea of pairing a bias with each step in the decision-making process. In their book *Decisive* they develop what they call the WRAP process for decision-making. The acronym WRAP stands for *widen* options, *reality-test* assumptions, *attain* distance before deciding, and *prepare* to be wrong. Each of these steps stems from what they call the four villains of decision-making: narrow framing limits options; confirmation bias compromises analysis; short-term emotion impedes the

---

1. Fox, "Economic Man," subhead Irrationality's Revenge, paras. 1–10.

ability to decide; and optimism bias blinds us from the need to reassess a decision.[2] While I think the approach the Heaths take in pairing biases with steps in decision-making is helpful, my starting point is the SDRM decision chain because I believe their steps are more thorough and actionable.

First, I pair the element of appropriate frame with what Chip and Dan Heath call narrow framing. Narrow framing refers to the temptation to transform complicated decisions with many facets into overly simplistic questions. Rather than assuming they understand the challenge at hand and rush to solution thinking, it's important for leaders to slow groups down to make sure they've considered every angle. When dealing with a challenge, groups I lead follow a process in which they move from restating the challenge to asking questions for clarification, and only after this step do they move on to posing solutions. This delay can be frustrating to the voices who want to go immediately to problem-solving, but short-circuiting this process often leads to good solutions to the wrong problem.

When it comes to creative, doable alternatives, leaders should be mindful of the anchoring heuristic. The anchoring heuristic causes us to get stuck on early ideas, which makes it difficult to think creatively. Firms such as Lexicon Branding don't use brainstorming, the staple of so many church boards, to avoid this impediment to innovation. The anchoring heuristic causes groups who use brainstorming to become overly focused on the first ideas offered. More effective processes include multitrack efforts in which the group splits up to work on multiple ideas at the same time.[3] At the end of the day, if a team has only one or two good options, they should not be satisfied but should search for more possibilities.

Confirmation bias, the tendency for humans to search out information that confirms their existing beliefs, poses the greatest threat to decision-makers getting good information. And gathering accurate information is one of the areas in which the church could improve the most. Even experienced pastors have seen only a small number of congregations. Yet, too often we make decisions informed by what happened at a single congregation in another time and place. Given we are especially prone to remember experiences that corroborate our beliefs, many boards make decisions based on little more than hunches and anecdotal experiences from a tiny set of data.

The affect heuristic, the power of short-term emotions to influence behavior, can lead groups away from the deep values that root them. When we are anxious or tired, common feelings among decision-makers, our physical states impact our perception in powerful ways. To counter the affect

2. Heath and Heath, *Decisive*, Kindle locations 294–98.

3. Ibid., Kindle locations 807–8.

heuristic, leaders should anticipate that anxiety makes us feel situations in extreme ways, and it is helpful for leaders to remember to consciously articulate the group's deepest values to keep on track. Countering the heat of short-term emotions is one area where the church should really shine in comparison with other institutions. Prayer and theological reflection are not only our birthright, but they are the very practices that help us slow down and remember that God is God and our fears are not.

SDRM acknowledges the importance of cognitive bias in the sound reasoning link of their decision quality chain. However, intelligent leaders often face the temptation of thinking that being aware of biases is enough to bypass their effects. One of the most common biases, the optimism bias, leads us to overestimate our abilities. When we consider the impact cognitive bias has on our thinking, we leaders need to keep the optimism bias front and center. Understanding bias doesn't make it go away. Dan Kahneman tells many stories about the ongoing power bias has over his own thinking in everything from grading papers to estimating how long it will take to write a book. Kahneman probably knows more than anyone else in the world about cognitive bias and yet continues to be hindered by it. Leaders should assume we will be, too.

Finally, we come to the last element of my modified decision quality chain: commitment to action. Here leaders must keep in mind the power of loss aversion. Behavioralists have shown that people are twice as unhappy losing an object or practice as they are gaining it. Change, in other words, is painful. Even good change means loss in some way. It's easy for us as leaders to become so focused on our brilliant and exciting solution that we forget that living, breathing human beings uninvolved in the decision-making process must be convinced to change, to possibly lose something important to them. If we solve an important challenge with no thought about how to persuade the rest of the stakeholders, we might have spent a great deal of time with very little to show for it.

The conflict between normative (rationalist) and descriptive (behavioral) decision theorists can become sharp, and it is worth taking a moment to talk about conflict within decision-making more broadly. Few of us wake up in the morning looking for conflict; however, as we saw in the second section on game theory, conflict can foster creativity and productivity. Is there a way to tell the difference between conflict that is likely to be destructive and conflict that leads to life?

According to researchers Pamela Hinds and Diane Bailey, the real concern with conflict is not necessarily how much conflict is present, although that is important, but what kind of conflict we are facing. We have to learn to examine conflict with greater precision and to identify and understand the strengths and weaknesses of three major kinds of conflict as described by Hinds and Bailey: task conflict, process conflict, and affective conflict.[4] Knowing what kind of conflict we are dealing with helps us know whether to encourage or discourage the behavior.

Task conflict boils down to questions such as this: is our institution doing the right things and are the right people doing the right things? In the book of Acts leaders faced a task conflict as the fledging church was growing. Two factions within the church, the Hellenists and the Hebrews, fell into conflict over the care of widows. Leaders were feeling stretched between the tasks of teaching and preaching and caring for human needs. Unfortunately, the Hellenists perceived that when push came to shove, it was their community that was receiving short shrift. The apostles, brilliantly realizing this conflict could easily devolve into chaos, focused not on the division between the Hellenists and Hebrews but on the division of labor. The right people, they concluded, were not doing the right jobs. And so they divided up the work of praying and tending to the word and the work of caring for the physical needs of the vulnerable (Acts 6:1–6).

This kind of task conflict—disagreement over whether our institution is heading in the right direction and whether the right people are perform-ing the right tasks—is often positive. Studies indicate that the presence of moderate task conflict in institutions corresponds with better outcomes, which makes sense given what we've learned. Vigorous discussion can mitigate the dangers of the anchoring heuristic and the confirmation bias, which can lead groups to fixate too narrowly and then discount disconfirm-ing evidence.

If only task conflict were the sole kind of conflict. Process conflict relates to questions regarding whether we're going about our tasks in the right way. Where task conflict focuses on the actions we're taking (the right jobs by the right people), process conflict revolves around how we arrive at these decisions and how we carry them out. Unlike task conflict, Karen Jehn asserts, process conflict tends to be more destructive.[5]

One of the ways religious institutions experience process conflict re-gards performance reviews and pay. Because religious institutions gather people from a variety of backgrounds, leaders bring assumptions from these differing work positions with them when it comes to thinking about perfor-mance reviews and pay. In the field of education, for instance, teachers tend to be highly suspicious and negative regarding attempts to tie performance to pay. Tenure plays a far greater role for them: the longer someone has been

---

4. Hinds and Bailey, "Out of Sight," 615–32.

5. Jehn, "Workplace Conflict," 24.

at an institution the more they should be paid. Tenure is definitely not the assumption many businesspeople bring when it comes to assessing performance and pay. Many businesspeople, on the contrary, come from forced ranking systems and rigorous, 360-degree reviews, and they are far more comfortable with linking pay to performance. When people from these different backgrounds collide in the church, negative conflict can and does arise. Unfortunately, when this conflict is not managed well, the substance of the review—how they feel about the performance of the staff and what people can do to improve—falls to the wayside. Less productive conversations regarding review philosophy take center stage. To mitigate process conflict, leaders need to have meetings about process before they attempt to have a meeting on content.

The third kind of conflict, affective or relational conflict, is almost universally destructive, researchers agree. It's what most of us think of when we think of conflict. With affective conflict people raise their voices, blood pressure soars, nasty looks dart across meeting tables, and church members not only disagree with but also actively dislike one another. At such fraught moments, nonviolent communication practices like those explored by Deborah Hunsinger and Theresa Latini in their fantastic book *Transforming Church Conflict* can really help.

My sense is the conflict between normative decision theorists such as Ron Howard and descriptive behavioralists such as Dan Ariely is largely a productive task conflict. While the behavioralist perspective speaks more naturally to me, there is an unhelpful tendency in the behavioral camp to point out the problems with our perceptions without offering a helpful way forward, which can leave people feeling paralyzed. The normative perspective of Ron Howard, with tools such as the decision quality chain and the decision complexity grid (which we'll see in the next chapter), pays more limited attention to biases but does provide in-depth guidance for better decision-making. The task conflict here is knowing when to listen to which side. We need to hear Dan's voice in our head when we're evaluating our perceptions, and we need Ron's impetus to action when the time to make a decision is upon us.

29

Making Decisions about Decisions

I noted in the chapter on the modified decision quality chain that one of the most challenging concerns about decision-making is knowing how much process to use. We can miss by applying too much or too little process. At times we breeze through a momentous decision only to regret this casual attitude later. At other times we ruin a meeting by going over insignificant, common-sense decisions in excruciating, pointless detail. I reiterate: judgment regarding how much process to use in the first place ranks right up there on the importance scale.

The leaders at SDRM utilize a simple but powerful chart to help leaders discern the appropriate amount of process. Imagine one axis that graphs the impact of a decision on the organization—the level of organizational complexity. How long might this decision impact the organization? How devastating might the consequences be if a mistake is made? Groups should treat low-impact decisions very differently than high-impact decisions. On another axis, picture a line that charts how complicated the decision is—the level of analytical complexity. How many people does the decision involve? Is the decision one that occurs often, or is it new in some way? How certain is the information we have? Just as we would give more thought to a decision with a high level of impact on the organization, we want to handle a complicated decision with greater care.

Decision-Making Complexity Grid

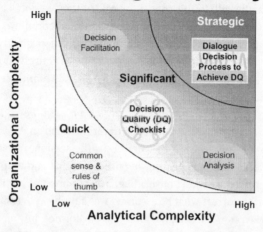

Decisions that are low in impact and complexity, what SDRM labels quick decisions, simply require common sense. Decision-makers should not spend too much time making these calls; they simply need to identify and make this type of decision. In some cases, these decisions need to become so routine they don't even feel like decisions any longer—leaders just react appropriately. What about more significant decisions with greater impact and complexity? Decisions with moderate amounts of complexity and impact can be thought of as medium-term decisions. These kinds of decisions can be made well in a few hours or days. They are complicated enough that decision-makers should use the decision quality chain to sort out decision quality from decision outcome, but they can probably make these decisions without implementing a full decision dialogue process (explained below). In contrast, decisions that are high in complexity and impact are known as strategic decisions. Organizations should treat these decisions with the utmost of care. These decisions not only require more time but demand a version of what SDRM refers to as a decision dialogue process.

In a decision dialogue process a decision leader heads a decision staff. The decision staff and the decision-making board, guided by the decision leader, work together through this multistep process. The decision leader facilitates a discussion during which the board agrees on the frame. With the frame in place the decision leader works with the decision staff, rather than a traditional committee, to develop creative, doable possibilities. Then, the decision leader presents these alternatives to the board for their consideration. With both the larger board and the decision staff in alignment on alternatives, the decision leader works with the decision staff to evaluate these various alternatives. The decision leader then goes back to the board with solid analysis for all alternatives and repeats the process until the board is ready to make the call. In this model the role of the decision leader is not to advocate for any particular position as a traditional committee does but to help the decision-makers achieve the highest decision quality possible given the time frame. The decision board participates actively in the whole process, rather than just being pitched one idea after a committee has done all the preliminary work.

The congregation I currently serve started in 1983. For reasons that are not entirely clear to me, the sanctuary never included an American flag. As far as I can tell the decision-making body, the session, never voted to exclude a flag. The issue was just never raised. It didn't come up until one new member noticed we didn't have a flag, became upset about it, and met with the session to correct what he assumed was simply an oversight on our part. Trying to sweeten the deal, he offered to pay for not only an American flag but a Christian flag as well. I have to admit that at that point in my life I didn't even know there was such a thing as a Christian flag. It turns out the absence of the flag wasn't an oversight. As soon as the issue came up, I could feel a pall of tension fall over the room.

Some in the session hoped I would just make the decision for them. Isn't that what pastors do? I won't say I wasn't tempted, but we agreed on another plan. Because this was a decision that would impact the entire congregation, we decided to make the decision after a series of meetings. I adopted the role of decision leader rather than decision-maker. I assigned various elders the tasks of researching the Scriptures, our *Book of Order*, and our *Book of Confessions* to see what wisdom they might offer. The Scriptures don't speak to the issue of an American flag per se, but they certainly do speak to issues of church and state.

We agreed to meet several times. As people got started on their research, we met a second time to generate ideas regarding alternatives. Were we really stuck with either accepting the flags or rejecting them? No, we decided there were several possibilities. Perhaps instead of just one flag we could purchase flags from many countries, showing God is the God of all nations and not simply our own. Or perhaps we could stick with the American flag but post it in our narthex, the gathering room right outside the sanctuary. Or maybe we could go to some effort and purchase a flagpole so that we could fly the flag outside. And, of course, we still had the option of just saying yes or no to the idea as presented. In the end we wound up with many options that could meet the desire for a small number of people to see a flag.

At the next meeting we listened to different elders report on what they learned from consulting the various sources of wisdom in our tradition. A review of the Scriptures revealed no clear answers, but it was helpful to our session to discover how rich the discussion is in the Scriptures and how few easy answers there are.

What ultimately carried the day was the insight of one of our most conservative elders, who spent time with our *Book of Confessions*. This elder, a man whose voice held a great deal of power in the group, had already shared he hadn't realized we didn't have a flag in the sanctuary and tended to agree with the suggestion to remedy the situation. I sent him home with the *Book of Confessions*, thinking he would probably find something to support his stated position, which would leave me stuck with a decision I didn't like. I couldn't have been more wrong. Not only did this leader read and absorb the Barmen Confession, written in Germany in 1934, declaring Christ to be the head of the church rather than any ruler or state; he also immersed himself in the Confession of 1967, which unequivocally states, "Although nations may serve God's purposes in history, the church which identifies the sovereignty of any one nation or any one way of life with the cause of God denies the Lordship of Christ and betrays its calling."[1] This elder read that statement to the group and then looked around the table. He said he had been sure he was going to be voting for a flag in the sanctuary, but reading the *Book of Confessions* changed his mind. Of all the options on the table, he now favored maybe posting the flag outside on a pole or perhaps in the narthex. I maintained my cool, but inwardly I was ecstatic—not so much celebrating his new position as thinking, "Seriously? You were converted by the *Book of Confessions*?"

The person who made the suggestion regarding the flags was less enthusiastic about all our creative, doable alternatives. When he realized we would welcome the flag pretty much anywhere but the sanctuary, he decided to rescind his offer. I wound up receiving an angry letter several weeks later complaining that all the churches he ever attended had flags and venting frustration about how people bring coffee mugs into the sanctuary. I was still so excited that anyone could be converted by a theological document that this cranky letter didn't even bother me. I wrote a pastoral response and moved on to other concerns.

Now, let's go back to the three different levels of decision-making: quick, significant, and strategic. The Scriptures brim with examples of all three decision types, but we'll just pull out three. When Jesus was sitting opposite the treasury in the temple (Luke 21:1–4; Mark 12:41–44), he

---

1. "Confession of 1967," 9.45.

observed people giving their offerings. The wealthy threw in large amounts, but what excited Jesus was the poor widow. She threw in only a few coins, but Jesus commended her for giving more than the rest since she gave out of her poverty while they gave from their abundance. There is no indication in the text that the widow hesitated or struggled in her decision to give. She simply walked forward and did what she had done a thousand times before. And therein lies the secret to decisions that shouldn't require much process: practice. Part of the power behind spiritual practices such as worship and prayer is that we do them so often and so regularly they form us into the people God made us to be. It is also what Paul is talking about when he uses the analogy of the games to describe spiritual practice: like athletes, people of faith must practice. Just thinking the faith isn't enough when it comes to routine decisions; they require practice.

Not all decisions are as simple as whether to be financially generous or not. Though the act of giving may seem difficult, even painful, generosity itself is not a complicated question. Some decisions are more complicated, though, and require additional thought. In Acts and Galatians we hear about a breakup between the Paul and Barnabas team. In Acts, it sounds as if the dispute is more about Barnabas wanting to take along John Mark, whom Paul perceived as a quitter. In Galatians, Paul hints that Barnabas might not have shared his Gentile inclusion views as zealously as Paul would have liked. Either way, Paul and Barnabas have to make a decision about whether to keep partnering or go their separate ways. Now, I'm not saying Paul and Barnabas whipped out their decision quality chain and worked through their options before settling on their decision to part company. What I am saying is that this decision was neither simple nor without consequence; but because it only involved a few people and could be changed in the future, it was a decision of moderate impact and complexity. Whether to partner or part ways is the type of decision that church leaders today often face. And much of the time such a decision calls for a moderate amount of discernment.

The decision that led up to the Paul and Barnabas split—the decision whether to enfold Gentiles into what had been a Jewish movement—was another story. Now *that* decision was as impactful and complex as it gets. The division between Jew and Gentile was as sharp as they come. As Amy-Jill Levine so eloquently reminds us, Jesus dressed like a Jew, ate like a Jew, argued like a Jew, and so on. The early movement was exclusively Jewish; but with Saul's conversion to Paul and Peter's vision of the sheet full of unclean animals, the movement experienced pressure to become more open and inclusive. Talk about high impact. No doubt the full inclusion of Gentiles would cause some within the movement to leave and others outside the movement to view it with suspicion. And once you open that door, there is no going back. And complicated? It involved the entire fledgling church, comprised of communities dotting the Mediterranean, each with its own unique culture. This kind of decision fell far beyond the scope of common sense or even just thinking through the decision quality chain. A council had to be formed to work out the details of this momentous issue; it was a decision that required a great deal of prayer, discussion, and time. And I can only guess that the actual decision was in reality vastly messier than the story Luke recounts in Acts.

Of course, as with most things in life, these clear distinctions between quick, significant, and strategic decisions are artificial. Every real decision falls somewhere in between. Some decisions even contain facets of all three. In the second section on game theory I shared the well-thought-out strategic decision our congregation made to retire its debt and how I made the less well-thought-out decision to light a symbolic mortgage on fire. My wife, Melissa, told me after the fact that she was going to ask me whether I had a plan but decided not to as she thought I would be testy about it. (I plead the fifth on that one.)

The entire decision to burn this mortgage could have benefited from just thinking it through. Did I know what I was doing? Had I thought about alternatives? Was I thinking as clearly as I could? Even a cursory run-through of the decision quality chain would have been helpful. But then, when the paper was burning in my hands, and I realized I needed to act quickly—then the moment took on the character of an immediate decision. Those kinds of decisions where you have to act quickly require training. And I had none. So, I panicked and held on to the paper as long as I could until it started burning my hands, then dropped it to the floor, where it left a mark on the carpet that remains to this day. I continue to be grateful to serve in a place where we laugh often and forgive generously.

30

When a Tornado Can Help

We now have two important tools in our decision-making toolbox: the decision quality chain and the decision complexity guide. In this chapter we'll look at another tool, one that is particularly helpful in setting financial priorities.

After a successful career in business my father-in-law became the business director of a fifteen-hundred-member congregation just outside of Portland, Oregon. Mark is a man of great wisdom and many quotes. One of his favorites is from Stephen Covey: "The main thing is to keep the main thing the main thing." When I first heard him say that years ago, I thought it sounded so obvious as to be pointless. Keep the main thing the main thing? Duh! Later, after pastoring a new church development and a vibrant, mid-sized congregation and chairing a presbytery committee, I learned why this quote was so meaningful to him. Staying focused on the main thing can be all but impossible to do.

Let's say your leadership body holds a successful vision retreat. Everyone leaves with a clear sense of where the Holy Spirit is taking them. But then, a month later a crucial staff member announces their surprise decision to retire. A month after that a significant (not to mention expensive) problem with the building surfaces. Then, on top of it all, one of your kids starts having trouble in school after years of good performance. And just that quickly all that focus you and your leadership team had on the main thing becomes little more than a faded memory. When these challenges pile up in my own ministry, I remember being told that leading a congregation is like trying to change a tire on an eighteen-wheeler while it barrels down the highway at full speed. Things go awry, but in a dynamic environment it's not as if you can call a time-out so you can concentrate on the problem at hand.

I suspect this distraction level is why the Scriptures so often emphasize the importance of focus. The prophet Habakkuk cries out to lift the vision up in such a way a runner at a distance can read it: make the vision plain and obvious, in other words. And how often did Jesus retreat to a deserted place, the first-century version of leadership author Ron Heifetz's advice to "get on the balcony" to gain a little perspective?[1] Once in motion it's incredibly difficult for us to keep the main thing the main thing. Good leaders try to find ways to keep their eyes on the prize.

But what if we don't even know what the most important things in our organization are in the first place? Theologically, the main thing is always following after the way of Jesus Christ. But in a concrete way, when it comes to taking care of his body, the church, it can be maddeningly difficult to discern how to prioritize the challenges in front of us and bring that theological truth to fruition.

As we've seen, a variety of cognitive heuristics and biases impede us from identifying the main things. The availability heuristic causes us to place too much importance on risks that alarm us viscerally. Sometimes negative trends are so gradual we fail to see their significance until it's very late in the game. Or sometimes loss aversion makes it hard to focus our attention. We're afraid of losing people, try to please everyone, listen to too many voices, and at times we just move from problem to problem with little overall forward motion. Finally, especially when it comes to financial decision-making, the bodies we lead are prone to what I might call understanding bias. They become overly focused on issues that are easy to see and understand regardless of how much the issues actually impact the overall mission.

To help with this understanding bias, leaders use what is known as deterministic sensitivity analysis. One tool they employ when conducting this kind of analysis is the tornado diagram, so-called because its descending horizontal bars—wider at the top and narrower at the bottom—look like a tornado. A tornado diagram is a simple but incredibly powerful tool for understanding how financially significant various aspects of an institution are to its overall operation. I should emphasize here that this analytical tool is primarily helpful for understanding financial impact. Because religious institutions are complicated organizations driven by multiple values, it's

---

1. See Heifetz and Linsky, *Leadership on the Line*, ch. 3.

absolutely the case that what has the greatest financial impact may not necessarily be what drives a decision in the end. But it's important for church
leaders to understand the financial realities in front of them so that should
they choose to make a sacrificial decision based on core values, they understand the material risk.

To understand how a tornado diagram works, it's helpful to think of
managing an apartment complex. Church leaders can gain insight from this
example because even though a congregation's buildings and grounds are
not exactly the same as those of an apartment complex, they are similar
enough to draw some meaningful parallels. Plus, it can be beneficial to understand a model using a neutral example before applying it to the church.

The power of a tornado diagram lies in its visual ranking of various operational cost factors according to their ability to impact the financial health
of the whole institution. In a tornado diagram for an apartment complex the
top horizontal bar, the most financially significant, represents the financial
impact of apartment vacancy: low vacancy rates, falling to the left side of the
bar, and high vacancy rates, rising to the right. The high vacancy end of the
bar shows the loss to the complex when the occupancy rates are extremely
low; the low vacancy end shows the profit as the complex moves toward full
occupancy. The significance here is that if vacancy is high, the apartment
complex will suffer a massive loss. If the vacancy rates are low, the revenue
will soar. Thus, apartment vacancy represents an incredibly important variable if you are responsible for making an apartment complex a sustainable
venture.

The impact of other variables, such as the rental rate, the cost of
maintenance, and the administrative expenses for managing the property,
fall below vacancy in terms of their impact, each bar smaller than the one
above. Tornado diagrams offer a powerful tool that allows a manager to see
at a glance the areas that have the biggest impact on financial success. So,
if an apartment manager tries to cut administrative costs for managing the
property, which lie on the bottom bar of the diagram, it won't matter much
whether the effort is perfect or a total failure. Even though these cuts might
be concrete and easy to do, changing anything on the lowest bar just won't
have much impact on the overall success of the operation. However, occupancy resides on the top bar, which means this variable has an enormously
powerful ability to impact the financial health of the whole complex.

Tornado diagrams sound great: just focus on the bars at the top and
ignore the bars at the bottom, and the institution will be OK. If only it were
that easy. Again, to lift up what I'm calling understanding bias, there is a
huge temptation for most of us to focus on concrete, achievable tasks such
as reducing waste. We can understand turning off lights and using less water.

We can directly control these things. And there is no argument that they are good practices. Who is going to argue against keeping costs low? On the flip side, things such as occupancy—or in the pastor's case, membership—are far more complicated and difficult to understand. No pastor can directly control membership, nor can anyone make more people magically show up to church or rent an apartment. So, even when the tornado diagram tells the savvy apartment complex manager that occupancy should be the area commanding most of the attention, it is easier said than done.

My guess is if we did this analysis for a church, attendance and membership are vastly more significant to the financial well-being of the body than controlling copying costs. But when it's the middle of a slow afternoon and a pastor isn't sure what to do next and notices a light left on that shouldn't be, it's easy to become distracted and start to work on a time-consuming plan to save energy. Again, hear me well. Energy conservation may be the right decision to make, especially if the concern of the pastor is creation care. This deep value may be worth pursuing even if it won't make a huge financial difference. Leaders do need to be aware of the choices they are making.

Here is a concrete example from the church I currently serve. In our denomination, the Presbyterian Church (U.S.A.), the district governing bodies ask individual congregations to pay a per capita gift on every member. This gift goes directly to help pay for staffing in the presbytery office as well as for higher governing bodies. Churches tend to pay this up front and then may collect it from individual congregants as a kind of tax. In 2015 the amount of per capita was $27.96. In a congregation of 250 with an annual budget of around $300,000, the total per capita amount would be just under $7,000, which represents right around 2 percent of the total budget. In the congregation I serve, leaders have spent hours debating per capita. Hours. Per capita tends to be poorly understood by the congregation. Some people pay more than they should, while others don't pay it all, which is frustrating to leaders. And I would be shocked if anyone at the church, leaders included, could articulate what per capita supports.

But let's say a member makes an annual pledge of $2,500 or even just $500. Do we really want to spend precious time and energy going after them over a mere thirty bucks? A simple tornado diagram shows that we would be vastly better off spending our time encouraging pledgers to pay their full pledge than going after per capita laggards. A tornado diagram shows that even if we had zero giving in per capita or perfect giving, it wouldn't impact our bottom line in any measurable way. And yet, per capita is something easy for leaders to lock on to. Every member is supposed to pay it, and leaders can see from month to month that we're behind. For some it's an emotional issue. It feels as if people aren't paying their fair share. And I will absolutely admit that when we remind the congregation, more per capita payments come in. However, even if every member paid their per capita, it wouldn't really make that much of a difference.

Worse, we have to remember what behavioralists call the pain of paying related to loss aversion. People will only write so many checks. One day a couple, two of our most generous contributors, entered our office. What were they there to do? Pay their per capita. How much did they owe us, they wanted to know. When told, they cut us a check for about sixty dollars. Sixty dollars. Every leader knows you can only ask people for money so many times. Rather than asking this family to make a gift that could tremendously impact a vital mission of the church, that day we settled for a check worth sixty dollars.

I'm pleased to say we've changed how we account for per capita now. Instead of devoting an entire line in the budget for it, we simply treat it as a cost of doing ministry and report it under another line item. It's still there, but it's less visible, which is as it should be. Also, we've stopped adding a line for it on our pledge card as we used to do. In comparison with the past, we don't spend nearly as much time talking about per capita. Now, I wonder what else we're spending our time on that could be directed in better ways. It makes me wonder whether we're keeping the main thing the main thing. And isn't that a question far more worth asking?

31

Choice Architecture

When We Choose Not to Choose

So far in this section we have focused on decisions in which leaders and the members of their institutions are consciously involved. When a decision-making board utilizes a decision chain, they become aware of their thoughts and feelings in a profound way. When a decision leader designs a decision dialogue process that enables a decision-making board to consider multiple alternatives with the goal of making the best possible call, the participants become more than usually aware of the issues before them. But leaders and institutions can't, and shouldn't, engage these in-depth decision-making tools all the time. Not only is it unrealistic to devote such attention given the limited time and energy real human beings have, but for many decisions it is overkill.

So, what about the many decisions people make all the time that shouldn't receive so much of our precious focus and attention? Cass Sunstein argues we should think about when it is wise to choose not to choose: "Sometimes the best choice is not to choose. Personalized default rules promise to make our lives not only simpler, healthier, and longer but also more free."[1]

In the first section we looked at how status quo bias makes default settings so powerful. Especially when people are tired, inexperienced, and

---

1. Sunstein, *Choosing Not to Choose*, 208.

pressed for time, they tend to choose according to the defaults given to them by leaders acting as choice architects. As a choice architect, a leader is not the one who makes the primary decision among various alternatives but the one who establishes the set of choices from which others will be selecting. How leaders structure these default choices can have enormous implications.

Remember the strange differences between organ donation rates in Europe? Those differences weren't due to varying religious, cultural, or philosophical differences among nations. The differing rates corresponded with whether the DMV in each country required drivers to opt in or out of organ donation. Countries that required drivers to take the extra step of opting in experienced terribly low participation rates, whereas countries that set their defaults to opt in enjoyed soaring levels.

Defaults like these can have massive economic consequences. I once lived in the Garden State of New Jersey, and my family hails from Pennsylvania. Although there is no love lost between fans of the Eagles and fans of the Giants, the truth is that there's no reason to believe the preferences of people living in each state differ dramatically when it comes to something like car insurance. However, Pennsylvania and New Jersey present different defaults. New Jersey offers drivers the default of a less expensive insurance plan but without the right to sue. Pennsylvania offers a more expensive default that comes with the right to sue. All drivers can opt out of the default plans and choose other options, but few do. The result is that drivers in Pennsylvania spend $140 million more dollars per year for car insurance than drivers in New Jersey.[2]

Pastors and other church leaders need to consider seriously their roles as choice architects. Not only can poor defaults have deleterious, unintended consequences, but there is every reason to believe that people are particularly prone to defaults in church and religious environments. We are prone to defaults when facing situations that are complicated and with which we have had little or no experience. Few people new to a congregation have any knowledge of the denominational polity behind practices such as membership. And when people experience the death of a life partner, it is often their first encounter with funeral arrangements. The stunning amount of paperwork and expensive funeral home options would be hard enough for someone who has experience and is not grieving. They are incredibly difficult situations for someone new to morticians and emotionally vulnerable.

Further, we are more prone to follow defaults without reflection when we are busy and our cognitive load is already great. Sunstein points out that

2. Ibid., 29.

the combination of time constraints and cognitive overload is one of the reasons the working poor are particularly vulnerable to bad defaults; thus, he suggests that choice architecture represents a justice issue. As a pastor, I can affirm that working families and active retirees in the congregation I serve lead incredibly busy lives that leave little room for poring over every decision.

Good leaders do the best they can within the constraints they are given; great leaders both question and change the defaults when they can. There's a great scene in *Men in Black* in which Will Smith's character is undergoing tests with a crew of other possible recruits to find "the best of the best of the best." Smith alone asks what will happen to them if they are selected. And then, when the group struggles to fill out the test in uncomfortable chairs, only Will gets up and moves this embarrassingly loud table over to his chair so that he can complete the test more comfortably. Smith didn't accept the defaults given to him. He questioned them and found a better way. Here I'd like to explore some of the defaults church leaders face and some ways we might faithfully navigate them.

In the Reformed tradition we observe sacramental defaults; we observe two sacraments, the Lord's Supper and Baptism, versus seven in Roman Catholic and Orthodox traditions. The Presbyterian Directory for Worship directs leaders to encourage parents to baptize children "without undue haste, but without undue delay."[3] This statement presents a clear default in favor of baptizing children. Personally, the practice of infant baptism is extremely important to me. One of our confessions, the Second Helvetic Confession, refers to baptism as "a perpetual sealing of our adoption."[4] While some traditions emphasize our choice for Christ, the Reformed tradition inverts this order by lifting up the importance of Christ choosing us. Our response to God's grace is important, but it is secondary. Our response is an act of gratitude. Infant baptism underscores this inverted order. Before a little one can think or respond in faith, in infant baptism we declare God has already named and claimed this person forever without reservation. I was baptized as an infant, my three children were baptized as infants, and my heart sings every time the congregation I serve surrounds a young family at our font as I present another member of the household of God.

But I remember the first time I encountered someone arguing strongly against infant baptism. I was in a seminary discussion session, known as a precept, when one of my friends—a friend I thought agreed with me most of the time—shocked me by leveling a feminist critique against infant baptism,

3. "Directory for Worship," W-2.3012(a).
4. "Second Helvetic Confession," 5.186.

likening it to a kind of rape. I couldn't believe my ears. What? Then, she thoughtfully explained that this action, while lovingly intended, manifested an act of will upon one who had no ability to voice a possible objection. Were this act a sexual one between two adults, she argued, this deed would be the very definition of assault. And, she wanted to know, wasn't a spiritual act every bit as important? I honestly had never thought about infant baptism that way before and was put off by the shocking nature of her comparison, but after sitting with this a moment I saw her point. The default of infant baptism with which I grew up was so natural for me as to become practically the only option, rather than one among many, and a potentially problematic choice for some.

I would learn my friend wasn't alone in her concern. No less than Karl Barth rejected the practice of infant baptism; he referred to it as a "wound in the body of the Church." Barth was less concerned with possible violence being enacted on a little one's soul than with the violence the baptized were committing in Nazi Germany. Barth rightly wondered how otherwise good and faithful Christians not only failed to resist the Nazi takeover of Germany but also participated in the extermination of six million Jews. For Barth, the default of infant baptism created incomplete Christians—men and women who identified as Christian but failed to internalize what it meant sufficiently to follow after the way of Christ in a time of great trial.

While I still practice infant baptism, I do so now with an awareness that it is a default option rather than a foundational reality. This awareness helps me to be a better pastor. One of the ways I experience the breakdown of Christendom in the extremely post-Christian landscape of the Pacific Northwest is by encountering families with either zero church background or a very limited one. Families come to me now not shaped as I was with the obvious default of infant baptism. These families ask really good questions. Should they baptize their infant? Why? What if the child wants to make a different choice later? Can we dedicate the baby instead of baptizing them? While I love serving parents who are traditioned and plan to baptize their infants without a great deal of reflection, it's incredibly exciting to be a pastor at a time when people are really giving their beliefs and actions more active thought.

Another default church leaders encounter on a regular basis is church membership. As Christendom continues to unravel, the decision whether to join a congregation becomes increasingly complex. What does it mean to be a member? Is it similar to being a member at Costco or Sam's Club? What does it mean to be a member of this particular congregation? If my family grew up Roman Catholic, is that pretty much just the same as being Southern Baptist or Methodist? And back to the baptism question: if I was baptized as a child, do I have to be baptized again? Or if I was baptized as a child but am not really sure what I believe about Jesus now, can I be a member or should I just attend and participate?

My sense is that the choices my tradition offers regarding membership continue to reflect Christendom more than the world in which we're living today. We have traditionally offered four categories: baptized members, active members, affiliate members, and . . . everyone else. Yet, the reality is that my congregants fall into a wider spectrum. I have members who show up once or twice a year, and I have folks who regularly attend and participate yet aren't interested in membership. The defaults in my situation are unhelpful. You're either a member or you are lumped into a category that includes people who show up every Sunday plus everyone else on the planet.

The absurdity of this situation became clear to me when a new couple (I'll call them Alice and Bill) began attending our congregation several years ago. Alice was able to affirm Jesus Christ as her Lord and Savior and answer all the other questions for membership, and she was interested in joining. Bill, on the other hand, wasn't quite sure he could honestly answer all of my questions to meet membership requirements, but he wished to join, too. The expression on my face indicated that that might be a problem. He quickly explained that his previous pastor told him the questions were a kind of formality and he could just say "yes" whether he really believed his answers. Horrified, I told him that our tradition and his beliefs deserved better.

I began to meet with Bill over coffee to talk about our faith and see whether he might be able to honestly affirm Jesus as his Lord and Savior. When it became clear that his affirmation wasn't going to happen anytime soon, I felt backed into a corner. I wanted to bless this man who faithfully attended our congregation and supported us with his time and treasure, but at the same time I wanted to honor the integrity of our polity as well as the meaningful struggle of his doubt. What to do?

At some point, I realized that our default choices were inadequate. The world I serve just does not break down neatly into Christian members who show up all the time and can affirm their faith in Jesus and . . . everyone else. I have members I hardly see. I have faithful people who come all the time, who love our mission and support it but still aren't entirely sure how they feel about our questions for membership. And I see people who can affirm the questions for membership but simply don't feel comfortable being members of any institution.

As one of my congregation's choice architects, I decided we needed more options. Having taken an oath to follow my denomination's polity, I knew we couldn't amend the categories of membership in our *Book of*

Order. However, I realized that our *Book of Order* didn't preclude us from adding a category.

We noted the practice of the first-century synagogues that affirmed Gentiles who participated in worship but did not become circumcised and full members of the community. The synagogue called these people "God-fearers." Deciding this term might be a bit much in our Pacific Northwest context, our session landed on the more neutral term "adherent" and began to welcome folks blessed as adherents into the life of our congregation. Per our *Book of Order*, our adherents can't vote in meetings, serve as officers, or be counted as members. But we do bless them. We do name them. And we do count them in the records we keep when we number our own.

When I meet with people who are interested in joining our congregation, I now have an extremely helpful choice to offer. In addition to Bill, we've blessed several others. Each time we bless new adherents, I give thanks that I have been called to serve a creative congregation that respects our polity but at the same time feels free to question the defaults we've been given. We are creating a choice architecture more in keeping with the beloved community.

Finally, let's examine defaults surrounding financial giving in the church. We live at a time when technology has greatly increased the number of ways people can financially give to religious institutions. Religious institutions everywhere are having really good conversations about financial choice architecture. Most Christian congregations continue to include an offering or collection on Sunday morning, but passing the plate is considered unacceptable in other institutions. Many synagogues follow a dues structure, although some innovative ones have begun experimenting with new models.[5] Most Christian institutions ask for an annual pledge as well as special pledges for things such as capital projects. But should institutions ask for money online? Should they encourage members and friends to give through direct deposit? Should they allow people to use their rewards credit cards for contributions, thereby getting something in return for giving? There are so many interesting issues to raise here, but I will confine myself to two: the defaults of pledging and the related issue of giving as an active choice versus giving automatically.

We looked at the Sunstein and Thaler retirement plan defaults example in the first section when we learned about the status quo bias; it is worth reviewing it again here. When Cass Sunstein and Richard Thaler were teaching at the University of Chicago, they saw a problem with the retirement plan. It wasn't the plan itself—the plan was great. The problem was with the plan defaults. Every year the enrollment period for the plans occurred during one of the busiest times for most faculty members. The default was set

5. Paulson, "Pay What You Want," paras. 1–35.

to no participation, even if you had been participating in the plan for years. If you missed filling out and turning in the complicated paperwork, you would miss contributing to your retirement plan for an entire year. Knowing what you know about defaults, what do you guess happened? Exactly. A ton of otherwise brilliant but busy professors weren't saving anything for retirement because of an opt-out default. Sunstein and Thaler simply proposed switching the default to opt-in so that if a faculty member failed to make an active choice, they would simply continue to contribute at their past level. Everyone was free to switch and contribute more or less. But if a faculty member did nothing, they would not be reset to zero. Unsurprisingly, retirement contributions dramatically increased, which was something everyone wanted.

Most religious institutions rely on an opt-out default when it comes to annual pledging. Every year scads of congregations endure the annual stewardship campaign in which a church leader lifts up various inspiring ministries, or some (hopefully entertaining) members speak about why they contribute. Then leaders distribute pledge cards, and people either fill them out or don't. And every year congregations struggle to find leaders willing to play the heavy who will follow up and telephone the laggards. In philanthropic circles religious institutions enjoy an enviable reputation, but is this opt-out model the best way for busy, generous people to give?

Sunstein advocates for what he calls a simplified active choice model; this model preserves the greatest amount of individual freedom and also allows people who don't want to squander their precious cognitive resources on certain decisions to choose not to choose. As an example, a religious institution might give people a one-time option to enroll in an automatic giving default: some might opt in to continue their existing pledge automatically each year, either at their present rate or at a slightly increasing rate over time; others might decline to participate in the automatic program and choose to fill out an annual pledge card or not. In this scenario people who know they want to keep financially supporting an institution can automatically enroll, taking this decision off their plate for years to come. Contributors who are uncomfortable with this automatic enrollment can continue to fill out an annual pledge card. Even if only a fraction of the congregation chooses the automatic default, I suspect it would simplify their giving as well as ease work for congregational volunteers.

We touched on Jeffrey Pfeffer's concept of evidence-based information when we learned about link three of the decision quality chain: meaningful, reliable information. In the next chapter we will expand that discussion and then finish out the section with a chance for you to apply your newly gained decision skills to a uniquely personal case study.

32

Evidence-Based Ministry

Testing God is normally a bad idea in the Scriptures. Except when it isn't. There is a fascinating story in the sixth chapter of Judges that Dan Ariely lifts up to demonstrate the biblical roots of an experimental way of thinking. Israel's enemies, the Midianites, Amalekites, and their friends, are threatening attack when the Spirit of the Lord falls upon Gideon. Rather than just rush into things, however, Gideon does something absolutely surprising. Gideon tests God, and God, oddly enough, appears to be OK with it.

First, Gideon tells God that he is going to put a wool fleece on the threshing floor; and if God is planning on supporting Gideon's efforts to defend the people, he would like this wool covered in dew while the floor around it remains dry. It's cheeky; but if he can put Bibles in every hotel room, maybe he knows what he's doing. Gideon sets the fleece on the floor, retires for the night, and then wakes the next day to find the fleece soaked but the floor around it dry. Awesome. Most leaders would be content with this single trial. But not Gideon. Realizing this first test could be a coincidence, Gideon devises a second one.

In the second trial Gideon tells God he would like to see the opposite condition. This time he wants to set the fleece out on the ground again and in the morning if the fleece is dry and the floor around it soaked with dew, it will be a sign of God's favor. God is obliging enough to meet this condition, and the next morning Gideon awakes to find the wool dry and the floor wet. With clear and indisputable evidence of God's favor, Gideon goes up against a seemingly overwhelming enemy force and wins. As Ariely puts it, "Gideon has all the proof he needs, and he has learned a very important research skill."[1] If only church leaders cared half as much as Gideon did for evidence-based decision-making.

Evidence-based decision-making—allowing the facts to drive our thinking—took an arduously long time to take hold in the medical world. George Washington died because he developed a sore throat and went to his doctor. Both doctor and patient were on board with the then commonplace practice of bloodletting, so they agreed to drain an enormous amount of blood from Washington to cure his infection. He died five days later. Unfortunately for Washington, just a few years later Pierre Charles Alexandre Louis conducted one of the very first evidence-based trials on pneumonia patients. Half of them endured the standard practice of bloodletting while half of them weren't treated at all. As you might imagine, the people who didn't lose enormous amounts of blood fared far better.[2]

Evidence-based management is in its infancy in the business world, but the conversation hasn't even been born in the church world. Yet when church leaders make decisions without facing facts, we run the risk of the ecclesial equivalent of bleeding people with leeches, a practice every doctor in George Washington's time believed was helpful even though the opposite was in fact the case.

Stanford professor Jeffrey Pfeffer, a leading proponent of evidence-based management, argues that when we don't rely on facts, we err in three main ways. First, we do what we believe worked in the past ("But we've always done it that way!"), without knowing whether it really did work or asking whether the current situation is different enough to merit change. Second, we make decisions based on imitating models that appear to be working, regardless of whether the circumstances in our situation equate to what we suppose must be the best practice. And third, we simply accept deeply held but unproven beliefs about what actions can and cannot work.

Leaders, especially successful ones, have the hardest time seeing how they and their organizations might lack the evidence that would cause them to make these three types of errors. Pfeffer writes, "There is a clear implication in all of this for selecting leaders—avoid at all costs the people who think they know everything. They don't. But worse than that, they are unlikely to embrace any facts that disagree with their preconceptions. This

---

1. Ariely, *Upside of Irrationality*, Kindle locations 3839–40.
2. Pfeffer and Sutton, *Hard Facts*, 13.

is why one of our favorite sayings is, 'When two people always agree, one of them is unnecessary.'"[3]

I vividly remember having a spirited discussion with my wife, an engineer and leader at Intel, about the practice in my denomination of a mandatory, lengthy interim ministry between installed pastorates. She questioned whether the loss of momentum was always such a good idea. Why did we make this mandatory rather than simply establish it as one tool among many? I immediately responded that we had to do this. "Why?" she pushed back. Multibillion dollar companies don't do this. But, I countered, the pastor of a church isn't entirely analogous to a CEO. Then I repeated what I had always been told: if you don't have a long interim ministry after a pastor leaves, even when they leave well, the next pastor is more likely to become an "unintended interim." Without missing a beat, she looked at me and said, "Really? How do you know?" "Well, I . . ." I sputtered.

And I suddenly realized that I didn't know. Not really. I was merely reiterating what I had been told so many times that I assumed it was the truth. But in that moment I had to admit that in all honesty, I really didn't know. Wouldn't it be fascinating for some doctoral student to look at the length of Presbyterian pastorates before and after the Presbyterian Church (U.S.A.) instituted this mandatory interim practice and also compare with the United Methodists, who don't traditionally use interims? My sneaking suspicion is that the data won't support the belief that the mandatory interim ministry dramatically improves the length of pastoral calls. But it will take evidence to know for sure.

Based on Pfeffer's work, evidence-based decision-making in the church would look like a constant, never-ending process of questioning the conventional wisdom by running small experiments and changing our practices based on the results. More new visitors become connected to the church when the pastor visits them. Really? Maybe it's true in your context. Maybe it isn't. Test it. You can't attract young people without radically changing your music and worship style. Really? I don't know. Test it. Advertising doesn't make any difference in how many people attend. Really? Test it. And so on and so on. Whenever someone offers up an absolute truth, rather than just accept it as I did in the case of interim ministry, take the opportunity to gently question it. Is it really true? How do we know? Is it just based on a feeling or one past experience, or is there data to support it?

To those who question this approach and say it may be appropriate in medicine or business but not for the church, I would say Jesus teaches us to seek the truth: "You will know the truth, and the truth will make you free"

---

3. Ibid., 31.

(John 8:32). Evidence-based ministry helps us make decisions grounded more firmly in truth. And to those who say we should "just have faith" and all this evidence-based decision-making sounds like we're crowding out God, I say faith doesn't mean checking our brains at the door. Theologian Dan Migliore says when people stop thinking and facing reality so they can just accept what feels like truth, this absence of reason isn't faith at all. Instead, Migliore says, it is fideism. Faith, rather, yearns for ever deeper understanding, which Anselm attempted to get at with his definition of theology as *fides quaerens intellectum*, or "faith seeking understanding." True faith always searches out understanding and is always willing to learn and deepen.

Churches are fantastic laboratories for testing. Not sure whether one type of pledge card may work better than another? Randomly select half the congregation to receive one appeal, and send the previously used card as a control to the other half. If the congregation is large enough, send multiple versions. Not sure if one element of worship is really working well? Announce a temporary experiment. Set up a free survey monkey to solicit feedback. Then run with it. People are incredibly forgiving when they know a change isn't a permanent loss but only a temporary experiment. The possibilities are truly endless.

In the second section I introduced you to my friend the Reverend Mike Mather, who currently pastors at Broadway United Methodist Church in Indianapolis, Indiana. Remember Mike's creative use of a leaderboard to playfully encourage his staff to get involved in their community? I first met Mike when I heard him speak at a conference and learned all about his interest in Jane McGonigal; I spent most of the evening eagerly learning everything I could from him over dinner. I discovered Mike's interest in McGonigal is typical of his voracious intellectual curiosity: Mike is interested in interesting people working on interesting projects no matter whether their work seems immediately relevant. Mike is drawn to creativity and exhibits an experimental mindset rare for most leaders and exceptionally rare in the church. If you ask Mike about his experimental bent, however, he doesn't think he's anything special. He just thinks he's living out the story of Pentecost.

The story of Mike's church, Broadway United Methodist Church, could be the story of many large urban congregations.[4] An enormous, thriving congregation in the forties and fifties, the church built a massive facility to serve their then twenty-three hundred members. Like so many other downtown congregations, they watched the need for this size evaporate as whites fled the inner city for the suburbs in the sixties and seventies. Today, Mike

4. See King, "Death and Resurrection of an Urban Church."

says with a sparkle in his eyes, they have about forty bathrooms for roughly seventy-five worshippers on any given Sunday. At least they have no lines.

For the longest time Mike was the model of an inner-city pastor organizing a massive social service effort. The project of which he was most proud for years was an after-school program that cared for around 250 kids. He was busy. The church was busy. Everyone felt great about what they were doing. He now laughs and admits he nearly broke his arm patting himself on the back. But he began to have doubts about what they were really accomplishing.

Then, within nine months, nine young men died from violence in the neighborhood. Some of these young men participated in the after-school program. Mike found himself wondering if what they were doing was actually helping anyone. What had been seeds of doubt grew into a full-fledged crisis of faith. He realized that although their intentions were good, there was a dark side to spending all of their time helping others. What they were really doing is seeing the people in their neighborhood as needs rather than as people, and their help often wasn't even helping. It was just a lot of work that made the church feel better without really solving anything. It would take Mike some time to heal and move from this place of recognizing the problem to seeing a solution.

In the meantime, Mike was sent to pastor a second Broadway United Methodist Church, this one in South Bend, Indiana. One Pentecost Sunday he experienced something of a revelation. They read the text from Acts 2 that quotes the words of the prophet Joel about the Spirit of God falling upon everyone: the young and old, male and female, and even upon the servants. The Spirit was poured out on everyone. All of a sudden it was as if Mike were hearing this text for the first time.

If this revelation were true, if the Spirit fell upon everyone in Joel's day and all the followers on Pentecost, then that same Spirit must be alive and at work in everyone today, too. And if it is true that God's Holy Spirit dwells in everyone, why doesn't our church treat people as if they are Spirit-filled? Rather than view the neighbors around them as fundamentally needy, what would happen if they saw their neighbors as bearers of the Spirit—gifted and blessed with something vital to share? Mike steeped himself in the work of John McKnight, a professor at Northwestern University who taught asset-based community planning. Asset-based planning teaches us to listen to communities and discover the gifts they have rather than focus all of our time and attention on what they lack.

Mike would see the real fruit of this emphasis on gifts when he returned to the first Broadway, in Indianapolis. Knowing he needed to try something different, Mike partnered with a member of the church, De'Amon

Harges, who also believed something needed to change. Mike hired Harges as Broadway's first Roving Listener to kick off an unlikely experiment that would in time yield incredible results. They decided to experiment by not helping people.

Harges spent all of his time visiting with people in the neighborhood. He talked to kids hanging out on playgrounds. He visited seniors at home. He listened to single moms tell him about what was going well in their lives and what was hard. Rather than focusing on their needs, Harges listened deeply for what their gifts might be.

While Harges was talking and listening, Mather was asking hard questions about some of the ministries the church believed were going well. For three decades members at Broadway tutored kids in the neighborhood. Yet, for three decades the dropout rate went up. What they were doing wasn't working, Mather concluded. So they stopped tutoring. It was the same way with their food pantry. For years, Broadway had a thriving food bank ministry; but when he started asking questions, Mather learned from local officials that hunger wasn't a serious problem in the area. Obesity was. Mather noticed that much of the food they were handing out was processed or canned—items such as peaches in heavy syrup. Not only were they not helping, Mather thought with alarm, but they were actively making the obesity problem worse.

Fortunately, Mike is one of those people who knows a crazy amount of things from a variety of disciplines. He knew all about loss aversion, and he knew you can't just take things away. You have to do something different instead. To figure out what to try instead, Mather and Harges started asking their neighbors three questions: What three things do you know well enough to teach someone else? What do you want to learn? And who, besides God and me, is walking with you on this journey?

Mike is a master storyteller, and one of his favorites is the story of Adelita. One day Adelita came to their food pantry looking for assistance. In the past, when the church thought their job was to be "helpful," they would, as Mike puts it, essentially ask Adelita how poor she was. They would ask what her monthly income was and what her expenses were, then note the discrepancy, writing it down on a sheet of paper. And what would they do with the paper? Well, what does any church do with a useless piece of paper? They filed it. They had stacks and stacks of such papers, all essentially recording people's poverty.

But not this time. With Adelita they asked her what she was good at, and she told them she could cook. With a laugh Mike said loudly, "Prove it!" He invited Adelita to come and cook Friday lunch for the pastor and staff. It was amazing. For the next nine months they called Adelita anytime people were using the church building and needed food. Then, the chamber of commerce asked Mike if they could meet at his church for an all-day meeting. Mike said absolutely, yes, but on one condition: they were welcome to meet there for free (and use all of those bathrooms) provided they used his caterer, Adelita. The church made one small investment in Adelita: they took twenty dollars and purchased one thousand business cards proudly advertising Adelita's "spunky Tex-Mex catering." The opportunity to cook for the chamber connected Adelita with the Women Business Owners of Michiana. A year and a half later she opened up Adelita's Fajitas on the corner of 8th and Harrison in Elkhart, Indiana. "Now," Mike reflects, "if we had asked her when she showed up tell us how poor you are, we would have all ended up poorer for it—and we would have missed a lot of great food."[5]

It's true that not everyone appreciated Mike's experimental attitude. Asking questions about whether ministries were bearing fruit meant that some groups, such as the tutoring program, needed to be retired or completely reconceptualized. Being experimental means that congregations will try things and some of them will fail. There will be programs—again, like the tutoring at Broadway—that appear to succeed but that, upon closer inspection, do not actually help. But through stories such as Adelita's and so many others, Mike demonstrates that the benefits of this new evidence-based, experimental approach far outweigh the pain in learning how to say goodbye to ministries that might have been appropriate at one time but no longer serve the needs of the community.

Another experiment in a very different context continues to bear incredible fruit. Lake Nokomis Presbyterian Church is a congregation that feels like déjà vu for many mainline pastors. After ninety years of ministry, Lake Nokomis Presbyterian Church saw its worship attendance dwindle from around five hundred in the 1950s to around thirty aging people in 2007. The church was facing death and entered into a year of discernment to determine whether they should close their doors or continue. They were looking at a choice so many congregations today face: keep on doing the same things and fade comfortably into dissolution or change and step into an unknown future.

When I was first starting out in ministry, I couldn't understand how this decision could be a difficult one. If a congregation faced certain death, why wouldn't they try anything they could? But that was before I knew about loss aversion. When a community isn't sure anything will work, it's incredibly painful to think about giving up cherished practices that have sustained them for decades. But this painful and courageous direction is

5. Mather, "Adelita's Gift," 4:19/4:29.

precisely what the people of Lake Nokomis decided to try. They sensed
God's presence still moving and called Pastor Kara Root to enter into their
sense of adventure and trust.

Root says no one quite knows how these key words emerged now, but
during the discernment period the community arrived at three touchstones:
Sabbath, hospitality, and worship. By honoring the Sabbath, Lake Nokomis
wasn't simply acknowledging their need for a break from the relentless
struggle in which they had been engaging—pretending to be the church
they had always been. It is true, though, that many congregations find themselves in this endless cycle of working and programming themselves back
into vitality, as if the future lies in their hands rather than God's wild Spirit.
The leaders of Lake Nokomis were asking deeper questions about entering
into the vulnerable, uncomfortable place of doing things differently by worshipping at a different time. Moreover, this question wasn't so much about
attracting new people to a time slot; it represented a conscious decision to
engage God in a different way. Underneath, they were asking a question
hardly any community dares to ask: what if we stopped trying to be the
people we once were but are no longer?

They decided to experiment with a different plan for gathering. For
a year, on the first and third weekend of each month, they would worship
on Sunday morning just as they had always done. But on the second and
fourth weekends they would gather on Saturday night for a quiet, contemplative time of worship and a meal, and then on the following Sunday they
would spend the day honoring the Sabbath by doing nothing from a sense
of obligation. During those rare months with a fifth Sunday, they decided
to join with St. Joseph's Home for Children, where they would worship
with the children on Sunday evening. Root says this experience has been
transformational. While other congregations support St. Joseph, the normal pattern is to send a pastor to lead a worship service. Lake Nokomis
Presbyterian is the only community that shows up as the body of Christ.
The entire church gathers with these young people who have experienced
various levels of trauma in their lives, and the experience has enriched the
lives of both communities.

When Lake Nokomis speaks of hospitality, Root says, they aren't
talking about Martha Stewart foodies and impossibly complicated meals.
Rather, they are living into the biblical practice of being present with and for
one another. When they meet with people interested in joining their community, for instance, instead of plying them with theological questions, the
leaders of Lake Nokomis meet with prospective members over a meal and
reflect on substantive faith questions. They talk about what they know to be
true and the questions with which they continue to struggle.

Hospitality, welcoming the other, has led the community into truly difficult waters. In our socially and culturally divided time, this historically progressive congregation had to ask themselves whether God could be speaking through their more conservative brothers and sisters. Especially when a community is feeling vulnerable and threatened, these are difficult questions to ask indeed. It's far easier to circle the wagons than engage the Other. But engage Lake Nokomis Presbyterian Church did. When the socially conservative Fellowship of Presbyterians (now The Fellowship Community) met in Minneapolis, Lake Nokomis agreed to open their doors and welcome participants to gatherings called Eats and Empathy. In these meetings liberals and conservatives met around table fellowship and entered into genuine conversation led by a facilitator (the same Theresa F. Latini, author of *Transforming Church Conflict*, which I previously commended).

What grounded all of these changes was worship. In worship, Root says, they remembered who they were and whose they were. And things changed. Unexpectedly, by worshipping less often on Sunday mornings the community found they were welcoming more children rather than fewer. I suspect what created this environment was a consistent effort to view young people as full participants with important things to offer. One of the changes Root led, for instance, was to retire the traditional children's sermon in favor of welcoming the children into worship for a time of sharing what they had learned in Sunday school. At one point the children crafted glasses on sticks to hand out to everyone. They explained that worship was about looking for God's presence; and while you could look for God everywhere, worship was the place where everyone really focused on it. The kids gave the adults the gift of these craft glasses to remind everyone to be on the lookout for God. These kids weren't just being taught; they were teaching.

The children also led worship by writing and offering prayer each week and serving on the ushering team. In time so many children started coming that the community began to experience growing pains. Some who used to complain about not having enough young people now started to voice concerns about all the noise. Root in her wisdom notes that every complaint is really God doing something wonderful and unexpected. In other words, Root reminds leaders that rather than pushing back on complaints or being defensive, they should view complaints as opportunities for wonder and engagement.

For Root the language of experimenting was crucial to their moving forward together. Because they were experimenting, they avoided the pressure of having to perfectly figure out what shape their new community was supposed to take. This openness toward changing and improving over time proved invaluable to the experiment from the very beginning. Root well

remembers the first experimental Saturday night worship. They tried contemplative Taizé music for the first time ever, using a questionable keyboard
accompaniment. They tried three minutes of silence when they had never
sat together for longer than a few seconds. Root said she believed the first
experiment was an utter disaster. But the next day she observed the Sabbath,
taking a long walk and a bubble bath with her two-year-old.

She remembers going to the follow-up meeting to discuss the Saturday evening worship experiment with this incredible sense of gratitude for
the Sabbath day, fully prepared to accept whatever decision the community
decided to make. While everyone agreed the worship needed work, all were
so restored by the Sabbath practice that there was no doubt they wanted
to move forward with the experiment. Perhaps the most important thing,
according to Root, is realizing that experimentation isn't a one-time thing.
Communities don't experiment once and then stop; they become experimental and enter into God's great, mischievous experiment of being with
and for us.

Root related the story of the Lake Nokomis church in her 2014 NEXT
Conference talk; expressing their experimental spirit, Root said she has no
idea what the future holds for the community. But what is so energizing is
seeing people willing to experiment and follow after where the Holy Spirit
is leading them. Like Mike Mather's community, Kara Root saw the people
in her care move from focusing on all the things they couldn't do, such as
building houses with Habitat for Humanity, to noticing all the new ways
they were serving their community: giving people rides to the hospital,
taking care of neighborhood pets, and creating banners for the Presbyterian General Assembly in Minneapolis. What is so life-giving about Kara's
leadership is her deep theological conviction, lived out through her experimental practice, that the church is not ours to anxiously protect; rather, the
church is God's, and we have a beautiful opportunity to take part in this vital
and living mystery.

33

Getting Real Part Three . . .
Really Real

The decisions in the two earlier case studies played out at the level of the local church and a regional governing body. What makes decision-making so fascinating, though, is how useful it is not just on these organizational levels but also on the personal scale. From the moment we wake up in the morning we make decisions constantly. Most of these occur below the level of our awareness, but many rise to the level of conscious thought. This personal application partly explains why what Cass Sunstein calls "second-order" decision-making—decisions about decisions—is so interesting for us. When we hear a story about a concrete decision and the way a leader or body goes about making it, we can't help thinking about personal decisions that we have made or that loom before us.

As I noted earlier in the book, my family lives just outside of Portland in a town named Tualatin. Tualatin sits about an hour and a half away from the Cascade Range and an hour and a half drive to the coast. Since I love the mountains and my wife loves the coast, Tualatin is a great place for our family to live. The first summer I was here, Rob, one of our backpacking and mountain climbing church members, asked me if I wanted to hike the Timberline Trail with him. The Timberline Trail circumnavigates Mt. Hood, running for forty-one miles generally beginning and ending at Timberline Lodge. The trail wends its way along every face of the mountain: canyons, old-growth Douglas Firs, alpine meadows, and high-desert, moonscape terrain. I was stoked.

I was also inexperienced. I had backpacked before, but the gear I had was old and heavy. I don't think I was ever as tired as when I made it to camp the first night. I woke up the next day feeling as if I had been hit by a train. I didn't complain too much, swallowed what Rob referred to as Vitamin I (ibuprofen) and followed after him. On the second day Rob tried to move my pack and nearly flipped out. What was I carrying in my pack, bricks? It was well over sixty pounds, and I learned that technology had greatly reduced the weight of most packs down to around half that.

Further, the wildness of Mt. Hood was new to me as well. I had backpacked in Pennsylvania, hiked parts of the Appalachian Trail in New Jersey, and day-hiked around Texas, but I had never been in a wilderness as remote as Mt. Hood. Around rivers, riverbeds, and high-desert areas the trail disappeared, making route-finding an essential skill. And we had to cross rivers without the benefit of bridges. We tried to cross most of them in the morning, before the glacial melt transformed them into raging torrents, but some, like Newton Creek, were dangerous at any time of the day.

Oh, I learned a lot on that trip. Easily my most significant new knowledge was what I learned about Rob's health. Over dinner one night, as we stared into the vastness of that landscape, Rob shared with me that he suffered from primary sclerosing cholangitis (PSC) of the liver. He explained that the ducts leading into his liver were abnormally narrow and that they would damage the liver over time, leading ultimately to liver failure. He was a young, fit, healthy guy. This disease has nothing to do with alcohol. It was just the unfortunate way his body developed. Rob didn't know when it would happen, but he knew that he was going to need a new liver at some point.

He and I didn't know it at the time, but "some point" was much sooner than later. Only a year or so after our hike, Rob began to develop symptoms of liver failure. His bilirubin count soared, making him itch and giving him a jaundiced, yellow appearance. He needed a liver fast. He was on the donor list in Oregon, but the question was whether he would live long enough to find a match. This waiting period led to one of the most moving and brilliant decision-making processes I've ever seen.

Rob and his wife, Jennifer, had one small child at the time. Rob's goal, he told me, was to live long enough to walk his little girl, Lauren, down the aisle. We were all wondering if he was going to see that wish come true. Not long after Rob shared his goal with me he received a phone call from his doctor telling him the transplant team had news. They had a donor, and the liver was a match for Rob. This was incredibly good news.

But the news was more complicated than anyone could have guessed. By then I knew all about the importance of blood markers and organ size. But I learned something new. It turns out the way someone dies also makes an enormous difference in whether their organs make good candidates for transplant. Brain death provides the best conditions for organ transplant. When the brain dies, the body can still function with assistance to supply organs with a steady stream of oxygen, which keeps them healthy right up until the minute they are taken. In this case the transplant team was working with a cardiac death, which means the potential donor's heart failed. Rob's doctor told him no one could know how much damage the organs had suffered from a lack of oxygen. Even when they harvested the liver and examined it, the damage would not be obvious.

The options open to Rob were limited. He could decide to take the risk that this liver was healthy only to find out later that he would need yet another transplant. Or he could choose to say no to this questionable liver and hope that his health would hold out until a new match became available. And—nothing like a little pressure to keep things interesting—he and Jennifer didn't have long to decide. The doctor said they needed to make a decision within twelve hours, or the organ would be given to another patient.

Adding even more tension to their decision was the fact that this was not the first phone call Rob had received notifying him of a potential liver. Patients with liver cancer were given the highest priority, meaning patients like Rob would get a liver only if something went amiss with the primary candidate. Three times Rob and Jennifer had rushed to the hospital for Rob to get prepped for surgery as a secondary candidate only to return home with no new liver.

So, how on earth were they supposed to make this decision? Despite the previous false alarms, they had to treat this phone call as if it were the first. But what if he accepted this liver, and it turned out to be more damaged than the one he already had? Or what if he didn't accept it, and it turned out the liver was fine? Could he hold out until another liver became available? And would Rob make this decision alone? It was his body and his liver, but Rob was married and had a child. His actions would have direct consequences for all of them.

Both Rob and Jennifer are engineers. As someone married to an engineer, I feel safe in saying that the process of becoming an engineer shapes how a person thinks and reacts to situations. Engineering is a habit of thinking carefully about problems and coming up with solutions that work. In this case their training led Rob and Jennifer to an amazing way of meeting this particular problem. Rob said they both talked about what they were thinking and feeling for a few minutes. They talked about the questions they had, and they put these questions to the medical team, who gave them the best information possible. But at some point they were going to have to make a decision.

Rob wanted to know Jennifer's opinion but feared that if he said what he was thinking first, she might agree just to be supportive. Jennifer had the same concern. She was worried that if she said which option she thought was best, Rob might agree when he really had misgivings. So here's what they did. They agreed to write down the decision they thought best on a piece of paper. Then they would slide the pieces of paper face down to one another across the table, pick them up, and read them at the same time.

Can you imagine that moment, how the two of them must have felt as they were writing down their first choices? As they passed them to each other across the table?

With relief they found that they agreed that Rob should take the risk and accept this liver, despite not knowing whether it was damaged or not. There was every hope that the liver would be fine. He was already living with a damaged liver, and based on what the medical team had told him it seemed unlikely that this new one would be worse than what he already had. And if he rejected the liver, he would lose this opportunity. No one could say if he would live long enough for another match to appear.

Though this episode was an intensely personal one for Rob and Jennifer, let's take a step back and look at what they did right. First of all, Rob and Jennifer did a great job assessing how much process this situation required. Immediate decisions that require a quick reaction are decisions that we encounter all the time and become familiar to us. This was definitely not that kind of decision. People don't make life-or-death decisions about organ donation every day. This decision was unique. It was frightening. And they also didn't have all the time in the world to make the decision—just twelve hours. So, too much process would have gotten in the way. As great as analysis is, you can definitely have too much of a good thing. So, first having a conversation about feelings, then recording questions, and lastly getting answers to these questions before settling on an initial decision was just right.

What makes this decision process particularly amazing is how they decided to go about getting authentic responses from one another. They were absolutely right to use more formality when it came to asking one another what they were thinking. So many factors made this an exquisitely difficult decision. Loss aversion looms powerfully over this decision. The call they received informed them that they had a liver. It was their organ if they wanted it. In addition to loss aversion, the endowment effect—ascribing more value to something because it belongs to you—complicated their ability to judge. Also the risk of this liver not being healthy and the prospect of losing Rob if they waited created strong emotions. As we have seen, we are not quite ourselves when under the spell of the affect heuristic.

The formal process they used, as simple as it was, allowed both of them to take some time away from the presence of the other. Taking time to breathe and still oneself and gaining a little distance are especially helpful when trying to minimize the affect heuristic. This process also offered the best chance of getting the most honest initial decision from each other. They had excellent, objective medical information from their team regarding the options. But in this decision it was vital that each of them knew what the other was really thinking. It's true that their final decision might have evolved quite differently if they had disagreed, but this disagreement would have been out on the table as opposed to being concealed.

Another thing I like about their process is that the slips of paper depersonalized this highly emotional decision in a way that was helpful, which would have been especially true if Rob and Jennifer had disagreed. By writing down the action that was their first choice, they kept potential conflict entirely at the level of task conflict. Remember that task conflict centers around the question, are we doing the right things? The pieces of paper quite literally embodied their thoughts, reminding them that they and their personalities were not the same as their beliefs about this decision. Now, I know Rob and Jennifer, and I can assure you they are nice people. But they are people. And they were people who were dealing with two high-stress careers, a young child, and a life-threatening illness on top of it. It's easy to romanticize how a loving couple might be able to just come together in a crisis and put aside differences; the reality is that this decision just put pressure on an already difficult situation. These are precisely the times when affective conflict, our frustration with each other, becomes heightened. Had they disagreed, the papers were a visual reminder to stay focused on the task at hand and not attend to the interpersonal friction alive and well in every loving couple, family, and team.

Another strong aspect of this decision, I think, is less what they did and who was present and more what they didn't do and who was absent. How many decision-makers does it take to make a high-quality decision? I agree with the wise folks at SDRM: as few as possible but as many as necessary. Especially given the time frame, Rob and Jennifer were wise to draw the circle of decision-makers tightly. In this case they had their medical team to provide expert information and just the two of them. How easy it would have been to call friends and family, but how potentially complicating it would have been. It's not difficult in situations like this one to think that simply because a decision will impact someone else, their input should always be solicited. Yes, this decision did impact friends and family, but the only reason to ask for help in this situation would have been if someone truly could have improved the quality of the decision. In this case I'd say the possibility that more voices would add unneeded confusion vastly outweighed the possibility that those voices would help.

The great news about this situation is that sometimes high-quality decisions do lead to good outcomes. While Rob has had some issues with the liver, he is strong, healthy, and thriving ten years later. When their son, Jonathan, was born I had the honor of baptizing him. On the Friday before his baptism I hiked back up to Newton Creek, one of our most challenging crossings, and brought back beautiful, clear mountain water to bless their new little one. With every step I took I thought about the first time Rob guided me around that mountain and all that I learned from him—and how grateful I was (and still am) to serve a congregation full of such wise members.

34

Ten Facets of Decision-Making
to Know

1. **Decision Quality vs. Outcome**: We tend to be outcome focused with decisions. If something goes well in a congregation, we say people made the right call. If it doesn't go well, we assume someone made a mistake. But this correlation isn't always valid. Good decisions don't always produce good outcomes, and poor decision-makers sometimes get lucky. Leaders should focus on decision quality rather than outcome.

2. **Behavioral Decision Quality Chain**: The behavioral decision quality chain is a tool to help decision-making bodies assess their perception of decision quality. The six "links" of the chain are as follows: consider whether you have the right frame, keeping in mind the problem of narrow framing; knowing the challenge that the anchoring heuristic can pose, come up with creative alternatives; make decisions based on facts, considering confirmation bias; watch for the affect heuristic as you evaluate decision possibilities based on deep, core values; constantly assess for all heuristics and biases throughout the decision-making process—especially the optimism bias; and finally, ask whether there is commitment to action in light of loss aversion.

3. **Three Kinds of Conflict**: Not all conflict is created equal. Task conflict refers to questions of whether we are doing the right things and is

considered to be generally positive. Process conflict asks whether we are doing things in the right way and is considered less positive. Affective conflict, also known as relational conflict, refers to visceral dislike among members and is always dangerous and requires management.

4. **Decision Assessment**: Decisions low in complexity and impact require common sense and should be made quickly. Decisions with more weight that can nonetheless be decided within hours or days require the decision quality chain. When decision bodies face complex, high-impact strategic decisions, they should employ a more thorough dialogue decision process. These distinctions are fluid and require judgment.

5. **Decision Leadership** and **Decision Dialogue Process**: Decision leaders work to lead decision-making bodies through a collaborative decision dialogue process. The decision leader touches base with the decision-making body regarding frame, alternatives, and analysis until a high-quality decision is reached. The most important aspect here is that decision leaders provide the decision-making body with the tools to make the decision rather than advocate for one particular outcome.

6. **Tornado Diagram**: The tornado diagram visually ranks financial aspects of an organization in terms of impact. Aspects like church membership, for example, have a greater ability to hinder or help most churches than operational expenses. This tool is crucial to assess the financial realities of the organization, but leaders still must decide how to spend their time and resources based on their core values and sense of where the Holy Spirit is leading.

7. **Default Choices**: A default choice is the apparent choice or choices an institution presents. For example, the default choices regarding membership vary significantly in religious institutions. When people are busy, tired, and inexperienced, they are more likely to accept defaults due to status quo bias, decision fatigue, or loss aversion.

8. **Choice Architecture**: While many decisions require conscious reflection, people make many more decisions without thinking about them. Choice architects focus on the default choices institutions present that guide these kinds of unreflective choices. When church leaders act as choice architects, they pay serious attention to situations in which people are asked to make active choices when defaults might be more helpful.

9. **Simplified Active Choice**: Cass Sunstein lifts up simplified active choice as one of the most important tools for the leader as choice

architect. Simplified active choice presents people with the decision to think for themselves or to follow defaults established by the institution. Simplified active choice powerfully balances our desire to choose with our need to be good stewards of our limited decisiveness.

10. **Evidence-Based Management**: Evidence-based management applies the scientific method to test the assumptions we make about what will and will not work in our context. This model encourages leaders to question beliefs constantly by running tests and changing practices based on the results.

Postlude

FLAME, SHAME, AND GRACE

Sermon given at Tualatin Presbyterian Church, January 26, 2014

John 7:53—8:11: Then each of them went home, while Jesus went to the Mount of Olives. Early in the morning he came again to the temple. All the people came to him and he sat down and began to teach them. The scribes and the Pharisees brought a woman who had been caught in adultery; and making her stand before all of them, they said to him, "Teacher, this woman was caught in the very act of committing adultery. Now in the law Moses commanded us to stone such women. Now what do you say?" They said this to test him, so that they might have some charge to bring against him. Jesus bent down and wrote with his finger on the ground. When they kept on questioning him, he straightened up and said to them, "Let anyone among you who is without sin be the first to throw a stone at her." And once again he bent down and wrote on the ground. When they heard it, they went away, one by one, beginning with the elders; and Jesus was left alone with the woman standing before him. Jesus straightened up and said to her, "Woman, where are they? Has no one condemned you?" She said, "No one, sir." And Jesus said, "Neither do I condemn you. Go your way, and from now on do not sin again."

This past week I took a decision quality class at Intel, an intense class designed to help leaders and decision-making bodies make better decisions. I shared my experience of lighting the symbolic mortgage on fire without any real plan of what to do once it was lit with my new friends and classmates . . . they all suggested I consider the extended version of the course.

Of course they had no idea how right they were. Truth is, this was *not* the first time I had set something on fire without thinking about the consequences. So, back in middle school (and don't the best stories always start with "back in middle school"?) all the drummers were getting bored in the percussion section. The woodwinds were working on something or other, and we were just sitting there. Then ol' Jay Wiley had this brilliant idea. He had this Binaca stuff, this breath freshener spray that's mostly alcohol, and he pours some of it into the top of an apple. And then—and I have no idea why any of us had a lighter, but someone did—someone lit the Binaca on fire. It was kind of like an apple candle with the Binaca giving off a nice blue, minty glow.

Now, this probably would have all stopped right there except that our very young band director saw what we were doing—and he smirked at us. It was his first year teaching. He was barely out of school, and he wanted us to think of him as "cool"—the kiss of death for a middle school teacher trying to maintain any semblance of discipline. Well, that smirk just emboldened us. After that we started burning everything, in particular these floppy rattan mallets we all despised.

It all came to a head one afternoon after school. We were all hanging out in the band hall like we did, with no supervision. And there were three of us in the big back practice room. And there was this stack of paper towels sitting against the wall. Now, I have no idea what part of my frontal lobes were not working, but I literally said something like, "Hey guys . . . I wonder what would happen if we set those on fire?" My more intelligent friends wanted nothing to do with it but encouraged me to try—and I lit those paper towels on fire. And it was like they exploded—they burned so fast and so high. Panicking, I didn't know what else to do but to kick them over and just stomp them out. Well, the practice room and the hall were full of smoke. And there was this large black scorch mark on the floor where the paper towels had once been. I looked around at my friends, and the looks on their faces expressed exactly what I was feeling—I was in terrible, terrible trouble.

But my middle school fire experience was nothing compared to the trouble the woman in our Gospel story finds herself in this morning. The Gospel story this morning is tantalizing. It's tantalizing because there are so few details. Who was this woman? Was she older, or was she just some kid married off before she was even in her twenties? And this adultery—was it just a mistake? A one-time kind of thing? Or was she in another relationship? Was she in love? And what about family? Did she have children yet, or maybe she was hoping to just leave and make a clean break? And what about her husband? Maybe he was cruel—some old man who treated her like property. Or maybe he was just a fool and trusted her, and she was playing him like a harp, or in this case, a lyre. Or perhaps she was a prostitute—maybe one who tried to leave the business, and the men were her angry clients. We don't know. We don't know anything about her, except that she was caught *in flagrante delicto*, literally "in the flame of the crime." And she was terrified. She was in terrible, terrible trouble.

I wonder if it wasn't the same for Jesus, too. He was up early, as we are this morning. He was up early teaching. The disciples were yawning, complaining about his energizer-bunny energy and grumbling about the fact that coffee hadn't even been invented yet. But then, right in the middle of one of his parables, all the disciples began staring at Jesus, as Princeton Seminary president Craig Barnes puts it, like the RCA dog with these puzzled expressions on their faces. Right in the middle of this story the rabbis came in, the pastors of the day, all wearing smiles like the cat who ate the canary. And they were dragging something with them—this woman. And they tossed her at Jesus' feet like a piece of poisoned meat. They told him, "Teacher"—how they loved calling him "teacher"—"we caught this woman in the act of adultery. The law says to stone her, but . . . what do you say?"

It was the perfect trap. They knew all about Jesus and his soft spot for people in trouble. They knew all about his penchant for talking about grace and forgiveness, and so they decided to test him. And it's a perfect test—if he says they should let her go, he's obviously in the wrong, and his reputation as a teacher is done. And if he throws her to the wolves, then he caves in front of his disciples, showing he can talk the talk but can't walk the walk.

And then shockingly (for Jesus) he doesn't have a reply. He doesn't have a "render unto Caesar what is Caesar's" or "love the Lord your God and your neighbor as yourself, and all the rest is commentary." He's got nothing. He just slides down into the dust, eyes down, his finger playing in the dirt. What on earth could he say or do? There was nothing he could say or do. And I imagine even Jesus at that point felt like he was in trouble.

So, the great thing about me is that I'm quick on my feet. I mean not quick enough to think, "Hey maybe this fire-burning thing isn't such a good idea," but quick like, "Now I'm stuck, what are my options?" Unfortunately, while I'm a pretty quick thinker, I'm not that great a repairman. What immediately came to mind is I remembered seeing these big cans of paint in one of the closets in the band hall. I have no idea what they were for. I don't remember ever seeing anyone use them. But I definitely saw them there. And one of them was blue—nearly the same kind of blue as the carpet. So, I ran down the smoky hall. And no, no fire alarms went off, *very* comforting, and I grabbed the paint and one of the brushes and brought it back to the room. And then—and to this day I marvel that I thought this could work—I tried to smooth the paint over the charred paper towels, making a nasty blue, chunky, paste . . . which, when I looked at it more objectively, wasn't really the same color blue at all. It was a mess. I had made a bad decision worse by trying to cover it up.

Jesus could have done this. He could have tried to cover over the woman's misstep. He could have said that her case was a special case, that the law didn't apply to her. He could have said that they just didn't understand her circumstances, that something about her life—maybe the way she was raised—excused her behavior. Or he might have said that you have to take the law with a grain of salt—sometimes you follow it, but other times, for complicated reasons, some people don't have to. He might have said something I was thinking when I read the Scripture text, something like, "I'll tell you about how the law applies to this woman if and when you go find the man she was with, and we talk about them together."

But he didn't. He didn't say any of these things. He didn't try to excuse her. He didn't try to pretend that her behavior was somehow, in the right light, actually OK. He didn't try to lift her up. Rather, sitting low in the dirt, and looking up at those self-righteous men, he realized they needed to come down just a little.

And so rather than defending her, rather than pretending she was in the right, he tried something totally different. Something I never would have thought of. He pointed out how they were all in need of grace. He said, "OK. Tell you what. You have a point about this woman here. So, here's what I say. Whoever here is without sin. Any of you. You go ahead and make her day. Anyone here entirely pure? Anyone here entirely unstained? Anyone?"

And one by one, the stones dropped to the sand. Thud after thud. And the men walked away. Sadder but wiser. And perhaps kinder.

It turns out back in the band hall that all of my anxious fixing only made things worse. When people who actually knew what they were doing came and assessed the situation, they figured out that the paper towels didn't really do any damage. They didn't actually burn the carpet—they never got that hot. They just made a mess. An inexpensive carpet cleaning could have solved the problem *if* I had owned up to my bad decision. Instead, the paint and the mess created a problem a simple cleaning couldn't fix. In this case, hiding not only didn't help, it made things worse. Had I been mature enough, both in moral and spiritual character, to stand in grace, I not only would have done the right thing, but I would have saved the carpet, too.

Now, the decision class we had this week, I loved it. And I certainly hope that my decision quality improves—personally and as a leader of this congregation. I certainly hope my decisions will be better with regard to fire.

Fire in buildings. Fire in buildings with carpets. But no matter how great our decision quality, one thing I know is that we will still make mistakes. We will. We can't avoid it. And when we do, if we face them with our heads held high and in Christ, we may have to bear consequences, sometimes heavy consequences. But we will do so with honor, integrity, and always, without condition, covered in the grace of Jesus Christ, who reminds us that none of us, even the best of us, are without sin. Amen.

35

Benediction

Go Forth and Be Irrational!

Sometimes, even with our newfound knowledge of cognitive heuristics and biases and game theory and gamefulness and decision chains and evidence-based decisions, we church leaders will still find ourselves or our churches in a bad game.

The David and Goliath game is definitely not one anyone wants to play, at least not if they're scripted to play the role of David. Who wants to go up against a juggernaut against whom you have no realistic chance? According to Malcolm Gladwell what makes David remarkable is not that he triumphed against all odds, but that he realized he was in an unwinnable game and decided to change it.[1]

Citing military historian Baruch Halpern, Gladwell relates that there are three main types of soldiers in the ancient battles between Israel and the Philistines: infantry, cavalry, and artillery (archers and slingers fall into the artillery category). Like rock, paper, and scissors, these different classes of combatants balanced one another out. Infantry with their long spears were effective against the mounted soldiers in the cavalry. The cavalry with their speed were able to evade and make gains against the artillery. The artillery

---

1. Gladwell, *David and Goliath*, 6.

with their incredibly powerful and accurate weapons were deadly against the infantry.[2]

In First Samuel when the two armies squared off in the Shephelah Valley, a bloodbath seemed imminent. The Philistines, a tough, seagoing people, had scored several victories against the Israelites over the years. King Saul, however, had gathered the full strength of his army. In order to stem the bloodshed, the ginormous Philistine warrior Goliath lumbered onto the field of battle to offer a challenge: whoever steps up to do battle with him would fight on behalf of all of Israel. If Goliath prevailed, the Israelites would become the servants of the Philistines. If the Israelites won, the Philistines would serve the Israelites. It was a classic *mano-a-mano* fight to the death. Personally, I like to imagine tumbleweed rolling by when Goliath roars his challenge and a Spaghetti Western soundtrack from Ennio Morricone playing in the background.

Of course, none of the Israelites were interested in stepping into the ring with Goliath. The guy was gigantic. In addition to his sword, Goliath had a spear as thick as a weaver's beam. Without having the language for a volunteer's dilemma, Saul must have known all of his soldiers were making the unconscious calculation that what might be good for the whole group might not bode quite as well for the one soldier who volunteered to fight Goliath. But then young David stepped up, boasting about his exploits as a shepherd. Saul argued against this mismatch, but no one else was willing to take the field. Thus, Saul reluctantly agreed to send David into battle.

Gladwell notes that everyone today thinks of David and Goliath as an epic mismatch in which an incredibly weak force goes up against an impossibly strong foe and against all odds wins, but he argues this isn't how to understand the story. What happens, Gladwell argues, is that David evens his chances against Goliath by changing the game everyone expected him to play.

Everyone expected David to engage Goliath as an infantry soldier. This is how man-to-man confrontations were conducted. Goliath and David would both wear heavy armor, hurl their heavy spears at one another first, and then slowly hack away with their massively heavy swords until one of them, undoubtedly David, made a lethal mistake. Saul even offered David his own armor and weapons to give David the very best chance at the game they all expected him to play.

But what's remarkable about David is not that he went up against Goliath as an infantry soldier and somehow triumphed. What made David remarkable is that he changed the game. The first thing he did was refuse

2. Ibid., 10.

Saul's heavy armor. He knew he wouldn't be able to move underneath the crush of that bronze. The second thing he did is stoop down to pick up those five smooth stones. No one yet suspected how David planned to attack.

Instead of slowly walking into battle lumbering under the weight of all that armor, David dashed into battle swinging his sling with one of those smooth stones faster and faster. All of a sudden it became clear to everyone watching that not only was David not the weaker power, but it was Goliath who stood no chance. If David had played the same infantry game Goliath was playing, the young man would have had no chance. But entering into the field of battle as a slinger, as artillery, changed everything. Everyone watching knew that infantry, no matter how big, didn't stand a chance against a slinger who was any good. And David was an amazing slinger, sinking that stone into Goliath's forehead and then severing his arrogant head. David triumphed not because he lucked out in a bad game; he won because he figured out how to change it.

So, if you find yourself or your church in a bad game, change it: change the game, change up some of the players, redesign the payoffs, or just stop playing.

Remember to sing to the elephants and teach the riders, knowing that we all have two brains—a System 1 and a System 2, an inner Esau and an inner Jacob.

Be on the lookout for cognitive heuristics and biases—those mental shortcuts and blind spots.

Honor the Schelling points you discover hiding among your church's sacred cows.

Look for ways to encourage cooperation and minimize defection in your church setting.

Play games in church.

Get in touch with your *jongleur de Dieu*.

Keep a decision quality chain in your toolbox.

Be experimental. Make glorious mistakes. Learn how to befriend failure.

And, above all, go forth and be predictably irrational in the best sense of Jesus and Paul! Amen.

Bibliography

Arendzen, John. "Docetae." In vol. 5 of *The Catholic Encyclopedia*. New York: Robert Appleton, 1909. http://www.newadvent.org/cathen/05070c.htm.

Ariely, Dan. *The (Honest) Truth about Dishonesty: How We Lie to Everyone—Especially Ourselves*. New York: Harper, 2013. Kindle edition.

———. *Predictably Irrational: The Hidden Forces That Shape Our Decisions*. Rev. ed. New York: HarperCollins, 2009. Kindle edition.

———. *The Upside of Irrationality: The Unexpected Benefits of Defying Logic at Work and at Home*. New York: HarperCollins, 2010. Kindle edition.

Attridge, Harold W. "Sin, Sinners." In *The New Interpreter's Dictionary of the Bible*, edited by Katherine Doob Sakenfeld et al., 5:263–79. Nashville: Abingdon, 2009.

Augustine. *The City of God* [*De civitate dei*]. Translated by John Healey. Edited by R. V. G. Tasker. 2 vols. Everyman's Library. London: J. M. Dent, 1947.

Axelrod, Robert. *The Evolution of Cooperation*. New York: Basic Books, 1984.

Barclay, William. *The Gospel of Mark*. Rev. ed. Daily Study Bible. Philadelphia: Westminster, 1975.

Barrett, C. K. *The Second Epistle to the Corinthians*. Black's New Testament Commentaries. Peabody, MA: Hendrickson, 2008.

Barss, Peter. "Injuries Due to Falling Coconuts." *Journal of Trauma* 24 (1984) 990–91.

Barth, Karl. *Church Dogmatics*. 3/2: *The Doctrine of Creation*. Edited by G. W. Bromiley and T. F. Torrance. Translated by H. Knight et al. Peabody, MA: Hendrickson, 2010.

———. *Church Dogmatics*. 4/4: *The Doctrine of Reconciliation*. Edited by G. W. Bromiley and T. F. Torrance. Translated by G. W. Bromiley. Peabody, MA: Hendrickson, 2010.

———. *The Humanity of God*. Translated by John Newton Thomas and Thomas Wieser. Richmond: John Knox, 1960.

Bauer, Walter. *A Greek-English Lexicon of the New Testament and Other Early Christian Literature*. Edited by F. Wilbur Gingrich and Frederick W. Danker. Translated by William F. Arndt and F. Wilbur Gingrich. 2nd ed. Chicago: University of Chicago Press, 1979.

Bazerman, Max H., and Margaret A. Neale. *Negotiating Rationally*. New York: Free Press, 1994. Kindle edition.

Beeley, Christopher A. *Leading God's People: Wisdom from the Early Church for Today.* Grand Rapids: Eerdmans, 2012.

Black, C. Clifton. *Mark.* Abingdon New Testament Commentaries. Nashville: Abingdon, 2011.

Bogost, Ian. "Gamification Is Bullshit." Position statement, Wharton Gamification Symposium, Philadelphia, Pennsylvania, August 8, 2011. http://bogost.com/ writing/blog/gamification_is_bullshit/.

Bonhoeffer, Dietrich. *Letters and Papers from Prison.* Edited by Eberhard Bethge. Enlarged ed. New York: Touchstone, 1997.

Bowman, Ray, and Eddy Hall. *When Not to Build: An Architect's Unconventional Wisdom for Growing the Church.* Grand Rapids: Baker, 2000.

Brafman, Ori, and Rom Brafman. *Sway: The Irresistible Pull of Irrational Behavior.* New York: Doubleday, 2008.

Brams, Steven J. *Biblical Games: Game Theory and the Hebrew Bible.* Rev. ed. Cambridge: MIT Press, 2003.

———. Interview by Austin Allen. *Big Think,* February 2, 2010. http://bigthink.com/ videos/big-think-interview-with-steven-brams.

Brown, Raymond, trans. *The Gospel of Peter.* http://www.earlychristianwritings.com/ text/gospelpeter-brown.html.

Brueggemann, Walter. "Biblical Authority." *Christian Century* 118.1 (2001) 14–20.

Buffett, Warren E. "Chairman's Letter." *Berkshire Hathaway Inc. 1990 Annual Report,* March 1, 1991. http://www.berkshirehathaway.com/letters/1990.html.

Byassee, Jason. "The Bishop's Dashboard: William Willimon's Experiment in Accountability." *Christian Century* 128.12 (2011) 26.

Calvin, John. *Institutes of the Christian Religion.* Edited by John T. McNeill. Translated by Ford Lewis Battles. 2 vols. Library of Christian Classics. Philadelphia: Westminster, 1960.

Capon, Robert Farrar. *The Third Peacock: The Goodness of God and the Badness of the World.* Garden City, NY: Image, 1972.

Carder, Kenneth L., and Laceye C. Warner. *Grace to Lead: Practicing Leadership in the Wesleyan Tradition.* Nashville: General Board of Higher Education and Ministry, United Methodist Church, 2011.

Cassian, John. *The Conferences of John Cassian.* Translated by Edgar C. S. Gibson. Rev. ed. Grand Rapids: Christian Classics Ethereal Library, 2009. Kindle edition.

Chaves, Mark. *American Religion: Contemporary Trends.* Princeton: Princeton University Press, 2011.

Chesterton, G. K. *St. Francis of Assisi (Annotated).* Boston: Andesite, 2011. Kindle edition.

Clark, Aric, Doug Hagler, and Nick Larson. *Never Pray Again: Lift Your Head, Unfold Your Hands, and Get to Work.* St. Louis: Chalice, 2014.

Collins, Jim. *Good to Great: Why Some Companies Make the Leap—and Others Don't.* New York: HarperBusiness, 2001.

"The Confession of 1967." In *The Constitution of the Presbyterian Church (U.S.A.): Part 1 Book of Confessions,* 9.01–9.56. Louisville: Office of the General Assembly, 2004.

Cox, Harvey. *The Feast of Fools: A Theological Essay on Festivity and Fantasy.* New York: Harper & Row, 1972.

Crossan, John Dominic. *Jesus: A Revolutionary Biography.* San Francisco: HarperSanFrancisco, 1994.

Crouch, Andy. *Playing God: Redeeming the Gift of Power*. Downers Grove, IL: InterVarsity, 2013.

"Directory for Worship." In *The Constitution of the Presbyterian Church (U.S.A.): Part 2 Book of Order 2013–15*, W-1.0000–W-7.7000. Louisville: Office of the General Assembly, 2013.

Dixit, Avinash K., and Barry J. Nalebuff. *The Art of Strategy: A Game Theorist's Guide to Success in Business and Life*. New York: Norton, 2008.

Dixon, Drew. "Videogames, Bibles, and Beer: An Interview with Game Church." *Patheos*, October 24, 2011. http://www.patheos.com/blogs/christandpopculture/2011/10/videogames-bibles-and-beer-an-interview-with-game-church/.

Duffin, Richard. J. Recommendation for John Nash, Carnegie Institute of Technology, February 11, 1948. Nash papers. Seeley G. Mudd Manuscript Library, Princeton, New Jersey. https://webspace.princeton.edu/users/mudd/Digitization/AC105/AC105_Nash_John_Forbes_1950.pdf.

Evers-Hood, Ken. "It's Never Just a Game." Sermon, Tualatin Presbyterian Church, Tualatin, Oregon, October 5, 2014. https://vimeo.com/108191659.

———. "Playing Church: Toward a Behavioral Theological Understanding of Church Growth." DMin thesis, Divinity School of Duke University, 2014. http://dukespace.lib.duke.edu/dspace/handle/10161/9471.

Fehr, Ernst, and Simon Gächter. "Altruistic Punishment in Humans." *Nature* 415 (2002) 137–40.

———. "Cooperation and Punishment in Public Goods Experiments." *American Economic Review* 90 (2000) 980–94.

Fisher, Len. *Rock, Paper, Scissors: Game Theory in Everyday Life*. New York: Basic Books, 2008.

Fox, Justin. "From 'Economic Man' to Behavioral Economics." *Harvard Business Review*, May 2015, 78–85. https://hbr.org/2015/05/from-economic-man-to-behavioral-economics.

Friedman, Milton. Interview by Phil Donahue. *Phil Donahue Show*, 1979. https://www.youtube.com/watch?v=RWsx1X8PV_A.

Gaiman, Neil. "My New Year Wish." *Journal* (blog), December 31, 2011. http://journal.neilgaiman.com/2011/12/my-new-year-wish.html.

Gilovich, Thomas, Dale Griffin, and Daniel Kahneman, eds. *Heuristics and Biases: The Psychology of Intuitive Judgment*. Cambridge: Cambridge University Press, 2002. Kindle edition.

Gladwell, Malcolm. *David and Goliath: Underdogs, Misfits, and the Art of Battling Giants*. New York: Little, Brown, 2013. Kindle edition.

Grant, Adam. *Give and Take: Why Helping Others Drives Our Success*. New York: Penguin, 2013. Kindle edition.

Haidt, Jonathan. *The Righteous Mind: Why Good People Are Divided by Politics and Religion*. New York: Vintage, 2012. Kindle edition.

Hardin, Garrett. "The Tragedy of the Commons." *Science* 162 (1968) 1243–48.

Hardy, Edward Rochie, ed. *Christology of the Later Fathers*. Library of Christian Classics 3. Philadelphia: Westminster, 1954.

Harman, Oren. *The Price of Altruism: George Price and the Search for the Origins of Kindness*. New York: Norton, 2011. Kindle edition.

Harrington, Joseph E., Jr. *Games, Strategies, and Decision Making*. New York: Worth Publishers, 2009.

Hawkins, Peter S. "Dogging Jesus." *Christian Century* 122.16 (2005) 18.

Hays, Richard B. *First Corinthians*. Interpretation: A Bible Commentary for Teaching and Preaching. Louisville: John Knox, 1997.

Heath, Chip, and Dan Heath. *Decisive: How to Make Better Choices in Life and Work*. New York: Crown, 2013. Kindle edition.

Heifetz, Ronald A., and Martin Linsky. *Leadership on the Line: Staying Alive through the Dangers of Leading*. Boston: Harvard Business School Press, 2002.

Hinds, Pamela J., and Diane E. Bailey. "Out of Sight, Out of Sync: Understanding Conflict in Distributed Teams." *Organization Science* 14 (2003) 615–32. http://web.stanford.edu/group/WTO/cgi-bin/wp/wp-content/uploads/2014/pub_old/Hinds_Bailey_2003.pdf.

Holmberg, Bengt. *Paul and Power: The Structure of Authority in the Primitive Church as Reflected in the Pauline Epistles*. 1978. Reprint, Eugene, OR: Wipf & Stock, 2004.

Howard, Ronald A., and Ali E. Abbas. *Foundations of Decision Analysis*. Upper Saddle River, NJ: Prentice Hall, 2015. Kindle edition.

Hunsinger, Deborah van Deusen, and Theresa F. Latini. *Transforming Church Conflict: Compassionate Leadership in Action*. Louisville: Westminster John Knox, 2013. Kindle edition.

Iersel, Bas M. F. van. *Mark: A Reader-Response Commentary*. Translated by W. H. Bisscheroux. London: T. & T. Clark, 2004.

Iverson, Kelly R. *Gentiles in the Gospel of Mark: "Even the Dogs Under the Table Eat the Children's Crumbs"*. London: T. & T. Clark, 2007.

Jehn, Karen A. "Benefits and Detriments of Workplace Conflict." *Public Manager* 29 (2000) 24–26.

Jinkins, Michael, and Deborah Bradshaw Jinkins. *The Character of Leadership: Political Realism and Public Virtue in Nonprofit Organizations*. San Francisco: Jossey-Bass, 1998.

Job, Reuben, and Norman Shawchuck. *A Guide to Prayer for Ministers and Other Servants*. Nashville: Upper Room, 1987.

Johnson, Eric J., and Daniel Goldstein. "Do Defaults Save Lives?" *Science* 302 (2003) 1338–39.

Johnson, Luke Timothy. *The Writings of the New Testament: An Interpretation*. Philadelphia: Fortress, 1986.

Jones, L. Gregory. "Traditioned Innovation." *Faith & Leadership*, January 19, 2009. https://www.faithandleadership.com/content/traditioned-innovation.

Jones, L. Gregory, and Kelly Gilmer. "Failing to Learn." *Faith & Leadership*, March 26, 2012. https://www.faithandleadership.com/l-gregory-jones-and-kelly-gilmer-failing-learn.

Kahneman, Daniel. *Thinking, Fast and Slow*. New York: Farrar, Straus and Giroux, 2011. Kindle edition.

Kahneman, Daniel, Jack L. Knetsch, and Richard H. Thaler. "Anomalies: The Endowment Effect, Loss Aversion, and Status Quo Bias." *Journal of Economic Perspectives* 5 (1991) 193–206.

Kallgren, Carl A., Raymond R. Reno, and Robert B. Cialdini. "A Focus Theory of Normative Conduct: When Norms Do and Do Not Affect Behavior." *Personality and Social Psychology Bulletin* 26 (2000) 1002–12.

Kee, Howard Clark, et al. *Christianity: A Social and Cultural History*. 2nd. ed. Upper Saddle River, NJ: Prentice Hall, 1998.

King, Robert. "Death and Resurrection of an Urban Church." *Faith & Leadership*, March 24, 2015. https://www.faithandleadership.com/death-and-resurrection-urban-church.

Kristof, Nicholas. "We Are All Egyptians." *New York Times*, February 3, 2011. http://www.nytimes.com/2011/02/04/opinion/04kristof.html?_r=0.

Krötke, Wolf. "The Humanity of the Human Person in Karl Barth's Anthropology." In *The Cambridge Companion to Karl Barth*, edited by John Webster, 159–76. Cambridge: Cambridge University Press, 2000.

Levine, Amy-Jill. *The Misunderstood Jew: The Church and the Scandal of the Jewish Jesus*. New York: HarperOne, 2007.

Levitt, Steven D., and Stephen J. Dubner. *Freakonomics: A Rogue Economist Explores the Hidden Side of Everything*. New York: William Morrow, 2005.

Liebert, Elizabeth. *The Way of Discernment: Spiritual Practices for Decision Making*. Louisville: Westminster John Knox, 2010. Kindle edition.

Lischer, Richard. *Open Secrets: A Spiritual Journey through a Country Church*. New York: Doubleday, 2001.

Locke, Samuel. Statement from Special Offerings, Presbyterian Mission Agency. January 12, 2015. https://www.pcusa.org/news/2015/1/12/statement-special-offerings/.

Longman, Tremper, and David E. Garland, eds. *The Expositor's Bible Commentary*. Vol. 9, *Matthew-Mark*. Rev. ed. Grand Rapids: Zondervan, 2010.

Lose, David J. "Mark 7:24–30." . . . *in the Meantime* (blog), June 23, 2012. http://www.davidlose.net/2012/06/mark-7-24-30/.

Marcus, Joel. *Mark: A New Translation with Introduction and Commentary*. Vol. 2, *Mark 8–16*. Anchor Yale Bible 27A. New Haven: Yale University Press, 2009.

———. *The Way of the Lord: Christological Exegesis of the Old Testament in the Gospel of Mark*. London: T. & T. Clark, 2004.

Martin, Roger. *The Opposable Mind: Winning through Integrative Thinking*. Boston: Harvard Business Review Press, 2009. Kindle edition.

Mather, Mike. "Adelita's Gift: The Value of Asking the Right Questions." *Abundant Community*, March 14, 2012. http://www.abundantcommunity.com/home/stories/parms/1/story/20120314_adelitas_gift_the_value_of_asking_the_right_questions.html.

Matthews, Peter, and Norris McWhirter, eds. *The Guinness Book of Records 1994*. New York: Bantam, 1994.

McGonigal, Jane. *Reality Is Broken: Why Games Make Us Better and How They Can Change the World*. New York: Penguin, 2011. Kindle edition.

———. *SuperBetter: A Revolutionary Approach to Getting Stronger, Happier, Braver, and More Resilient—Powered By the Science of Games*. New York: Penguin, 2015. Kindle edition.

McLean, Bethany, and Peter Elkind. *The Smartest Guys in the Room: The Amazing Rise and Scandalous Fall of Enron*. New York: Portfolio, 2013. Kindle edition.

Migliore, Daniel L. *Faith Seeking Understanding: An Introduction to Christian Theology*. Grand Rapids: Eerdmans, 1998.

Moltmann, Jürgen. *Theology of Play*. Translated by Reinhard Ulrich. New York: Harper & Row, 1972.

Murphy-O'Connor, Jerome. *The Holy Land*. 5th ed. Oxford Archaeological Guides. Oxford: Oxford University Press, 2008. Kindle edition.

Nasar, Sylvia. *A Beautiful Mind*. New York: Touchstone, 2001.

Niebuhr, H. Richard. *The Kingdom of God in America*. New York: Harper, 1959.

Nowak, Martin A., and Roger Highfield. *SuperCooperators: Altruism, Evolution, and Why We Need Each Other to Succeed*. New York: Free Press, 2011. Kindle edition.

Partnoy, Frank. *Wait: The Art and Science of Delay*. New York: PublicAffairs, 2012. Kindle edition.

Paulson, Michael. "The 'Pay What You Want' Experiment at Synagogues." *New York Times*, February 2, 2015. http://www.nytimes.com/2015/02/02/us/the-pay-what-you-want-experiment-at-synagogues.html?_r=0.

Peterson, Eugene H. *The Pastor: A Memoir*. New York: HarperCollins, 2011. Kindle edition.

Peterson, Martin. *An Introduction to Decision Theory*. Cambridge Introductions to Philosophy. Cambridge: Cambridge University Press, 2009. Kindle edition.

Pfeffer, Jeffrey, and Robert I. Sutton. *Hard Facts, Dangerous Half-Truths, and Total Nonsense: Profiting from Evidence-Based Management*. Boston: Harvard Business Review Press, 2006. Kindle edition.

Piketty, Thomas. *Capital in the Twenty-First Century*. Translated by Arthur Goldhammer. Cambridge: Belknap Press of Harvard University Press, 2014.

Poundstone, William. *Prisoner's Dilemma*. New York: Anchor, 1993.

Rand, David G., et al. "Religious Motivations for Cooperation: An Experimental Investigation Using Explicit Primes." *Religion, Brain & Behavior* 4 (2014) 31–48.

Robertson, Margaret. "Can't Play, Won't Play." *Hide&Seek*, October 6, 2010. http://www.hideandseek.net/2010/10/06/cant-play-wont-play/.

Rowe, C. Kavin. "Failure as Christ-Shaped Leadership." *Faith & Leadership*, November 7, 2011. http://www.faithandleadership.com/c-kavin-rowe-failure-christ-shaped-leadership.

Rubinstein, Ariel. Afterword to *Theory of Games and Economic Behavior*, by John von Neumann and Oskar Morgenstern, 633–36. 60th anniv. ed. Princeton: Princeton University Press, 2007.

———. *Economic Fables*. Cambridge: Open Book, 2012. Kindle edition.

Russell, Bertrand. *Common Sense and Nuclear Warfare*. London: George Allen & Unwin, 1959.

Sample, Steven B. *The Contrarian's Guide to Leadership*. San Francisco: Jossey-Bass, 2003.

Sanders, E. P. *The Historical Figure of Jesus*. London: Penguin, 1995.

Scanlon, Leslie. "Special Offerings Campaign Draws Criticism." *Presbyterian Outlook*, January 12, 2015. http://pres-outlook.org/2015/01/special-offerings-campaign-draws-criticism/.

"The Second Helvetic Confession." In *The Constitution of the Presbyterian Church (U.S.A.): Part 1 Book of Confessions*, 5.001–5.260. Louisville: Office of the General Assembly, 2004.

Seidman, Dov. *How: Why How We Do Anything Means Everything . . . in Business (and in Life)*. Hoboken, NJ: John Wiley, 2007.

Shani, Ayelett. "What It Feels Like to Know What We're All Thinking." *Haaretz*, April 5, 2012. http://www.haaretz.com/weekend/magazine/what-it-feels-like-to-know-what-we-re-all-thinking-1.422824.

Shepherd, J. Barrie. *Whatever Happened to Delight? Preaching the Gospel in Poetry and Parables*. Louisville: Westminster John Knox, 2006.

Sivers, Derek. "Fish Don't Know They're in Water." June 19, 2011. http://sivers.org/fish.

Skyrms, Brian. *The Stag Hunt and the Evolution of Social Structure.* Cambridge: Cambridge University Press, 2003. Kindle edition.

Sparks, Susan. *Laugh Your Way to Grace: Reclaiming the Spiritual Power of Humor.* Woodstock, VT: Skylight Paths, 2010. Kindle edition.

Stanovich, Keith E., and Richard F. West. "Individual Differences in Reasoning: Implications for the Rationality Debate?" *Behavioral and Brain Sciences* 23 (2000) 645–726.

Steinberger, Michael. "Psychopathic C.E.O.'s." *New York Times Magazine*, December 12, 2004. http://www.nytimes.com/2004/12/12/magazine/12PSYCHO.html?_r=0.

Sunstein, Cass R. *Choosing Not to Choose: Understanding the Value of Choice.* Oxford: Oxford University Press, 2015. Kindle edition.

Thaler, Richard H. *Misbehaving: The Making of Behavioral Economics.* New York: Norton, 2015. Kindle edition.

Thaler, Richard H., and Cass R. Sunstein. *Nudge: Improving Decisions about Health, Wealth, and Happiness.* Rev. ed. New York: Penguin, 2009. Kindle edition.

Theissen, Gerd. *The Social Setting of Pauline Christianity: Essays on Corinth.* Edited and translated by John H. Schütz. 1982. Reprint, Eugene, OR: Wipf & Stock, 2004.

This American Life. Episode 556, "Same Bed, Different Dreams." Hosted by Ira Glass. Aired May 1, 2015. http://www.thisamericanlife.org/radio-archives/episode/556/transcript.

Tierney, John. "Do You Suffer from Decision Fatigue?" *New York Times Magazine*, August 21, 2011. http://www.nytimes.com/2011/08/21/magazine/do-you-suffer-from-decision-fatigue.html.

Tversky, Amos, and Daniel Kahneman. "Rational Choice and the Framing of Decisions." *Journal of Business* 59.4, part 2: The Behavioral Foundations of Economic Theory (1986) S251–78.

Tyrrell, George. *Christianity at the Crossroads.* 1910. Reprint, Whitefish, MT: Kessinger, 2010.

Ward, Hannah, and Jennifer Wild, eds. *Resources for Preaching and Worship—Year B: Quotations, Meditations, Poetry, and Prayers.* Louisville: Westminster John Knox, 2002.

Weems, Lovett H., Jr. *Church Leadership: Vision, Team, Culture, and Integrity.* Rev. ed. Nashville: Abingdon, 2010.

Werbach, Kevin, and Dan Hunter. *For the Win: How Game Thinking Can Revolutionize Your Business.* Philadelphia: Wharton Digital Press, 2012. Kindle edition.

Williams, Bri. "The Mary Poppins Principle: The Behavioural Economics of Should and Sugar." *SmartCompany*, March 20, 2015. http://www.smartcompany.com.au/people/46160-the-mary-poppins-principle-the-behavioural-economics-of-should-and-sugar.html#.

Williams, H. A. *Tensions: Necessary Conflicts in Life and Love.* Springfield, IL: Templegate, 1977.

Wines, Michael. "Reaction to Ferguson Decision Shows Racial Divide Remains over Views of Justice." *New York Times*, November 25, 2014. http://www.nytimes.com/2014/11/26/us/after-ferguson-announcement-a-racial-divide-remains-over-views-of-justice.html.

Witherington, Ben. *The Paul Quest: The Renewed Search for the Jew of Tarsus.* Downers Grove, IL: InterVarsity, 1998.

Index